Life In China

My Story

Jean M. Life

To order additional copies of this book, contact:
Xlibris Corporation
1-888-795-4274
www.Xlibris.com
Orders@Xlibris.com
94841

Contents

Acknowledgments

This book would have never been written if it had not been for the persistence of so many people who said I should write it, but the one who was the catalyst to give me the final push was my godson Jack Griffith. Thank you, Jack, for being the one who made me start—and finish it. Also a special thanks to Janet Holliday who worked in the Human Resources Department at American Electric Power in the Columbus office. She was our guardian angel as we lived out our years in China. If we ever had a question or a problem, we turned to her, and she always had an answer or a solution almost immediately. Thank you so much, Janet, for all your help and support. Others who were instrumental in encouraging me were my husband, Ralph, whose job made this adventure possible and whose computer help was invaluable; our daughters Sarah and Amanda; my mother-in-law and father-in-law, Ruth and Granville Life; my sisters-in-law Mary Garrett and Jane Smith; my brother-in-law Dennis; my cousin Rosalyn Hensley, who has always supported me in all my decisions no matter how crazy they were; my friend Jane Huff, who was my first proofreader and advisor; my friend Keith Pratt, who also proofread, gave great input, and encouraged my efforts; my friend Brent Davis, who is a published author himself, who not only proofread it and gave me advice but gave me much information about getting my book published; our friend Roy Wilson, from London, who shared two years of our Nanyang experience and has provided help with remembering events correctly; all the foreigners who shared some of our time in Nanyang; and finally, so many of our friends who kept saying, "You should write a book!" And so, at last I have. I hope you will discover and enjoy a glimpse of the "real China," or "the frontier," as we fondly called it. May it encourage others to embark upon their own amazing adventure.

The Beginning

It all happened so quickly. Ralph came home from work one evening in the spring of 1998, walked in the door, and said, "Think about moving to China," immediately followed by, "I'm going to play golf." With that he was out the door, and I was left with my emotions in turmoil. We have moved many times during the course of our marriage, so I was used to moving and change—just not to a third-world country and half a world away from family and friends. I had a million questions and could hardly wait until he answered them.

A few hours later, he returned to explain things. As it turned out, his employer, American Electric Power, was asking him to consider going to China as general manager of a joint venture power plant. AEP was then in the foreign investment phase of the company and co-owned a plant with Henan Power Bureau in the Henan Province of China. This project was called Nanyang General Light and Electric Company (NGLE). I learned that we would be living in a small city named Nanyang, in central China, where there was very little development in 1998 and the people were still very traditional in their approach to life. It was a poor area in modern times but had been rich in the early history of China. The only Americans the people there had ever seen were the engineers and others sent to work on the project in the beginning stages of the venture. I would be the first American woman to actually live in Nanyang. It was a lot to absorb, and we both had a lot of thinking to do.

After graduating from Virginia Tech in 1972, Ralph had begun his long career with AEP. He had started as an engineer and through the years had advanced to the point of becoming plant manager at the Kammer-Mitchell power plants in West Virginia. When he first learned of this new joint venture project several years prior to this, he had expressed an interest in going to China. But as the years went by and no mention of his working on this project came up, we no longer thought about it—at least I didn't—until now.

Even though our daughters Sarah and Amanda were very supportive when we told them about the possibility of moving to China, I'm sure they had some reservations about our going so far away to live. Sarah was a graduate of The Ohio State University School of Pharmacy and was working and living on her own. She had recently become engaged to Patrick Metzger and was in the process of planning her wedding. Amanda was finishing her junior year as a mechanical engineering student at West Virginia University Institute of Technology and would graduate the following year without our presence. They both assured us they would be just fine if we accepted the offer. So after much thought, prayer, and angst, we finally decided we would go. Although our families wished us well, I think they thought we were absolutely crazy, as did most people we knew. We were literally besieged by many pleas of "don't go!" After all, both of us came from Elkton, Virginia, a small town in the Shenandoah Valley of Virginia. We were the only ones on either side of our families who had ever left home. So what in the world were two middle-aged people with no experience of living in a foreign country, let alone China, thinking? With visions of the Tiananmen Square incident firmly imbedded in their minds, the general consensus was "It's dangerous over there!" I'm sure they thought we were going to our imminent deaths at the hands, guns, and tanks of the Communists. Some tried to discourage us with any derogatory news they read or heard about China, but most just said, "I wouldn't go!" One neighbor, an elderly woman who had lived in Italy at one time in her life, was the most vocal and persistent about our not going. Almost daily, she would come across the street to tell me about some life-threatening circumstance she was sure would happen to us there. So doubts began to replace the optimism we first experienced, and our fears grew about this move to China—"of all places."

Ralph began making trips to China to see the project and to familiarize himself with the lay of the land. We began making plans to sell the house and car and get our financial affairs in order. My mother agreed to keep our cats for us, which took a big load off my mind. All the other details of the move began to fall into place.

The day Janet Holiday called from AEP Human Resources in the Columbus, Ohio, headquarters to tell us that a cross-cultural training session had been arranged for us in Chicago was the beginning of the reality that we were indeed going to go to China. We had an intensive two-day marathon of different classes on the culture, habits, behaviors, and history of the People's Republic of China (not to be confused with the Republic of China, which is Taiwan). We also received instruction on how we would be received, the hospitality of the Chinese people, and suggestions on how to handle the inquisitiveness of the Chinese about our personal life (such as their wanting to know our age and/or weight and especially how much money we made). We were given the advice to get a box and put some things inside. These items we could pull out on the day we realized we were there to stay and would need the comfort of a touch of home—my box consisted of my favorite book, popcorn, and pictures.

Those two days were exhausting for both of us as we tried to absorb and remember all the information we had received. But by the time the classes were over, I realized I had once again started to believe in our ability to handle this challenge.

Initiation and Goodbyes

Ralph was to make the move to China to begin his job as general manager of the project in January 1999. I was graciously allowed to go along to assess the situation of living there before I made the actual move. Traveling with us were Glenn Davis and Frank Van Pelt, who were engineers involved with the joint venture; and Helen Sun, who was from Beijing but was employed by AEP as an accountant. She told me I would find China harsher than life in the U.S., which proved to be more accurate than I wished to believe at that time. This trip, however, was short and hurried as we tried to get over jet lag, travel to Nanyang via plane and motor by car for three hours down what I came to call the Suicide Highway. We attended dinners, saw as much as possible of where we would be living, and last of all attended a wedding. It was quite an overwhelming whirlwind of activity and cultural shock. Plus it was a bit unnerving being stared at by the people of Nanyang, who had never seen a white woman before. Some would actually stand in front of me and look into the first set of non-brown eyes they had ever seen. The wedding was fun but involved much toasting to the bride and groom and to each other with the most unusual and potent alcoholic product I believe exists on the planet.

Before the wedding festivities were over, Glenn and I had to catch a plane at the local airport to get back to the U.S. By this time, both of us were rather intoxicated from all the toasting with the rocket fuel. And on top of that, we had to ride to the airport in the "wedding car"—a black sedan decorated with a plastic bride and groom on top and artificial flowers all over. I came to find that this was the customary transportation for a bride and groom on their wedding day. So I kissed Ralph goodbye with the promise to be back as soon as possible and rode to the airport in grand style. When we got out of the car at the very small Nanyang airport, the local people could hardly believe their eyes as two middle-aged foreigners emerged from a traditional wedding car. A first in all of Nanyang history!

We managed to complete our journey, and I arrived back at our home in West Virginia to finish up the process of moving. Thankfully, Granville, my father-in-law, and Mary, my sister-in-law, came to New Martinsville to help in the packing up and getting our household goods ready for storage. They not only helped me with whatever work that needed to be done but also gave me moral support while there. And so, one more step toward leaving was done.

Before Ralph had left for China, many friends came to visit with us—either to wish us well or to see if we had actually lost our minds. Our godson Jack and his wife, Stacey, traveled all the way from Memphis, Tennessee, which was a real gift to us since we had not seen them for several years. They were there for the dinner our friends at the West Virginia AEP Kammer & Mitchell plants had for us. It was a wonderful evening, thankfully kept upbeat and happy as, by this time, we were getting a bit apprehensive over this whole China thing.

Then came my goodbyes to our families in Virginia, friends from New Martinsville, Pt. Pleasant, and Winfield in West Virginia, and from all the other places we had lived. The house and car were sold, the furniture packed up and in storage. The things we were taking to China were on the way there. I finally said goodbye to our neighbors and friends at First Presbyterian and sadly realized that I probably would not see some of them again. It was a bittersweet time, giving us many memories to take with us on our journey.

The only thing remaining was for me to be with our daughter Sarah as she chose her wedding dress for her upcoming wedding to Patrick Metzger in September. Once that was done, there was nothing left to prevent my departure. Amanda drove me to Columbus, and she and Sarah took me to the airport in March of 1999. We tearfully said goodbye, and I was off to China—leaving Sarah to plan her wedding without me and Amanda to finish college with no mom or dad for moral support. I was by myself and scared to death—all my courage and bravado absolutely gone. At this point, Ralph wasn't sure he could come to Beijing to meet me, so that added to my fears.

Arrival

The plane landed in Beijing and I didn't know what to expect, but there was Ralph waiting for me and I felt safe again. Bernard Hu, who was in charge of the AEP office in Beijing, was with him. Bernard, an American citizen from Taiwan, was to become a very dear friend over the time we spent in China, and he always looked after our well-being.

We went to the Great Wall Sheraton Hotel, a very nice five-star hotel, and checked in. Immediately afterward, and in keeping with the tradition of AEPers going to China, we quickly went across the street to the Hard Rock Café—for the last hamburger we would have in a very long time. The next day, we went to the Hongqiao (hongchow) Market, and Ralph bought me a beautiful strand of pearls from Ding Xuefei (shufay), beginning a jewelry relationship that would last for many years. After two more days in Beijing and two dinners with bankers from Shanghai, where I learned very quickly, but maybe not so correctly, how to use chopsticks, we boarded the plane for Zhengzhou, the capital of Henan Province. There, Bernard told us, we would have a formal dinner. "What would be the difference from the very nice dinners we had in Beijing?" I asked. "You'll see," he replied with a twinkle in his eye.

We landed at the Zhengzhou airport and were met with beautiful bouquets of flowers from the employees of Henan Power and many stares from those waiting for other passengers to arrive.

We were taken to a waiting car complete with driver. From there we went to the hotel named Speed Dragon (humorously called the Speedy Dragon by the engineers), which was owned by Henan Power Bureau, AEP's co-owner in the joint-venture project. Not as nice as the Great Wall Sheraton but comfortable. The further you get from the major cities in China, the more "rustic" things get.

That night, we went to the dinner, and I immediately saw what Bernard had meant about a formal dinner. Upon entering the banquet room, I saw a long table with a golden yellow velvet cloth running down the center of the entire length. By now, I was aware that in ancient China, yellow was the color of the emperor and only he, the empress, and the Buddhist monks could wear this color. I already knew that Mr. Li (lee), who was head of the power bureau, was a very important man and was quickly finding out that this was indeed a formal occasion. In my excitement, I had forgotten about the significance of the thimble-sized small cups at each place on the table and the taste of the concoction they would hold. Mr. Li entered the room, and everyone took their place at the table. I was sitting on the opposite side of the table but near Mr. Li's seat, so I could see him with no trouble—and he could see me.

The etiquette of banquets is that "cold dishes" are placed on the table, but no one eats anything until after the first toast. There are always young girls stationed around the banquet tables. Not only was it their job to tend to the people's dining needs, but they also were in charge of the small white pitchers which held one of the most expensive and famous brands of Chinese liquor called Moutai (maw-tie). Finally, the time came for dinner to begin. Mr. Li stood and made a toast, after which he said, "Ganbei!" (gahn-bay) I knew this meant "bottoms up," so I downed the contents of the little cup in one gulp. All eyes were on me and were watching to see my reaction to the brew. The taste in my mouth said, "Turpentine and kerosene!" and my mind said, "Keep it down," which I was able to do and received applause and approval from everyone. From then on, it was known that I could handle their favorite toasting beverage and would thereafter be expected to drink copious amounts at the many banquets we attended during our stay in China. After the first cup is drunk, everyone begins eating the cold dishes. Then the host says, "Second cup," followed soon thereafter by the third. By this time, everyone is feeling very jovial, happy, and friendly. So then the toasting begins in earnest—with everyone jumping up and going to toast someone else with the inevitable little white pitcher in hand. Now this is where it gets interesting: the custom in the Henan Province is to ask the one being toasted to drink three cups alone and then one with the person doing the toasting—four cups total with each toast. Good bargaining skills can sometimes reduce the number of these toasts, but not often. I eventually learned to pour green tea or water in my cup, and if no one was watching, I occasionally got out of drinking a few toasts per evening. This toasting process is repeated during the remainder of the banquet for all of the following reasons: (1) it is traditional, (2) it shows hospitality, (3) they actually like the stuff, and (4) everyone relaxes and enjoys the evening more. But sometimes, it is used to get guests drunk and then call a meeting to discuss business—a means of getting the better part of the deal, especially since the host has had water put in his little white pitcher.

The next day after the banquet and our stay at the Speed Dragon, we got in our car and headed—blasted off is more like it—for Nanyang. I was learning that you have to relax and let the driver do his job, but I have to admit that I was still getting used to the driving style of the Chinese. There are no rules—or that was what it seemed to me at the time. My right foot was soon tired from trying to slam on the brakes a thousand times during our three-and-a-half-hour trip. We flew down a road that wound through villages and small towns with animals and people appearing in the road at any moment, cars and trucks using whichever part of the road they wished, and toll booths interspersed along the way. As it got dark, I discovered that car lights were optional, and the wearing of illuminated clothing was nonexistent. As time went on, I did find that traveling this highway was a good way to see much of the rural life of China, but at the time, it was only a hazardous blur of the countryside and village life. I quickly named this road "the Suicide Highway" as I had already determined it was a miracle to survive any trip made on it.

We arrived in Nanyang late in the evening. It was so dark—no street lights to mark the way, only our headlights and a dim bulb occasionally seen in a small shop along the darkened streets. We followed a big truck filled with animal skeletons, and as our headlights shown on this spectacle, it seemed like an ominous sign in the dark. After the events of the previous few days and such a long, dangerous trip, I was pretty tired, and things weren't looking so good. Soon we arrived at our apartment building, climbed the sixty dusty concrete stairs to our doorway, and entered our new home. Well, here we were, together again and in Nanyang—in a less than well-decorated and even less clean apartment. I unpacked my suitcase, picked a paperback book from the well-stocked bookshelves left there by the previous AEP engineer, and got in a bed the size of Asia to read. The bedside lamp had about a twenty-five-watt bulb in it, which was yet another reminder that as long as we lived here, we weren't going to be able to enjoy the standards of the good ol' USA and life was not going to be as "nice." After watching some sports on TV, Ralph came to bed. I lay awake for a long time that first night thinking, "I can't do this for three years, but how can I tell Ralph?" Thus, our life in China began.

Ralph, Dennis, Bernard, Eric, Glenn meeting with Mr. Li
who was head of Henan Power Bureau

First Day

After Ralph left for work, I went back to sleep for a short time, waking once again to begin my life in China. **Thud!** My heart sank as I quickly realized there was no heat and no water in our concrete and steel apartment. I crawled back into bed to keep warm and wondered how in the world I was going to endure living here. Soon the phone rang, and it was Ralph telling me that everyone wanted me to come to lunch at the hotel where his office was. I told him I couldn't shower and had no heat, but he said, "I'll send a driver with a company car to pick you up." Okay, I would be ready—somehow. I got a pan of water out of our water cooler, washed my face, and brushed my teeth. I dressed and began to feel human once again. Soon our driver Mr. Bai (bye) and our translator Linda arrived in the promised car and off we went to have lunch with the people of NGLE. As I was being whisked through the cold, dirty, crowded streets of Nanyang, I tried to get used to Linda's English and not be distracted by all the activity of one kind or another going on in the streets. But soon, we arrived at the hotel, and I made my entrance into the unheated dining hall. Of course, I was the center of attention, so I just tried to pretend I did this sort of thing every day and did not notice their curiosity. I let them stare as I looked over the buffet table and tried to find something to eat that looked vaguely familiar. I did find some vegetables that I recognized and some noodle soup, which was delicious and quickly became my favorite Chinese food.

I learned that more wheat than rice was grown in our province, so, consequently, people in this part of China ate more noodles than rice. That was just fine with me, since I had never been much of a rice fan. My opinion on this was to change, however, as I soon found that the sticky Asian rice is much tastier than our enriched rice here at home.

At that time, Frosty Cunningham, one of the AEP project engineers, was still working at the plant, and he ate lunch at our table. I learned that he lived in the apartment above us, and Eric Chan, Bernard Hu's friend from Taipei, Taiwan, who also worked with Ralph, lived in the apartment below us. Then I was introduced to all the people who worked in the office building, and they were all very friendly.

Soon, Mr. Bai and Linda took me back "home," and I found that I had heat and water again. I was left on my own until Ralph got home that evening. I spent the rest of that day washing down the walls of our kitchen, which were coated with the gray dust that continuously found ways into the apartment. This dust came from the pollution of the motor vehicles, the burning of the charcoal bricks used for cooking, the manufacturers who had no environmental laws to obey, and even possibly from all the cigarette smoking which was a national pastime. During my labors, I did a lot of thinking about my new set of circumstances. Ralph, Eric, and Frosty got home about 5:30, and we all ate dinner with Eric in his apartment. He had employed a local woman to cook for him, and so far, those were two things I didn't have to worry about—shopping for and cooking Chinese food. Eating with Eric became a routine that was to last for several weeks.

That evening, I discovered that we had two English speaking channels called Star World and Star Sports on our TV. Star Sports covered mostly European and Asian sporting events—soccer, rugby, and Formula One car racing. Star World carried mostly '50s, '60s and '70s shows. More current offerings included *Larry King Live, Tool Time, Law & Order* and the soap opera *The Bold and the Beautiful.* Okay, not a great TV lineup, but I could live with this.

Besides, the bookcase was well-stocked with reading material, and I figured I had plenty of time to take advantage of that.

I was learning very quickly that I wasn't "in Kansas anymore" and to keep my expectations of cleanliness and quality products at a lowered level. I was beginning to cling to hope—you know it really does spring eternal. After all, today, I had made some huge steps—I had survived being assessed by a room full of strangers, I had met a new circle of friends, I found I wasn't going to starve, and currently, I had heat and water. I was not dead yet, and although at this time I wasn't really enthusiastic about this whole "adventure," things were starting to look promising.

The first two questions people usually ask me when they learn I have lived in China are "Why did you go?" soon followed by "Why did you stay?" The first one is easy. Ralph and I had grown up together, attending the same church and school. We had married in 1969 and had always been together since, so the "for better or for worse" part of the marriage vows was a fact and not an option. I must admit, though, that I do have a bit of adventurous spirit and had always gone wherever the job took us. The second one is more difficult. I just didn't know that every ounce of that adventurous spirit and more was going to be needed to accomplish this move. So I guess the answer to the second one is I determined that I would survive this ordeal or die trying.

Settling In

With Ralph at the office all day, my time in the apartment was spent at the computer, in the kitchen futilely trying to clean the gray dust off those white tile walls, looking out the windows at the events in the streets, watching a little TV, or reading. I had been warned by the translators not to go out on my own as it could be "very dangerous." At the time, I totally believed this, not realizing that if anything did happen to me, the people who worked with Ralph would be held responsible.

From the bedroom window on the front of the building, there was much to watch. This became my "window on the world"—well, at least the world I was living in at that time. I watched cows being killed and butchered across the street at an outdoor restaurant. This was done by tying the cow's legs together and bringing it down to the ground. Then a big pan was put under the cow's head and a long knife was used to cut the throat, allowing the cow to bleed to death. After several minutes, the cow was dead and the pan was full of blood, which was poured into a big plastic container. Next, the head was cut off and laid aside and the legs were cut off and thrown into a pan. Then the skin was cut down the belly and laid out to finish the butchering process. After the insides were removed and saved, big hunks of meat were hung on hooks and displayed for either cooking at the restaurant or for sale to customers. Once all this was done, the hide was folded up and put aside. Before the day was over, people would come to purchase the meat, blood, hide, head, intestines, or other parts of the animal. Nothing went to waste.

I also watched the metal workers across the street. Several times a week, they would have a sheet of metal that needed to be flattened. Instead of spending much time and energy on this chore, they just threw the metal out in the street and let the cars and trucks do the work for them. Noisy, yes, but I had to admire their resourcefulness.

Since the people spend most of their time in the streets, there were also the street dramas to entertain me. I was told soon after we got there not to interfere with any fights I may see as this was none of my business. Even men beating women was off-limits, and I did see this quite often. The fights always drew crowds with everyone watching but no one interfering in them. One of the most humorous fights I saw from my window involved a saleslady who had spread out her shoe inventory on the street under my window. For some reason, a young man was arguing intensely with her. I don't know if he insulted her, her merchandise, or what, but he had obviously managed to enrage her to the point of getting physical. She gave him a big push and he pushed her back, causing her to fall to the pavement and roll around moaning and holding her head in her hands. Suddenly and very dramatically, she recovered from her injury, jumped up, grabbed a stick, and went after the young man with a vengeance. He laughed at her, which only enraged her more. Wielding her stick and pursuing him, she, he, and the crowd moved on down the street and out of my sight, taking their fight and my entertainment with them.

One day, I was working at the computer when I heard loud squealing sounds. Not knowing what in the world was going on, I ran to the window. Well, it turned out that a huge pig had been dumped into the street from a three-wheeled tricycle cart. A very small man was trying valiantly to put the pig back into the cart, but the pig was bigger than the man. The harder he worked, the more the pig squealed. Finally, another man stopped to help, and, eventually, they were successful in their endeavors. So on went man and pig, one pedaling diligently and one riding contentedly in the back.

From the windows on the other side of the apartment, I watched a colony of rats scurrying around in the empty lot in the back. The garbage chute was located in the back of the building, and the local "recycling man" would gather up the plastic bags of garbage and then dump out the contents. The bags were then taken up the street to an empty lot and spread out to dry so that he could then make a little money from them at the recycling place. These rats in the lot were well fed. Little did I know then that these rats would soon become our roommates.

I could also keep track of the activities of our gatekeeper who lived in a storage shed with his wife. This shed was about six feet by eight feet. To supplement his meager income, he kept chickens in the empty lot behind our building. Besides being a source of food, he sold the chickens as well as the eggs. Along with the rats, I watched the chickens as they grew and raised their families. This gatekeeper was a great entrepreneur as he collected anything made of metal, wood, or glass and sold these treasures. I would take them food gifts on holidays, and although we could not verbally communicate, I found that smiles and nods worked wonders. I considered them my friends. They had a traditional bamboo bed and would put it outside on hot summer nights and sleep there with mosquito netting protecting them from the bug bites. For people who had so little material goods, they seemed to be genuinely happy.

Also, in the back was another apartment building to our right. On the porch across the way from our side windows lived a rooster. Very early every morning, he crowed delightedly and continued to crow almost the entire day. Guess he didn't have a lot to do but strut around that porch flapping his wings and crowing, most likely at all the gatekeeper's chickens in the lot below him. I named him Mao. Well, about the time I thought I would go crazy with all the crowing, it suddenly ended. Most likely he wound up in the wok that evening as supper.

A major disappointment happened about the same time of the rooster's demise. Our Star World station went digital, so we had no English-speaking TV except for the sports station, which didn't carry any sport of interest to me. "Someone" was trying to find a way to get us another English-speaking channel. That "someone" turned out to be a Mr. Wang, who made several profitable, although unsuccessful, attempts to procure us English-speaking TV before he suddenly disappeared from Nanyang. At least Eric could not find him anywhere. We found out later that he had been installing temporary promotional programming, which only lasted about a week at a time; but he wasn't telling us this and continued charging us for his services. I called him Mr. Wrong.

The streets were a theater of constant activity. As I was driven through the streets of Nanyang, I thought it probably was a good idea for me not to venture out alone since I didn't know if I could maneuver through all this movement without getting hurt or possibly killed. Everywhere you looked, something was going on. Traffic was a chaotic mess compared to anything we knew stateside. The mass of humanity that was in motion either on foot, bicycle, or in motorized vehicles was overwhelming, and the cacophony of the considered necessary horn blowing was nerve-racking. Then there were also the dogs, cows, and goats added to the mix. Just riding in a car was a test of nerves, since you had to totally depend on your driver to be able to see and contend with it all. As time went on, we initiated first-time visitors by putting them in the shotgun seat to experience the miracle of actually reaching a destination alive. Mr. Bai, who was our usual driver, saved our lives more than once during our four and a half years' stay in Nanyang, as did Mr. Bian (bee in'), who occasionally drove us. I was in awe of their ability to see and to react quickly to different situations. But I learned soon after I arrived in Nanyang not to mention anything that captured my attention, or our driver immediately turned the car around in the middle of the street, parked on the sidewalk, and escorted me to whatever I had mentioned.

After several weeks, we hired a cook for our evening meal. She was a young girl with a two-year college education who couldn't find a job. I learned that in China, ability does not count for much in the job-hunting process. Getting a job depended on three things:

1. Having a degree from a major university
2. Knowing someone who could get you a job
3. Having someone in your family pay the bribes necessary to find employment

There is a fourth way, illegal as it may be, and that is paying for a diploma that was not earned. This whole system can be disastrous because often an employer winds up with workers who can't be fired even if their skills are nonexistent. This is because everyone is related to or has "a relationship" with someone in power.

At any rate, this young girl did not have the connections she needed in getting a good job. However, she was the daughter of friends of one of Ralph's coworkers who recommended her to us since she "spoke a little English." Xiao Hang (Show Hahng) was her name, and she was scared to death of us foreigners and could barely remember the "little English" that she did know when we first met her. Scott, one of the translators, came with her one Saturday to show her the kitchen and help her get over her fear of us. The intent was for her to show me how to cook Chinese style, but she was so nervous when I tried to watch her that I soon just left her alone and let her prepare the meals by herself. Neither of us knew at the time that she would be with us for the entire time we stayed in China. This worked out quite well for her since she was always assured of a paycheck on payday, which was not a guaranteed reality for many in China. Plus, her salary was as much as most people made.

Soon, the days were turning into weeks and then into months. I was relaxing and absorbing as much of this new and much different culture as possible. Within a week or so, I had stopped trying to shrink up into a small ball when riding in those dirty taxi minivans. I had learned that I was not going to have heat and water every day and that I could live a while without a shower, even though I did so appreciate and enjoy them when possible. I remember the day I had a trickle of water coming out of the shower head and I said a fervent, "Thank you, God." Immediately, the trickle disappeared and the water went off for most of the day. I was beginning to think I was jinxing the place! I was learning lessons in patience and endurance on a daily basis at inconveniences of life in China.

I benefited from the advice and information we had been given in Chicago and also began reading *Fodor's Exploring China*. I even tried to learn some of the Chinese language, a feat I would never really accomplish. The same words said in different tones mean entirely different things. I could learn the words but could never manage the proper tones, which meant I never said what I intended. Once I practiced all day on one sentence: "I want to buy a dozen eggs." But my tones were evidently horribly incorrect because after I proudly said my sentence to Xiao Hang that evening, she looked at me with surprise and asked, "Why do you want to buy a little duck?" That put a damper on my efforts for quite a while, and I went back to relying on the translators to do my verbal communicating.

Ralph's office at that time was in the town's only three-star hotel, which was owned by the local government. This was the best hotel in Nanyang at the time we arrived, although it was not even considered a one-star by most western standards. When the first AEP engineers arrived, they didn't have washcloths, and so the guys went shopping and finally were able to find some. I'm sure this was a novelty to the staff and caused some lively conversation about the foreigners, but soon thereafter, washcloths did appear in the rooms. Occasionally, the staff was caught in the rooms going through the drawers to see what the Americans had because they were always interested in anything we bought, had, or did. The beds were as hard as the floor, since the "mattresses" were only boards with a quilt covering. It was wise not to forget this because if you plopped yourself down on one of these beds, you could give your body quite a jolt and a headache to boot.

Underneath the hotel was a karaoke bar, which had been dubbed "The Hole" by the engineers. Karaoke bars also had rooms for other activity beyond the singing and dancing room. In those rooms, young, pretty girls "worked" in this Communist country that claimed they had no prostitution. Usually, these girls came from the villages and entered into this profession to earn enough money to get married. Whenever there was a national holiday, the karaoke bars would close for a few weeks. This way, the girls could go home for the holidays, and there would be no prostitution "in a country that has no prostitution" during this time. The Hole became a familiar place to us as we would go dancing after almost every banquet. Mao had liked ballroom-style dancing, so everyone we knew loved to dance. Also, the Chinese love to sing, and most do it very well. The saying was, "The Japanese created karaoke, but the Chinese made it famous." So it was a place to go to relax and enjoy an evening out as well as being a safe place for us to go since it was a government-owned hotel, the offices of NGLE were there, and the manager of

The Hole knew us well. It was also a place we always took visitors to let them get a look at a part of the culture they would never get on a tour.

Soon after our arrival, the hotel hosted a talent show. All the employees were invited to perform. I discovered that almost all Chinese people love performing, and when given a microphone, their rule must be to yell loudly into it. Well, Ralph and I were not only invited to the show but given front row seats—right next to the loud speakers. I spent the evening being blasted with booming voices in my right ear. The employees all performed according to their talents, whether they were musical, comedy, or cooking. While most people sang or danced, there were some comedy routines which went over well with the crowd. Last but not least were the chefs' performances, where they showed how quickly they could prepare the food and how fresh the food was. First, they held up a live chicken. Then they turned the chicken's head to the side, cut its throat, thrust it into boiling water dunking it up and down a few times, plucked the feathers, chopped it up, threw it into a wok for a minute, and then invited us up to have a bite. I thought I was going to throw up at this three-minute chicken! But after a most insistent invitation, I did go on stage, take a piece with chopsticks, manage to get it into my mouth and keep it down—to great applause from the huge crowd. This was my first public performance in China.

Saturdays became a day for me to go shopping with either Scott or Linda. I'm sure they got tired of this routine but would never make any indication to me that they did. These shopping trips were not only a way to escape the walls of our apartment but became cultural learning experiences. I learned which bread was sweet and which was not and found peanut butter, crackers, and other foods that were fairly common to our tastes. Although the peanut butter was certainly not Jiff or Skippy, if you added some honey, it made a nice sandwich. I learned which supermarkets were run by the government and which smaller ones were privately owned—private ownership was fairly new in China at that time. I learned which streets had the best shopping opportunities at both indoor and outdoor markets. And most of all, I learned to just let the people stare at me without feeling uncomfortable. After all, most of them had never seen "one of us" before and probably thought they never would. There was usually at least one person who would openly look in my basket at the things I was going to purchase.

I also discovered that besides all the other noise and activity on the streets of Nanyang, there were musical competitions held frequently on Saturdays at various supermarkets. It was deafening if the competitions were across the street from each other, but they drew large crowds, which I suppose was the purpose. One particular Saturday, we had one of those rare sunny days with blue skies. It was Linda's turn to take me shopping. Meixi Lu (may-she lu) was our favorite shopping street, so we decided to go there. The weather was perfect, the sun was shining, and I was having a good hair day. After a while, Linda suggested we stop and rest a bit with a "co'-lah" (cola). The street vendor handed one can to Linda and then one to me. Linda opened hers with no trouble, but when I opened mine, it erupted, spewing "co'-lah" all over me. The vendor immediately grabbed the gray rag he had been using to wipe things up and patted my face with it. Since I knew he was doing what he thought he should, I stood there and let him do it, trying not to think about where that rag had been all day. So much for my good hair and my perfect day, but another lesson in tolerance was learned.

I began learning a little Chinese, such as how to count from one to ten, how to say thank you, hello, and goodbye, and which numbers were lucky and those that were not. Lucky numbers are 3, 6, 8, and 9; but 4 is not a good number because the word for 4 is "se" (suh) and is also the same word as death when spoken in a different tone. I still could not master the tones and could not detect them when the Chinese spoke to each other. I did eventually learn several words that I could say well enough to be understood, and that sufficed in helping me get around town and a little in conversation at all the dinners we attended.

One day, a big package arrived from Ralph's sister Mary and brother-in-law Phil, which contained many "essentials" for cooking and daily living—at least things considered essential for life in the U.S. Among canned foodstuffs, there was a package of twelve rolls of Bounty paper towels, which immediately became one of my most highly prized possessions. I had already discovered that no such quality paper products existed in Nanyang. I put them out of sight in a closet and only used them when I was cooking or cleaning by myself. I was so frugal with these paper towels (which I used, hand washed, dried, and reused once or twice more before discarding) that I had four rolls left years later when we returned home to live. I gave these to other western friends who were as happy and grateful to get them as we were when they arrived.

Since our furnished apartment included a VCR, we eventually had the brilliant idea of asking friends and family in the U.S. to tape TV shows and send them to us. Ralph's sister Jane and our friends Rose Bridgeman and Dr. David Rice, from New Martinsville, West Virginia, faithfully taped and mailed recorded shows to us during the entire time we lived in Nanyang (*ER, Law & Order*, and comedy shows among them). Those were happy days when the tapes arrived! I doubt Jane, Rose, and David will ever know how much we appreciated their efforts and the joy those tapes gave us. As with the paper towels, we rationed them carefully, only watching for an hour each evening as we enjoyed being briefly transported back into a more familiar world. When other westerners arrived, we shared the tapes with them, and they also enjoyed a reprieve from the daily life of Nanyang.

First Apt.—Street side, where I watched the
street dramas from bedroom window

First Apt.—In Back—where chickens
and rats lived 160 & 161

First Apt.—Stove with oven—bought in Zhengzhou

A Job for Me and More

Several weeks after moving to Nanyang, Scott approached me about helping the students at his alma mater, the local university, with their English-speaking skills. I found out later that it was not officially a university yet but did attain that status before we left China. I agreed to take the "job," and Ralph and I made a visit to this university named Nanyang Institute of Technology (NIT). We first went to a classroom in the building where I would be working. By western standards, it was a grim and utilitarian place, all concrete and steel. But this was what they were used to and, for some of the students, much better than the high schools they had attended. Most of the students there had not scored well enough on the college entrance exam to attend a "better university." Most of them had also come from poor villages and small towns where the schools reflected the communities around them, and their education suffered because these schools usually did not have the best teachers. As time went on and they felt more comfortable around me, many students came to tell me they were so upset with themselves because of their failure to test higher and get into a better university. I always told them not to limit their hopes and dreams to what college they attended. If they wanted something badly enough, they would find a way to achieve success—and several of the students in my classes did go on to further their education and find good, well-paying jobs. I always hoped I gave them the encouragement to do so.

On that first day, we went into a classroom devoid of pictures, maps, and wall decoration. The walls were painted but were dirty, and the windows were covered by the inevitable gray dust. The teacher's desk, a blackboard, and about sixty to eighty student desks were all that the room contained—not a pleasant environment for learning. The room was full of students and teachers, and, of course, both Ralph and I had to speak and answer questions from the students, all of whom I am sure were handpicked to attend this auspicious occasion. After this, we were taken on a tour of the computer room and the teachers' offices and met the people who would be "taking care of me" during my days at the university. They said they could not pay me much, but I insisted that I would not accept any payment whatsoever. I would be glad to volunteer my time and efforts. This earned me much favor throughout the province the entire time we were in China.

My first day "on the job" was a warm, sunny day, and we met outside on the grass. This was a much better environment than the classrooms since the grounds had been landscaped with flowers and trees. Most of the students had never seen a westerner before. Consequently, they were afraid of me at first and hesitant to use their English. I later found out this was because many of them had had teachers who could only teach them to read English but could not teach them how to pronounce the words since most of them had never heard a native English speaker before. I also learned that many Chinese teachers use their position and power over the kids to be abusive by belittling and even hitting them. So I began to build their trust by speaking slowly and using what I consider Standard English, although I'm sure some people here would say I did so with a slight "Southern accent." In my defense, most of them told me they preferred American English over British. I also smiled a lot and treated them with respect and kindness. Once they trusted that I would not laugh at their pronunciations or yell at them, they began speaking more freely. They said they tried to listen to Voice of America at night but could not always hear it well. So for the time being, I was their only source of hearing English spoken on a regular basis, if at all.

During this time, they mostly asked questions about America and, of course, asked me to sing a song—they always want you to sing a song. So I sang the "Bicycle Built for Two" song adding the verse where Daisy refuses Michael's marriage proposal since he only had a bicycle and not a carriage. Well, to my surprise, one of the quieter students spoke up and said, "A bicycle is all you need," putting a perspective on the song that I had never considered and made me realize that this was indeed the case of most people in China. The village people were so poor that having a bicycle was a treasured necessity—a motor scooter being the new status symbol and an automobile just a dream.

When we moved inside the building due to the weather turning cold, I discovered that the classrooms as well as the dormitories had no heat, so I learned to wear several layers of clothing on those cold wintry days. Still, the cold from those concrete floors would seep through my shoes and two layers of socks and I would go home chilled to the bone. It took a long time to get warm again, and I couldn't imagine living in such conditions where there was no place to get warm except to go to bed. My sympathy for the students increased.

Upon moving inside to the classrooms, I found that the easy conversation outside did not translate well to the classroom setting. In this setting, the kids were not so vocal and became more reserved. I soon began searching the Internet for lesson plans and ways to encourage them to use their English. I tried to help them pronounce sounds that were difficult for them. They could not say the words "usually" or "casual"—these translated as "urally" and "carol" (as in Americans wear more "carol" clothes than the Chinese. It took me quite a while to figure out what carol clothes were). I tried to teach them to practice saying the "Fuzzy Wuzzy Was a Bear" rhyme to get them to be able to say the "z" sound. Another sound that many of them had trouble with was "th" as in "think" or "thank" which was mostly spoken as "sink" or "sank," so I showed them the placement of the tongue or lips as they tried to master the difficult words or sounds. I told them to watch their mouths in a mirror as they practiced their English. Another piece of advice I gave them was to try to spend at least ten minutes a day speaking nothing but English with a friend. And I taught them simple songs to help them have a fun way to practice the English language. They always said "colleague-ers" instead of "colleagues," but no matter how hard I tried, I was never able to get them to change their pronunciation of this word.

Chinese teachers usually spend the entire class time telling the students what they need to study or memorize as they sit there quietly trying to absorb it all. I began to break up the hour and a half class time into twenty-minute segments, changing from one thing to another so that they did not have time to get bored and fall asleep. One of my twenty-minute segments consisted of finding an interesting article on the Internet, having Ralph make enough copies of the article at his office for each student, and asking several students to read a paragraph aloud. In this way, I could help them with words they had trouble speaking. They seemed to enjoy this as it not only helped them practice their English speaking and comprehension, but gave them a glimpse of life in the U.S. I would then ask the students questions on these news items and try to get them to think outside the box. One such news item involved a murder, so I asked what they thought should be done to punish the murderer. Their quick answer was, "Kill him!" which was the usual response whenever there was a murder in China. Then I asked them, "What if the murderer was mentally ill or it was self-defense?" This made them stop and think in a way they would never have done before. They loved being able to take these papers with them. I asked other questions also, and the best and most eager responses came when I asked how they would change the educational system in China. They all had ideas about that which they were very willing to share and could not speak fast enough on this. The biggest complaint was the testing system, which determined which ones could go on with their education or had to stop and "go to work." Only the best were rewarded with further educational opportunities. The second was that they never really learned what they were memorizing for the testing since they had to be ready to start memorizing the material for the next test.

These kids were under so much pressure to succeed since so much money was being spent on their education, and their futures depended on it. The days of "cradle to grave government care" were long over. The competitiveness they constantly endured was of major concern to them. Since there was no heat in the dorms in the winter, they had to study under their quilts with a flashlight in order to stay warm, often into the late hours of the night. Sometimes they would come to class with frostbite.

My class was not mandatory, but they came as often as their schedules would allow, and I usually had between forty and sixty people each session. Since I was there on a volunteer basis and was only there once or twice a week, I did not grade them, although I found that they graded me and learned from Bonnie and Michael that I was receiving good marks.

In spite of all the pressures of college life and the less than comfortable living conditions, these kids were so innocent and lacked the sophistication that most kids their age in the U.S. possess. If they told you they loved you, they meant it with all their heart. It was easy to quickly become very fond of them. They would think a fun time was taking a walk along the river with their girlfriend or boyfriend on a sunny day. One boy told me he loved going home to his village where the skies were blue and he could climb a tree and play his flute. He was twenty years old. Not many kids that age in the U.S. or any western country would think that was a fun time. Of course, they also had their parties where much beer was consumed, but most of them soon realized that they couldn't afford to party often because too much depended on their grades.

Each American holiday gave me an opportunity to tell how and why we celebrated these events. They were very eager to learn about our festivals. On Thanksgiving, I showed them a picture of a cooked turkey, pointing out to them that there was no head or feet on this bird as is done in China. They asked, "Why not?" I replied that we did not think these parts of the bird looked attractive. They immediately cried out, "But those are the best parts!" At Christmas, I told them Christians celebrate this day as the birth of Jesus but many nonbelievers also celebrated Christmas because it was a fun and festive time of year. I had to be careful not to inject my own religious beliefs and only answered their specific questions about Christianity. Every school and organization has a Communist Party secretary, and I am sure I was monitored closely. I had a few Bibles at home but would wait until I was asked for one and have that student come to our apartment to get it.

I asked Janet Holliday at the AEP offices in Columbus if she could find a way to contact Voice of America and ask them if they could send any tapes or other learning materials for the students. Soon a box with materials for learning to speak English arrived. The teachers and students alike were very appreciative and could hardly believe these things were free. Janet also got permission from AEP to give several magazine subscriptions to us to pass on to the students. I finally learned to keep the magazines in the classroom before passing them on to the teachers, because if I didn't, they would be put in a "library," and I discovered only the teachers had access to that room. Go figure! I guess there was just too much information about life in a free society in those magazines or possibly there was some criticism of Chinese policy.

Soon I was asked to go to the middle and elementary schools to speak and maybe help them learn some English. A friend, who was the Communist Party secretary at a very poor school, once asked me to come to her school at 3:00 PM as she put it "for a class." I prepared enough material for an hour. Well, an hour passed with no sign of class being over, so I soon ran out of prepared subjects and had to conjure up some improvisational material.

Finally the class was over due to the fact that it was National Children's Day and they were having an assembly in celebration. I was then taken into the huge, packed auditorium and handed a red scarf to wear—just like the ones the students were wearing. Soon after the opening ceremony, I was asked to go on stage and "sing a song." I'm thinking, "Okay, what am I going to do now?" I sang. For some reason, a song with motions popped into my head—"In a Cabin in a Wood, Little Old Man by the Window Stood." As I sang, and not too well either, I did the motions with my hands, and I must say it was well received and applauded long and loudly. Then I was asked to teach this song to a few handpicked children and sing it again with them. After this, I was taken to observe other school activities and then ate dinner in a room with the teachers. Next came pictures with several classes, and I finally said I had to leave. It was now 8:00 PM and some classes were still in session. I got home about 9:00 PM totally exhausted but wiser concerning the time I would agree to devote to school visits.

I was also approached by several people who wanted either themselves or their child to come to our apartment to practice their English. They began bringing family members and other friends with them. Sometimes I had eight to ten people show up on a given day. It was a total exercise for my mind as I tried to understand their English and make my own understandable for them. I had my "regulars," and one of them was a teacher who was very inquisitive about everything. This required my explaining things to her constantly in simple English that she could understand. She especially wanted to learn as much about America as she could. I think this was because her grandfather lived in the U.S. He had fought for the Kuomintang Army during the revolution and had abandoned his wife and family to go to Taiwan when the Communists won the war. This was not an uncommon thing during that time, as many families were abandoned when the men who fought for the Nationalists fled mainland China. He eventually made it to the U.S. and remarried. Her grandfather had recently contacted his son, her father, and tried to make amends. Her father was still angry, though, and would not reconcile with his father. So her questions went on and on about the U.S. and they were mostly about daily life here. She said her dream was to come to America. Once she said, "I heard that in America people's garbage is picked up and carried away." I told her that was true, and she was completely amazed. In Nanyang, most people would just throw their garbage outside their doors and let the goats or rats or other animals take care of its disposal. One day, I showed her a Bounty paper towel, but I could not convince her it was indeed paper. She insisted that it was cloth. Having had some experience with their paper products, I could understand her disbelief completely. She was my most faithful and persistent "student" and was with me to the end of our stay in China.

Added to the school visits and in-home students were the occasions where I was invited somewhere not realizing that I would be called upon to speak. I was discovering that in China, you quickly learned to speak in public at a moment's notice and would be expected to continue to talk as long as you would or could, especially if you were not charging a fee. At that time, any westerner who could be found was invited to attend functions and was asked to speak—and/or sing—and we all did so for at least an hour or two without ever understanding where our ability to do this came from, especially for so long a time. We talked about life in the U.S., our travels through China, what foods we liked best, the school system in our country, and any subject that came to mind. They just wanted us up in front and talking, not seeming to care what we said as long as we kept a steady stream of words coming out of our mouths. Of course, we finally figured out that only about 30 percent of the people listening intently to us understood much of what we were saying, so that made it a little easier.

Jean at NIT

Jean at a middle school in Nanyang

Jean at the oil field school

Jean visiting school on Children's Day (note red scarves)

NIT—Student Dormitory

NIT students who came to our first apt. for hamburger/ hotdog dinner

NIT students in Luoyang

Venturing Out

I finally reached the point where I felt I could venture out by myself on the streets near our apartment to do some vegetable shopping. I still could speak virtually no Chinese and was very apprehensive at first. The street I watched from our bedroom window was lined with vendors, usually women, displaying their potatoes, celery, carrots, onions, tomatoes, cabbages, and other vegetables either in their tricycle carts or on the ground. Some also had eggs, which were put into thin plastic bags for carrying home. So I gathered up my courage and went down to do my first street shopping alone.

I walked along the street and surveyed the produce until I made up my mind where and what to buy. I would point to what I wanted, and they would give me a plastic bag to put the amount of the chosen vegetable into. Then they would use a handheld scale and weigh the bag for the kilogram weight. Nothing was priced by amount, only weight. They would always tell me the cost—in Chinese, of course—and I would just nod my head, hold out my yuan, and they would take the correct amount of money, giving me change if necessary. This method of shopping frustrated Linda and Scott since part of the shopping process was to bargain your head off at the street markets. Well, I didn't have this ability, and the food was so cheap by American standards that I felt I was already getting a great bargain. Besides, these people were struggling to make a living in a city with a bad economy, and I admired their work ethic. Only once in the entire time we lived there did I ever feel I had been cheated, and that was when I held up the yuan I had and a woman took an amount, then took some more, and then took more. I figured there's one such person in every group, but that was the first and last time she had an opportunity to do that again.

Eventually, I chose my favorite vendors and usually just went to them if they had what I was looking for. My confidence in my ability to function in our new home was increasing every time I pushed myself to overcome any fears and to adapt to new ways of doing things. There were days when I didn't want to venture out because I just didn't want to deal with all the staring and attention, but there were also days where I didn't mind it at all and just smiled and laughed with them. If I heard someone call out "lao wai" (foreigner), I would just answer back with one of the few Chinese words I knew, "Meiguo ren" (American), which sometimes embarrassed them that I understood what they had said. Occasionally, they would rub their small noses, which meant "long nose," another word for us foreigners. I was definitely quite a sight for these people who had never seen a westerner, or at least a woman westerner, before. I'm sure I gave them much material for conversation those days.

Upon returning to the apartment, I always washed the produce in water with the detergent "White Cat," which had been developed for washing vegetables and dishes. Since everything was grown in soil using manure for fertilization or had been exposed to the pollution in the city, I had been advised this was necessary. I kept this rule the whole time we lived there, although after a year or so, I did come to believe that Americans are way too rigid in many of our food and sanitation regulations.

As I went in and out of the apartment, I noticed that the people who lived across the hall from us were littering the hallway with their garbage. Sometimes they would take it to the garbage chute but not bother to toss it in. Gum wrappers and other trash were dropped on the dirty, dusty concrete steps. Once we even had to dodge their vomit, which they never bothered to clean up. When Eric's wife, Zhou (Jo), came to visit us, she spent a morning with a hose trying to clean the hallway and steps. Then she went to our neighbor and asked the woman if she liked the way the hallway looked. She said she did, so Zhou asked her if she would like to help in keeping it clean. She quickly said, "No, I have to take care of my baby and don't have time!" No multitasking for her! I was just becoming aware of the Chinese characteristic of only being concerned with their personal living space. Anything outside of that did not concern them much.

Our First Visit Home and Our First Wedding and Honeymoon

In August, I returned home to help our daughter Sarah finish her wedding preparations. Ralph couldn't take that much time off work, so he stayed in China until two weeks before the wedding. When I first got home, I remember looking out at the streets of Columbus, Ohio, from an AEP office and marveling at how clean they were. The sky was blue, the air was fresh, and there were hardly any people on the streets. Oh, what a lovely place Columbus was!

But I couldn't spend too much time enjoying the beauty and normalcy of things here since there was much to do and we had to get busy. Besides taking care of all things related to the wedding, I went to see all my doctors and our dentist to make sure I was medically sound in the hopes of preventing my needing medical care in China. It was definitely a whirlwind of activity, which included a bridal shower, shopping for the cake and favors, making the favors, and finding a dress for me to wear. We accomplished a lot in a short time, and finally, the big day arrived. It was a beautiful wedding at Dublin Presbyterian Church, and a friend told me later she thought it was the most perfect wedding she had ever seen. The following reception was the great party they had hoped it would be—good food, great music, and lots of dancing. Everyone seemed to enjoy themselves thoroughly.

The day after the wedding, Sarah and Patrick boarded the plane with us for a honeymoon in China. It was their first time flying business class and a treat for them. Since they didn't have time to go to Nanyang, we stayed in Beijing at the Great Wall Sheraton, our usual five-star hotel. The night we landed, we checked in, and, as tradition demanded, we walked across the street to the Hard Rock Café for some "close to American fare."

In Beijing, there are several historical places to visit, and we had chosen to tour the Great Wall, the Forbidden City, the Summer Palace, the Temple of Heaven, and Tiananmen Square.

The Great Wall of China was our first destination. The next morning, we headed to the site of the Great Wall that is called Mutianyu (moo tee ahn' yu) which is about forty-five minutes away from Beijing. It was not only their first visit to the Great Wall but ours also. It was also our first education about the history of what is called the Great Wall and learned that it was begun by the first emperor Qin (chin) and was built using rammed earth in the flatlands and stones in the mountains—the following dynasties normally used stone and bricks. The purpose of the Wall was to protect China from invasions from the north. This section was mostly restored, but there are sections that are not and are not officially open to the public. However, Ralph, Eric, and Glenn once went to one such site called Simitai (sim'uh tie) and were able to pay a young man from a nearby village to take them up to the wall and walk/climb on it—dangerous, yes, but the challenge was too great to resist.

We had a beautiful day—perfect for being able to walk along the top of this wall for several miles and absorb the wonder of such an amazing construction having been built by manual labor so long ago. Upon seeing the steep and forbidding mountaintops of the Mutianyu site, we could not imagine how the building materials were brought up to the top. Neither could we understand how any invaders were able to get over these mountains, let alone overtake the soldiers living on and manning such a monumental barrier.

The wall was wide enough in some places for four horses to walk side by side upon it. We learned that the smoke signals used to warn of impending invasions could be seen in Beijing.

After we had spent the entire morning and part of the afternoon on the Wall, we headed back to Beijing, stopping on the way for a McDonald's hamburger—the tasty treat most Americans seem to crave soon after arriving in China. This was our first visit to a McDonald's during their stay. We managed another visit to a McDonald's in the city of Beijing while they were there because you can only eat so much Chinese food before you start wanting a taste of home. McDonald's and KFCs are all over Beijing and are loved by the Chinese as well as westerners. I wish tour guides would realize this and plan a stop at one of them for westerners after the tour has had a few days of nothing but Chinese food.

That evening, we took them to a German restaurant named Schillers, which was not far from the hotel. It was a favorite place for all western foreigners staying in that area of Beijing. There were business cards and money from many countries decorating the walls. It was a fun place to spend an evening, especially since we could sit outside as we enjoyed some good German food.

We spent the remaining days touring the following ancient historical places:

Forbidden City—this city is also called the Imperial City and is the walled-in palace where the emperors lived with their families, concubines, eunuchs, servants, and all those who served the emperor and the court in any capacity. We did not have a tour guide since we could read the captions at all the buildings within the city and didn't want to commit ourselves to more time than necessary or the cost of a guide. It is a huge place that seems to go on forever—building after building, courtyard after courtyard. At that time, they had not repainted the structures, and the pollution of Beijing had taken its toll. However, you could still get a sense of the grandeur and intrigues that had once taken place within these walls. I heard later that before the 2008 Olympics came to

Beijing, the renovation to restore and repaint the Forbidden City was completed.

Temple of Heaven—the temple where the emperors of the Ming and Qing dynasties went to pray to heaven and make sacrifices for good harvests. It was built during the Ming Dynasty between 1406 and 1420. The ancient Chinese believed heaven to be round like a dome, and so the Temple of Heaven was built as a round structure made entirely of wood without the use of any nails. The Echo Wall, which surrounds the Imperial Vault, is so named because of its acoustical abilities. If you whisper something on one side of the wall, it can be heard from the other. Sarah and Patrick tried this and found it to be true.

Some additional information on the Temple of Heaven was told to us by Eric. At the end of the war between the Kuomintang and the Communist Party in China, it became apparent that the Communists were in a position to win the war when they reached Beijing. The members of the Kuomintang, including Eric's mother and father, were holed up in the Temple of Heaven as the Communist soldiers surrounded them. Trees were cut down on one side of the temple, and airplanes were brought in to take them out of Beijing to Taiwan. Eric's parents were on the last plane out before the Communist soldiers were able to make it inside the temple. Since I knew his mother, I got chills when I thought about what her fate could have been if they had not been on that last plane out.

The Summer Palace—This is a gardenlike park in the typical Chinese style. It was first built in 1750 and called the Garden of Clear Ripples. The emperors spent the hot summer months there. It was totally destroyed by Anglo-French Allied Forces in 1860. The Qing Dynasty began rebuilding it in 1886 and was then called Garden of Health and Harmony as well as the Summer Palace. It also served as the summer resort for the empress dowager Cixi. It was destroyed again during the Boxer Rebellion, and restoration began again in 1903. When the Republic of China won the revolution in 1911, it was opened to the public, and after the last Qing emperor PuYi was forced to leave the palaces, it was turned into a park. We had a fun day walking through the gardens, climbing Longevity Hill to see the Buddhist temples, walking the entire length of the Long Corridor, which is beautifully painted with murals depicting stories of battles and mythological events, viewing the marble boat permanently resting on Kunming Lake, which is a manmade lake, and generally seeing as much of the park as we could. Many elderly people go there to relax and visit with friends, some of whom entertain the crowds by playing musical instruments, singing, or showing off their other talents. Although the Summer Palace was originally built for the enjoyment of the emperor only, now it is open to millions to enjoy each year.

The celebration of the *50th Anniversary of Communist Party Rule* occurred during their visit, so Beijing had been cleaned up and beautified. The beggars and transients had been banished from the city, no big trucks were allowed in the city in the daytime, and most industrial plants had stopped production so the air was clean and the skies were blue. Therefore, Sarah and Pat saw Beijing at its very best and did not get to experience the city as usual.

On October 1, the actual day of the anniversary, everyone not invited to attend the parade and other festivities was told to stay in their homes and hotels. Of course, this was done to prevent any disruption of the "glorious" anniversary of the People's Republic of China. We complied and watched it all on TV in our rooms. We watched their display of military might as jets put on an air show. We saw the jets take off on TV and then saw them as they passed by our hotel-room windows. This show was most likely not only for the pride and entertainment of the people of China but also used as a warning to the government of Taiwan.

The next day, as we toured *Tiananmen Square*, we joined the immense crowd of mostly Chinese tourists who had come to Beijing for the holiday. The entire open-air space of the huge plaza was covered with people. This square dates back to 1651 and was enlarged to its current size (one hundred acres) and paved over in 1958. The Tiananmen Gate on the north leads to the entrance of the Forbidden City. The Great Hall of the People sits on the left side of the square and the National Museum of China on the east side. On the south side is a huge gate called Zhengangmen, which, in olden days, protected the Forbidden City from direct entry. In the center is the mausoleum of Mao Zedong in which his preserved body is displayed daily for public viewing—an exhibition we did not choose to see. During our time there, Sarah and Patrick were often asked to pose with the young people who were most likely from outside of Beijing and wanted a picture of themselves with foreigners.

One evening, we had dinner in *Bei Hai Park Restaurant* where the emperors had dined long ago. The people working there were in the character and dress of ancient China which included the wearing of high platform shoes. Our friend Helen was with us and did the ordering. Most of the food was very good, but I was not fond of the texture or taste of the deer tendon—it reminded me of an unsweetened rope of gelatin with a rather funky taste. We got some good pictures of us at this famous ancient restaurant and pictures of the girl pouring tea into our cups from a copper teapot with a neck spout about three feet long. The technique used was to stand away from the table, use one hand to pour from high above the cup while not spilling a drop. It took much practice to be able to be skilled in the art of using such a teapot. After dining, drinking tea, and touring the restaurant, we decided it was time to return to the hotel. On our way out, we had to cross a bridge where an elderly man was leaning against the side of the bridge. He began rolling his hips in a circular motion as if he were winding up his rear end and I thought, "Oh, no! He's not really going to . . ." which is as far as my thought got before he let loose with the loudest and longest backside yodel I think I have ever heard. However, we were the only people who seemed to take notice of this noisy, gassy emission. Bodily functions are considered normal in China, and the Chinese don't seem to find them offensive, rude, or crude.

One night, we dined on the top floor of our hotel, which gave us a fantastic view of the city. I think this was some of the best Chinese food we had while Sarah and Pat were there. We all especially enjoyed a spicy shredded beef.

Of course, we took them to the Hongqiao Market for shopping and to introduce them to Ding, my jewelry girl. The Hongqiao Market is a huge building and sells just about anything you could imagine. On the first floor, you could buy fake watches such as Rolex, telephones, calculators, Chinese clothing, scarves, shawls, cosmetics, souvenirs, etc. The second floor sold mostly clothing and suitcases. The third floor sold jewelry and souvenirs. The fourth floor was devoted strictly to jewelry, but was a much calmer environment and a much more expensive place to buy jewelry. There is a picture of then president Bill Clinton as you ride the escalator between the second and third floors. He had visited the Hongqiao Market on one of his trips to China. Combined with all the merchandise, the insistent manner of the sales people, and the tedious bargaining process, it can be an overwhelming experience at first. We also went to the Silk Market (often called the Silk Road), which at that time was an outdoor market that sold the same type of merchandise as the Hongqiao. It just so happened that the American embassy was on the same street as the Silk Market, so we were able to see a little of the U.S. and the American flag occupying a bit of Chinese soil.

When it was time to return to the hotel, I told Sarah it was her turn to negotiate a price for the taxi. We found a driver outside his parked taxi near the embassy and approached him with our hotel card. After looking to see where we wanted to be taken, he nodded his head yes indicating he could take us there. Sarah began negotiating with him as he knew the English words for the monetary amounts. She was quite masterful in her bargaining skills and was able to get the driver so rattled that when she gave him a fairly low price, he said, "No!" and then gave us an even lower price than Sarah had said. Sarah jumped on that quickly and said, "Okay!" We all burst out laughing—even the driver, but he honored the fare he gave us and we got back to our hotel very cheaply, laughing the whole way.

All too soon, it was time for them to leave for Columbus and for us to return to Nanyang. They seemed to enjoy their experience and, we hoped, had good memories of their time in Beijing. We certainly enjoyed spending the time with them and showing them the history and culture of a country far different than the one they knew, although I think Beijing is no better a measure of the real China than New York is of the real U.S.

I never thought we would go on our kids' honeymoons, but we not only went on Sarah and Pat's in 1999 but on Amanda and Nick's also in 2001. I will tell about that honeymoon later.

1st Honeymoon—Tiananmen Square,
50th Anniversary of Communist Party Rule

1st Honeymoon—Tiananmen Square,
Building is Great Hall of the People

1st Honeymoon—The Great Wall, Mutianyu Site

1st Honeymoon—Schiller's German restaurant
near our hotel

1st Honeymoon—Tiananmen Square,
Workers (or People's) Statue

1st Honeymoon—Tiananmen Square,
Temple of Heaven

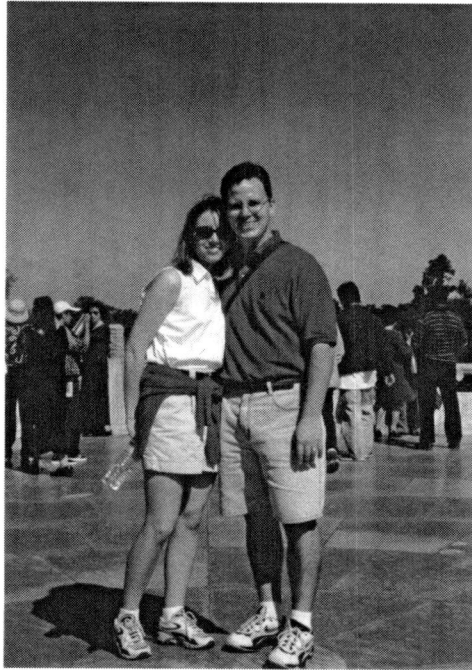

1st Honeymoon—Sarah and Patrick
at Tiananmen Square

1st Honeymoon—Young man asked to
take a picture with them

1st Honeymoon—Beijing, Forbidden City

1st Honeymoon—Great Wall, Mutianyu Site

Unwelcome Roommates

After the lovely wedding and happy honeymoon, the "real" China was waiting for us in Nanyang. We had hoped for many visitors to come to see us in China. But the first ones that showed up were not given an invitation. As time went on, the rats that I watched running around the empty lot beneath our living room window began coming into the outside hallway and up the stairs of our building. Soon we heard them running across the ceiling. Eventually, they finally made it into the apartment. We would be watching TV and see them running across the floor, or worse yet, our feet. One day I opened the linen drawer in the kitchen and took out a dish towel. It felt funny so I shook it. To my surprise, a rat fell out onto the floor and ran under the stove. These "guests" had come with the intention of staying.

We tried local remedies to get rid of them, such as sheets of sticky paper and did catch one using this method. When I found it, it was firmly stuck to the paper but was still alive. Mr. Bai, our driver, came to my rescue and asked for a chopstick. This was what he used to kill it; how he did it, I don't know because I didn't watch. They use chopsticks for lots of things, but I never suspected rat execution to be to be one of them.

Soon after this episode, we did some traveling, and when we got back, the rats had gotten back in, built nests in our closets and had eaten all our houseplants. I was getting to the point of not knowing how much more I could stand. The next time we went back to the U.S. for a visit, I returned to China armed with D-Con to put around the apartment. This proved somewhat effective as we saw fewer rats for a while—until the day I found one bleeding on my bed. This was the rat that got us our new apartment. AEP finally decided we did not need to be living with rats or in bed with them, so they gave us permission to begin looking for a new apartment. As with all things in China, it was a much slower process than it would have been in the States. So we continued to live in this apartment for quite a while, battling the rodent problem, the dust and dirt, and the incessant horn blowing on the street outside our bedroom window.

Very Welcome Houseguests

After our daughter Amanda graduated from West Virginia University Institute of Technology in 2000 as a bona fide mechanical engineer, she returned to China with us after our Christmas visit home. Not being used to such living conditions as we had then, she had a rather difficult time dealing with the rats and many of the other inconveniences.

I think the evening we spent at the Nanyang Institute of Technology, our local university, was one of the longest evenings of her life. We were invited to dinner by the head of the Language Department, but first we were taken to a room for the obligatory meeting prior to dining when having "important guests." It was January and a very bitterly cold one at that. We sat on one side of the room and he and the other people from the university sat on the other. By means of translators, we began talking. There was not a drop of heat in that room, and after sitting and talking for about twenty minutes, the cold from the concrete floor had crept into our feet and our legs. After about an hour of this, we were so cold we were almost shaking. Finally, they signaled this part of the evening was over, and we were given a walking tour of the campus—in the wind and rain, no less. Of course, they had on their long johns and probably many more layers of clothing where we only had on normal winter clothing and a coat. By the time we sat down to dinner, we were so cold we were beginning to feel sick.

But we endured, the room was heated, and in the end, the dinner was very pleasant.

Before she left to return home, she was able to attend a Chinese wedding, visit the ancient capital city of Kaifeng, have her picture taken in traditional Chinese clothing at a local park, tour the famous Shaolin Temple, and survive a minor car wreck with no injuries. She also experienced the drinking ritual at several banquets and celebrations but never acquired a taste for the baijiu. I think by the time she left, she was probably looking forward getting back to living a "normal" existence, never suspecting at the time that she would be returning a couple of years later to honeymoon in China.

Another guest came in October when the weather was starting to improve. This was my friend Bonnie Turner. We knew Bonnie through her daughter Terri and son-in-law John Lester, who had worked with Ralph in West Virginia. Once when I was visiting with Terri, she told me her mother was so happy to learn that someone she knew was going to live in China. Bonnie was going on a tour of China and wanted to visit us when her tour was over. We said she was definitely welcome to come to visit us. She had taught about China as a schoolteacher and wanted to dip her feet into the Yellow River, from which it was thought that Chinese civilization had begun. She said she wanted to "immerse herself in the culture," and I thought that Nanyang was definitely the place to do just that.

She landed at the airport in Zhengzhou, and Mr. Bai drove me up the Suicide Highway to meet her. That was her first private car ride in China—what an initiation she had as we alternately zoomed along through countryside and villages at great speed, braking often to avoid other vehicles, animals, and people. We stopped at a roadside "rest area" (and I use that term very loosely) to use the restroom, and she was treated to her first outdoor toilet in China. These were concrete buildings with the squatter commodes or else those with just a trough over which to squat. The stench was staggering, especially if these toilets were filled almost to the brim with human waste. Sometimes a stream of water was running though these outhouses to take the waste out into the fields where the crops grew. There was a water spigot outside for washing hands, but there was no soap. Her immersion into the culture was in full swing.

I have to say that during the time she spent with us, Bonnie was a real trooper and possessed a sense of humor and adaptability that is so necessary to living in China. Whenever one of our dimly lit lamps suddenly went out and I would move the chair against the plug to turn it back on, Bonnie would just laugh and giggle at my "fixing technique." She also had a great laugh over my use of binoculars to survey the merchandise of each of the vegetable vendors on the street outside our bedroom window. I told her this was how I knew where to shop to get what I needed that day. We were having a little lull in the rat infestation at that time, so she didn't have to deal with that like Amanda did. But at the many dinners she attended during her visit, she refused to ever drink the "rocket fuel" and survived her entire time in China without doing so.

I took her to the university with me each week, and she got to experience a Chinese classroom. Of course, she fell in love with the kids, and they loved her back, so it was no surprise to me that she was asked to come back to Nanyang to teach at the university. Although she was retired from teaching, she readily agreed to come back to China to teach these kids and to further her cultural immersion.

One day, Bonnie said, "Let's go for a walk." At first I told her that I was told not to do this because it was dangerous. She replied, "You are a prisoner in your own home!" I thought, "Well, how true!" After all, I went down on the street around our apartment to do vegetable shopping all the time, and I certainly wasn't afraid of the people there. Also, after riding around Nanyang for so long, I knew certain areas of the city well and how to get around. So off we went to the street that sold handmade baskets. It was so nice to be able to get out of the apartment on days other than Saturdays when Scott or Linda took me shopping. We passed the cows and goats on the street that were there as a source of fresh milk and the cows and goats that were waiting to be killed and eaten. We passed restaurants, markets selling vegetables, baskets, plastic wares, and other necessities of life. Other than giving the people quite a sight to behold, we survived our walk without incident and returned to the apartment intact. This was the first step in my getting back some of the independence I had lost after moving to China.

When it was time for Bonnie to return home, I went with her to Beijing to catch her flight. We had a couple of days to shop before she left for the U.S. I introduced her to Ding, "my pearl girl," and the overwhelming Hongqiao Market shopping experience. She would return in late summer to teach at NIT and begin her own China adventure.

1st Apt.—Bonnie and Jean hanging out

Amanda's visit to Nanyang—Night at NIT University

Amanda's Visit to Nanyang—Night at NIT University

New Apartment

Eric began the search for a new apartment almost immediately after we were given the go-ahead. After a few months of looking, he finally found a new complex being built just a couple of blocks up the street from our current place. Then he began negotiations for an agreeable price for three apartments—one for him, one for us, and a third for Helen Sun from Beijing who would come once a month for a week or so to attend to accounting duties. We finally got to the point in the negotiations where we found three apartments on the second floor of a building still under construction. The only drawback was that the third apartment was already owned by someone else. It was agreed that we would pay the complex management for the apartment and they would pay the current owner his price.

At this point, the apartments were nothing but concrete walls and floors. We hired a renovator from Zhengzhou, who was familiar with better construction methods than what was done in our current place. And finally, the work began—and went on and on. After what seemed forever, we were finally ready to move in. We hired some men with the two-wheeled carts, and Scott negotiated a price for their services to move us up the street. The total charge was thirty-five yuan—about five dollars at that time. To earn this, the men climbed the forty steps to Eric's apartment, sixty steps to our apartment, and eighty steps to Helen's apartment to carry our refrigerators, furniture, boxes of clothes, dishes, personal items, etc., down to their carts. Then they had to pull all this stuff two long blocks up the street, carry everything up to the second floor and place it where we wanted it. It took them three trips, and although I had not had a say in the negotiations, I thought they were grossly underpaid.

There was one glitch in our moving experience. Our and Eric's apartments were finished before the apartment for Helen was done. As the renovations went on with that apartment, the previous owner would show up occasionally and tear up the floors, or other work in progress. We finally found out that the management of the complex had not paid the owner for the apartment and he was taking his revenge by destroying as much as he could of the renovations. We were all caught in the middle of this mess, and Eric confronted him one day when he came to do more damage. Eric's mother was visiting at the time, and for some reason, the man horribly insulted her. Eric's mother handled the situation like the lady she was by asking him how he could call himself a human being after saying such things. But this insult to his mother was not to be borne lightly by Eric, and they got into quite a verbal battle which we were afraid might become physical. This did not happen, though, and the man finally left. Eric then went to straighten things out with the management, who eventually paid the previous owner his money, and the apartment was finished in due time. Business as usual in China.

Compared to the old apartment, and in the opinion of most people in the area, we were living in luxury. Of course, this was one of the places the "people with money" were moving. I would not attempt to tell you we were actually living according to U.S. standards, but it was 99.9 percent better than our old digs. Instead of an old couple who lived in a storage shed being our gatekeeper, we now had uniformed young men who kept a close eye on all those coming and going. We also had a parking garage, clean streets, and even some grassy areas with not one rat occupying the premises—at least none that I ever saw. There was no street noise, and the garbage was routinely picked up and carried away.

Double-paned windows had been installed, which kept out the dust and pollution. We had two bedrooms, a computer/dressing room, two bathrooms, a kitchen/dining room, and a living room. The floors in the dining room and hallway were wood laminate, tile in the kitchen and bathroom, and carpet in the bedrooms and living room. The closet doors actually stayed in place and moved easily, we had heat and water almost all the time, and we had a glassed-in porch for storage. We had a front door with a peephole, but because robberies were the biggest crime in Nanyang at that time, we also installed a heavy-metal security door in addition to this one. The only thing we didn't do was have bars put over the windows because (1) we felt fairly safe here with the guards at the gate, (2) the security door was in place, (3) we were on the second floor, and (4) we didn't want to feel as if we were in prison. Our lack of foresight about this matter proved to be a mistake, which I will tell about later.

This apartment became a sort of "refuge" for many of our western friends, as their apartments at the various schools were very basic and utilitarian. They could escape the dirt, pollution, and noise of Nanyang here and also enjoy western food. When they came to visit us, they could even lie on a carpeted floor as we watched movies on DVDs (pirated if bought in China or not if brought back from the States), sporting events (usually soccer or rugby), or other programming (tapes of American TV shows that our friends Rose Bridgeman and David Rice so faithfully sent to us). Sometimes we had them over for brunch—which usually lasted most of the day. Other times we would have them for lunch or dinner. They said our apartment gave them a feeling of being back in a familiar world with the added bonus of food that was a taste of home. We too immensely enjoyed these times of visiting and eating together. While we loved our Chinese friends, it was good to be able to spend time with people who shared a cultural bond even if we were not all from the same countries.

2nd Apt.—Inside gates of complex

2nd Apt.—Construction, Glenn inspecting progress

2nd Apt.—Moving in,—master bedroom

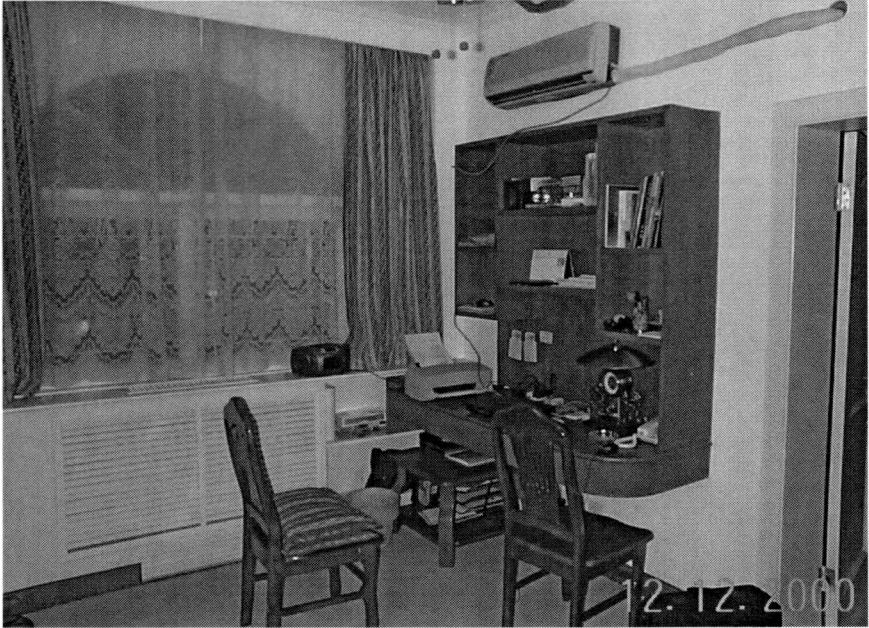

2nd Apt.—Moving in,—computer/dressing Room

2nd Apt.—Moving in, kitchen

2nd Apt.—Moving in, dining room (2)

2nd Apt.—Moving in, dining room

2nd Apt.—Moving in, living room (2)

2nd Apt.—Moving in, living room

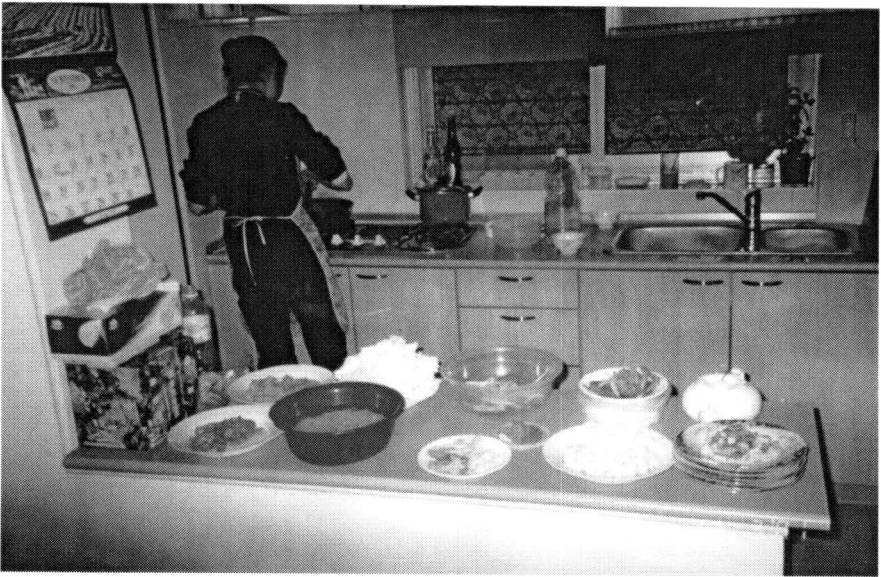
2nd Apt.—Xiao Hang cooking dinner

Henan Province

Let me tell you about "our" province. The Henan Province (not to be confused with Hunan Province) is located in central China and has a five-thousand-year history. It is also the most heavily populated province with approximately one hundred million people. Our city of Nanyang is located at the southern end of the province. The Yellow River runs through the northern part of this province and is considered the cradle of Chinese civilization. The name of this province comes from He (meaning river) and Nan (meaning south), resulting in Henan, meaning "south of the river." In ancient times, Henan was also a very prosperous part of China and is home to three of the earliest capital cities of China before China became a united country: Luoyang (loy yahng'), Kaifeng (ky fung') and Anyang (ahn yahng'). Now, however, it is one of the poorest areas of China due to the natural resources being used up by the huge population and the many wars fought there so long ago. Also, most of the industry and development is in the eastern and southern part of the country and in the larger cities.

Henan Province is an agricultural one, with wheat and sesame being the major crops followed by rice, cotton, and maize. Coal production and electricity generation are the major industries of the province. The majority of the people are Han (hahn) Chinese (99 percent) and the Hui (whay) make up approximately 1 percent.

Although we did see some changes during our four and a half years there, this is a very traditional part of China with things done pretty much as they always have been done.

Traveling

Traveling inside and outside of Henan was accomplished by bus, train, automobile, and airplane. Most people traveling-long distances used the trains. This was mostly due to the fact that it was the fastest and cheapest way to travel. Also, the trains ran on time—always. The cost depended on which type of ticket you bought:

1. The cheapest being for just a seat, which in holiday times or during the times for college students going to and from home could be so crowded people sometimes died from hot, crushing conditions
2. A medium-priced ticket was for a hard bed, which was in a car with several rows of beds bunk-bed style, usually three beds high
3. The most expensive ticket was for a first class compartment, sometimes known as a soft bed, which was a four-bunk compartment shared by people whom you might or might not know

Buses were normally used if you only had to travel a distance of about three to four hours and were an economical way to travel. However, these buses were usually very crowded, and there was the risk of getting one of the kamikaze drivers to boot.

At that time, cars were only owned by government offices and companies. The general population could not afford to own automobiles—motor scooters were the status symbol then. Now, that has changed, and private ownership of cars is becoming more common, which is most evident in the larger cities. Ralph's company, NGLE, owned a few automobiles, and we were able to travel in this manner while being chauffeured by a driver. These drivers had a great responsibility as they were accountable for the safety of their passengers and could easily lose their jobs if they were involved in an accident. Whenever Mr. Bai or Mr. Bian avoided an accident by their skillful driving and watchfulness, we always gave them a pat on the back and said "good job!" Only once did I almost lose my life while being driven by Mr. Bai. We were going through a roundabout and a big truck came barreling through without yielding the right-of-way. If it hadn't been for Mr. Bai's superb driving skills, the truck would have slammed into the side of the car where I was sitting. I don't know how Mr. Bai was able to avoid our getting hit, but he did manage it by the tiniest of margins. I had never seen him so angry, and I know he was using the foulest language he knew, even though I couldn't understand a word he said. To this day, I am wary of roundabouts as I remember how close I came to dying in one in China.

Traveling by air was the best way to go if you could afford it and if you were traveling long distances. We were fortunate to have a small local airport in Nanyang, but we only had flights departing and arriving two days a week. Although it was small in size, it was huge in security. We were put through more security measures at this airport than we were in Beijing before 9/11. Of course, since the employees were less busy than their Beijing counterparts, they had more time to devote to their jobs. I was amused by their attentiveness to duty in making sure we foreigners in Nanyang were obeying all the rules since there were so few of us at the time.

Unless we were lucky to be traveling on a day when there was a scheduled flight at the local airport, we had to be driven by car to the Zhengzhou airport to catch a flight. This meant enduring a ride on the Suicide Highway. Once I was used to the erratic driving practices of everyone using this road and learned to "let the driver do his job," I actually took some naps or observed the rural culture during the ride.

It was not uncommon to see dead livestock in the road as we zoomed along. If not tied up in the villages, they sometimes wandered into the road, which was a certain death sentence as the traffic was swift and constant. Once, I didn't go to Zhengzhou when Ralph went to a meeting there and he said he is fairly certain he saw a dead human in the road. This was probably the body of a mentally ill person because the mentally ill were usually beggars who roamed about with their few possessions tied in a bundle they carried on their backs. We would see them walking along the highway fairly often. By wandering around this way, the odds of their survival were slim, and I am assuming one of them met his fate that day. No one stopped, and the traffic kept flying over and around him. Had he been someone with a family nearby, the family would have donned white cloths tied around their heads and would have been out stopping traffic to beg for money to bury him. White, not black, is the color of mourning in China.

If we did travel by car, Linda or Scott often kept the driver or us entertained with stories and other conversation. Linda told us of how her father knew how important it was for her to get an education, but she never told me how many of her brothers and sisters were also educated. At least one sister grew up during the Cultural Revolution when the schools were closed, so I know she was not educated. Sometimes, other people in the village derided her father for his belief in education by asking, "If everyone rides in the car, who will drive the car?" He prophetically replied, "My children will ride in the car and your children will drive it." She said she had to live at the school she attended when she was small because it was too far from her village to walk back and forth each day. She told us how she would go home on weekends and how her mother gave her sweet potatoes to take back for her to eat during the week. She said, during lunchtime, she would run to a nearby village, ask a woman there to cook a potato for her, and then run back to the school before classes resumed. She said the meals at the school cost very little, but they didn't have enough money to pay for them. She ended this story by wistfully saying, "And I was just a little girl . . ." I could tell by the way she said that how truly poor she had been and what a difficult time it was for her to get her education. Later, she would go on to become a nurse in traditional Chinese medicine, go to Singapore to study Western nursing methods, then was able to learn English well enough on her own to become a translator and land a job with NGLE. On Sundays, sometimes we would go shopping or to a local park called Liberation Park to watch the people fly kites. This was because Sundays seemed to be the day that relatives and other people from her village would come to ask for money. Although she always gave them money because she said she remembered how difficult life was in the countryside, she tried to avoid them if possible.

AIDS in Henan

In my opinion, the worst thing to happen to Henan Province in modern times was the arrival of AIDS. China was forced to recognize that AIDS had invaded their country in the 1990s when a contaminated blood supply was given to people in central Henan. This contamination was the result of inadequate sterilization procedures. Consequently, the devastation of this disease was begun, and, in many villages, almost the entire population is HIV positive. Many of these villages are so remote that the sick cannot travel to hospitals for treatments. There is also the stigma of being HIV-positive, and many have been refused entry to hospitals and schools because of the fear of catching this disease from them. At that time, the government was not admitting to having homosexuals in China, so that added to the stigma of having AIDS. Henan Province is not alone in having so many people suffering from AIDS. I heard that due to much drug-trafficking, AIDS was also prevalent in the Yunnan Province, which is located in the southwestern China.

Perception of Henan People

At the time we lived there, the people of Henan Province were held in fairly low esteem by those in the more developed cities and provinces. This was due largely to their level of poverty, their dialect, their adherence to traditional ways, and the lack of development there. Another reason was the attempted cover up of the AIDS epidemic, which after it became known nationally added to the negative feelings about Henan Province. There was also the "problem" of the house churches, which are fairly numerous in Henan. Some people would say to us when we told them where we were living, "People of Henan are famous for their drinking!" I guess you could say we were considered the hillbillies of China. I have heard the people of Henan called mean, dishonest, and backward, but we quickly found that we preferred the people of Henan to those who lived in places that were more modern and prosperous.

Henan Historical Museum in Zhengzhou, outside

Henan Historical Museum in Zhengzhou, ancient
musical instruments

Henan Historical Museum in Zhengzhou, ancient
musical presentation

Henan Historical Museum in Zhengzhou, ancient
musical presentation

Henan Historical Museum in Zhengzhou, ancient
musical presentation

Wheat Crop

Wheat Crop, tossed in road for cars to
run over to thresh

Tanghe Village near Nanyang

Tanghe Village near Nanyang (2)

Tanghe Village near Nanyang (3)

Tanghe Village near Nanyang (4)

Henan Province, noodles at noodle factory

Commonly used broom; also used to sweep streets

Luoyang, Longmen Grottoes

Luoyang, Longmen Grottoes (2)

Luoyang, Longmen Grottoes (3)

Luoyang, Longmen Grottoes damaged during Cultural
Revolution

Luoyang, Longmen Grottoes damaged
during Cultural Revolution

Ancient architecture style

Re-enactment of ancient trial at nearby town

Re-enactment of ancient trial at nearby town (2)

3. 4. 2000

School in Xixia partly funded by AEP

Hydroelectric power plant near Xixia in Henan Province

Our City of Nanyang

Our city of Nanyang is considered a small city by Chinese standards. We only had about a million people living there. I was also informed that in China, a city is larger than the county, which lies within the city—another flip-flop on what I considered logical. We were located in the southern end of the Henan Province about three hours southwest from our provincial capital of Zhengzhou and not far from the Hubei Province to the south. However small it was considered to be, it was teeming with the business of daily living.

Most of the major historical sites of early Chinese history are in Northern Henan, but there are a few places of interest in or near Nanyang. Most visitors are proudly taken to these two places in the city:

1. The Hut Temple of an ancient wise man named Zhuge Liang who was also a military strategist, scholar, inventor and statesman
2. A replica of a seismograph invented by another ancient named Zhang Heng who was known as a scholar, astronomer, inventor, and mathematician among many other attributes.

A little northwest of Nanyang is the county of Zhenping (jen ping') which has a huge jade market. We used to go there occasionally to shop the large variety of sculptures and jewelry available in the numerous shops. Traveling northwest from Zhenping takes you to Xixia (she'shah) where dinosaur eggs were found and are seen on display there. Also in Xixia is a school that AEP's contributions helped build. The AEP logo is displayed prominently on top of the building. Eric took us there once, and we were certainly given the royal treatment as we were the representatives of AEP that day.

Street Life

Nanyang was a busy place. There was constant motion of all kinds going on from dawn to late at night. When we first arrived, there was little to no order in the movement of traffic. It just seemed that cars, motor scooters, bicycles, and pedestrians went where they wanted, when they wanted, and however they wanted. This seemed to work for them, but it terrified anyone from western countries where we have strict laws concerning driving in lanes, obeying posted signs, and most of all, staying on the roads and off sidewalks. I had to get used to the rhythm of the streets before I ventured out for walks. The people walking and the bicyclers all seemed to have a certain speed at which they moved. I always seemed to walk much faster than they did and would usually pass them. I did learn to be alert at all times if I wanted to get to my destination without incident. I managed to avoid getting hit by motorcycles, bicycles, and taxis, getting spit upon due to the inevitable spitting habit of everyone, and even dodged getting peed upon by a naked baby boy being held by his mother. I suppose my near mishaps were due to daydreaming and not paying proper attention to my surroundings. I almost did get hit by a taxi once as I was walking on the sidewalk in a busy part of town. I wasn't as alert as I should have been to this activity until I suddenly heard a noise behind me. It was a taxi traveling on the sidewalk as the driver was trying to take a shortcut around all the traffic in the street. Luckily, I heard him and jumped out of the way before he hit me. I learned also to watch where I walked if I didn't want to step in globs of spit or animal or human waste because both children, and even some adults, and all those animals used the streets as a toilet. Babies and young children don't wear diapers because the mothers quickly learn the body language of their babies indicating when they are going to void. When the children show these signs, the mothers hold them over a toilet or away from their bodies for them to "go." Toddlers wear pants with a split bottom and no underwear, allowing them to just squat wherever they happen to be when the urge to void comes upon them. I do have to admit the sight of the little butt cheeks peeking out of their pants is really cute. Besides tradition playing a big part of the no-diaper policy, there is the expense of diapers. Also, the problem of disposing of all those diapers in a country with such a huge population would be monumental.

The streets were very noisy as the drivers of automobiles and trucks blew their horns constantly as they drove about the city. I don't think they could have driven automobiles if they couldn't blow those horns. Added to this was the cacophony of firecrackers going off all the time. Firecrackers were used in celebrations of the opening of new stores, moving into a new home, weddings, or just about anything you could think of to celebrate. With so many people in the city, the noise of these instruments of celebration was a constant in our lives.

In the early morning, there was the rush of automobiles getting their occupants to work, the taxis looking for fares, the street vendors setting up their carts or arranging merchandise on the street, groups of people busy at Tai Chi, old people exercising by walking backward, children walking to schools, and employees lined up outside restaurants or other businesses appearing to listen intently to whomever was standing in front of them lecturing. I never did find out what they were telling the employees, but I suppose it had something to do with either their evaluation or procedural plan for the day.

Then as the day wore on, there were the shoppers out to get fresh foods for lunch, the inevitable bargaining for anything being bought or sold, children going home for lunch, and restaurants preparing for the lunch crowd, which included killing any animals they were going to cook that day. Walking right before lunchtime or dinnertime was not for the faint of heart. Animals were being slaughtered in the street in front of the restaurant that was going to serve those animals for the next meal. You might see several goats lying on the sidewalk with their throats cut, heads hanging over the edge of the sidewalk, bleeding out into the street. Or you might see a cow being butchered, or a little lamb tied up outside a restaurant, bleating pitifully. Once as I was taking a walk with one of my students, I saw a cow ahead of us getting ready to have its throat cut. I said, "Let's cross the street." Of course, he wanted to know why, and I told him I didn't want to see the cow being killed. He immediately said, "But we like to eat them!" I told him I liked to eat them too but didn't want to see them kill the cow. I don't think he understood that at all since he had grown up in Nanyang and saw this as a normal practice. I grew up in a rural area too where there were designated "butchering days," but we preserved our meats to last for a while and did not have to have "fresh meat" on a daily basis.

After lunch, there was a lull in the activities because of the long nap most of the Chinese took after eating. Whenever we had people in the apartment to fix something such as the air conditioner/ heaters, they left promptly at noon and did not return until 3:00 PM. It seems that this eating and sleeping on time is so traditionally ingrained in them that they cannot function well without doing either. The people at Ralph's office were convinced to work an American work-day schedule by having NGLE pay for their lunch at the hotel. But as soon as they finished eating, they rushed back to the office to either play ping pong or take a much needed nap. Ralph said that if he had a meeting soon after lunch, some people would just naturally doze off during the meeting. The street vendors would usually drape a cloth over their wares and would lay their head on the cart to nap. After a new large supermarket named Three Doves Supermarket (numbers are frequently used in the naming of things) opened up within a twenty-minute walk of our new apartment, I did my shopping at this time since there was less street activity after lunchtime and before 3:00 PM.

Many times, I would pass people who were just lying down on the sidewalk sleeping and even some who were napping on piles of coal. I used to say they could sleep on anything when the urge came over them.

By 3:00 PM, the activity of daily life was back into the rhythm of the streets. People were shopping, visiting, working, playing games such as mahjong, chess, and cards, and going about their daily business. This would continue throughout the afternoon, with a break for dinner, and then continuing until everyone decided to go home to sleep. Most of their waking hours are spent in the streets, as it makes them feel comfortable to be surrounded by the mass of humanity. One of my students, who came to practice English on Saturdays, went to the U.S. to visit a relative. Upon his return, he told me that he had been very lonely as no one was outside or came to visit. I tried to explain that Americans have made their houses very comfortable and like to enjoy being in their homes. Also, I told him they probably didn't visit as they were either busy with their schedules or else thought they were being considerate of allowing him to visit his relatives without their interference. Being invited to someone's home instead of-stopping by seemed to be a new concept to the Chinese. Many times in Nanyang, I would have unexpected guests who appeared to have a two-hour visitation limit. Once they had accomplished what they came to do or this time span was over, they were up and out the door as unexpectedly as they had arrived.

Taxis

The only industries who were making money at the time we arrived were the alcohol manufacturers and the cigarette companies. People were doing whatever they could to survive. Many who had lost jobs due to the poor economy had begun driving the three-wheeled taxis, either motorized or pedal-powered, to make a living. This upset the drivers of the licensed yellow minivan taxis to no end. They said they had to pay fees to run their taxis as opposed to the owners of the tricycles, who did not. Eventually, the owners of the decrepit yellow vans decided they were going to caravan to the capital city of Zhengzhou to make their protest. Ralph and I just laughed and said, "Let them go—not one of them will make the trip due to their condition." Unfortunately for them, they were stopped at the city limits by the local police at the orders of the party officials, and a fight erupted between the drivers and the police. Fighting with the police was common since no one respected them because of the corruption among their ranks. Besides, they had no guns, so that fear factor was missing. At any rate, the "protest caravan" was prevented, but soon the tricycles were banned—only to be quickly replaced by motorcycle "taxis" roaming the streets looking for customers.

Ah, those yellow taxis! Although they were a decrepit fleet of automotive nightmares, they were a necessity in helping to keep the city going. Having been outlawed in the bigger, more prosperous cities, they had been banished to the smaller, more rural areas where there were poorer people—and fewer tourists. These vehicles were already worn out, polluting dirty pieces of machinery when they reached places such as Nanyang. However, the upside was that you could haul whatever you wanted in them if it would fit. During the time our friend Frosty, an AEP engineer, was still in Nanyang, he bought a large table to use as his desk and transported it back to his apartment in one of these. A couple of years later, our friend Michael Zargarov, who was teaching at the university, was riding his bicycle one day and was surprised to see a goat get out of a taxi, closely followed by two men. I laughingly told Michael the men must have been the translators for the goat. In all probability, the goat was probably going home for dinner—as the main course, that is. Many of these taxis did not have proper floorboards but only had heavy cardboard in place. Often you could see the streets where the cardboard had moved. After becoming used to riding in these pieced-together and repeatedly repaired pieces of machinery, I didn't think twice about riding in one—as opposed to the hesitation I had upon my arrival.

The drivers, however, seemed to come in two varieties: those who masterfully maneuvered these taxis around the city and those who were the kamikaze drivers. The latter would scare the pants off the bravest and most stoic of passengers as they seemed hell bent on driving as fast as possible, weaving about and dodging all things in their way and only slamming on the brakes when absolutely necessary. With those drivers you just held your breath and held on to anything that was stabilized in the taxi, all the while hoping you got out of there alive.

I eventually figured out a system to regain more of my independence by using these taxis. I asked Linda to type out the names of the places I normally went in both English and Chinese characters and then my return address in both Chinese and English. All I had to do then was present the card to the taxi driver, pointing out the place I wanted to go, and he had no problem knowing where I wanted him to take me. I also had her do a menu of things I liked to eat so that I could meet western friends for lunch and order by pointing at the items we wanted.

A couple of years later, when a group of English teachers from many countries arrived, we would sometimes meet for lunch at various restaurants. After eating and visiting together, we all took taxis back to our respective apartments. One day, after one of these lunches, I hailed a taxi and proceeded to get into the back seat. Well, the driver was absolutely thrilled to have one of us lao wai (laow' wye), which was the word for foreigners, in his taxi. He would look at me in the mirror, laugh, and say things to me in Chinese. Of course, I couldn't understand his words, but I could understand his glee at his good fortune. Finally, he stopped the taxi and patted the front seat beside him. I got out and got back in beside him—all to his immense delight. He was completely overjoyed and could hardly contain himself. He continued talking to me and laughing. I just sat there and smiled at him. Then he saw some friends of his working on one of the broken-down taxis and immediately pulled in beside them to show off his "prize."

They were not nearly as impressed with me as he was, but then they had the critical job of fixing their vehicle so they could earn more money that day. We reached our apartment complex and he was still laughing. I got out and handed him the proper fare plus a little for a tip. He tried to refuse anything, but I insisted he take it, and finally he accepted the money. What a story he had to tell that evening—a lao wai passenger and a tip to boot! I was happy too because I had just made a person's day and all I had had to do was just exist and be friendly.

I rode all over Nanyang in this manner with no problem until the day Eric's wife Zhou Zhen (jo jin') and I got in the back seat of a taxi with Zhou in the opposite seat facing me. There was a metal partition between the passenger's and driver's side. We proceeded to move along until we came to a street where the traffic was moving slowly—mostly due to pedestrians crossing the street at the wrong place. I wasn't paying any attention to the driver, but he was evidently paying too much attention to me, Zhou said later. Suddenly, the driver braked sharply, throwing Zhou into my seat and me into the metal partition. Zhou began trying to pull me to my feet, and I was trying to help her in her efforts. Neither of us could understand why I couldn't get up—then I realized my necklace was caught in the metal partition. We freed the necklace, and she and I exited the taxi to learn that the driver had hit a pedestrian!—all because Zhou said he had been watching me in the mirror. Of course, the boy who was hit was crying and milking the situation for all it was worth, but we had hardly been moving, and I doubted he was hurt very badly. The cops were there by then, along with a huge crowd that had formed to watch the goings on. This was the first street drama where I was a participant, and I'm thinking, "What do we do now?" Zhou said we would get another taxi, and I asked her whether we should pay the driver. She emphatically said no to that, and we left the scene of the accident without a word to anyone. Since there were so few foreigners in the city at that time, I'm sure we wouldn't have been hard to find if the police had needed us, but neither Ralph nor I ever heard from them about the incident. Zhou and I arrived home, and other than some stiffness and a few sore places in my shoulders, I was fine. I couldn't convince Ralph's coworkers, though. They made calls and visits and sent fruit and flowers as if I had been severely injured.

Bicycles and Scooters

There was a multitude of bicyclers during the daytime in Nanyang. Unlike the motor vehicles, they all moved at the same rhythm and speed, with no one disrupting the orderly movement of the herd. Of all the vehicles in the city, it seemed as if they observed more safety rules than any other method of transportation—including walking.

It was amazing to me to see up to three or four people riding peacefully on one bicycle. With one person doing the pedaling, the passengers were free to engage in whatever activity they wished including reading, sleeping, eating, or singing joyously. A bicycle helmet rule was nowhere to be found as young children often stood on the back carrier with their arms around their mother or father who was pedaling. Sometimes they only had their hands on the head of the person pedaling, and I never saw one of them fall off or even seem to lose their balance.

Dogs and cats often rode in the bicycle baskets, enjoying the passing scenery with all the smugness of their special status and seemed to enjoy the passing scenery. A common sight was ten or more chickens tied by their legs to the handlebars or attached to the back carrier as they made their way to a market.

There were motor scooters and, eventually, motorcycles in the city. These were the alternatives to the bicycle and were status symbols to the people who could only dream of owning a car. There was a law that required the riders of these vehicles to wear helmets, but most people ignored this law as deliberately as they ignored the "no horn blowing" and "no smoking" signs.

Shopping

Just about anything you wanted to buy could be found somewhere in Nanyang; well, that is, except a hamburger. There were the large outdoor markets which mainly sold vegetables, meats, herbs, eggs, dishes, and live animals, which would be killed and butchered for you if desired. There were also sections that were comprised of the same type of merchandise, such as the furniture section of town where you could buy a finished product or have your furniture made to specifications. There was the pharmaceutical area, where you could buy both traditional and modern medicines, such as amoxicillin, although it was questionable if the amoxicillin was the same strength as what could be bought in the U.S. Many markets catered to those shopping for clothing and others where you could find hardware or construction materials for the constant renovating that was being done. If we needed something in particular, we just asked Eric, Linda, or Scott, and one of them was sure to know where to go or could find out where to go. Fruit and vegetable stands were everywhere as well as small shops that sold alcoholic products and cigarettes. If you wanted to buy fabric or have clothes tailor made, there were shops for that. And then there were the large government-owned department stores interspersed throughout the city. Most of the shops were small and provided services such as beauty shops, framing shops, the bread/cake/pastry shops, and shops that sold the necessities for funerals. Eventually, privately owned shops became more numerous and competed successfully with the government owned shops.

One of the best places to find electronics, DVDs (mostly pirated copies), cookware, and just about any item sold in the city was the market at the train station. Eric would often take us there on Sunday afternoons, and we would usually come home with a treasure or two, including our DVD player, a toaster oven and, of all things, an electric pizza pan.

We even had Avon shops in Nanyang—no Avon lady, but actual shops where you could buy real Avon products. We didn't buy anything to do with body lotions, though, as there was a whitening agent in the creams. Chinese women avoided getting much sun at all and would use these whitening creams and wear big hats and small silk capes in the summer to avoid darkening their skin. I think one reason they did this was to avoid looking like the peasants who worked outside in the fields with little or no protection from the sun and, of course, had much darker skin than that of the city folk. I found it sad that people who moved from a village to the city just a short time earlier were already looking down their noses on the farmers, who were not only already at the bottom of the economic chain but also considered socially inadequate as well. Once I was asked by the students in my class at the university if I liked the farmers. I quickly answered, "Yes, I like the farmers! If we don't have farmers, we don't eat!" I could tell by their faces that this was not the expected response, but I said many things that were outside the box of common thought. There were some, though, who appreciated the clean air and peacefulness of country life.

I would be remiss if I didn't add the "street shops" to the business life of the city. If a bicycle broke down, there was someone set up on the street nearby to repair it. There were people with sewing machines set up on the street to make or repair clothing; likewise with shoes or belts. Just about anything you wanted repaired could be done right there on the street. You could also get a haircut on the street, buy fresh milk from the owner of the cow or goat on the corner, buy shoes or clothing, or dine at an outdoor restaurant without ever entering a shop or store.

I had brought some egg cartons back with me on one of our visits home and began to take these when I wanted to purchase eggs since they were normally just put in a thin plastic bag. At first the street vendors were surprised at these curious things and would examine them closely. They didn't know what to do with them until I put some eggs in to demonstrate what they were for. I even allowed them to include the weight of the cartons when weighing the eggs, resulting in their making a little more money for themselves. I'm not sure if they were impressed with this practical way of carrying eggs or if they thought how strange Americans were that we had to have something like this—just for eggs.

About a year and a half after we arrived, items began appearing in the supermarkets like Dove candy, M&M's, Oreo cookies, Pringles, and Lays potato chips, Coca Cola, Magi dry soup mixes, and saltine crackers that went by the brand name of Pacific. Soon these were regularly stocked items and easy to find. Life was improving, and so was the economy of the city. I found a sausage that resembled Polish sausage and bought that often, but I usually gave money to Xiao Hang each month to do the meat shopping and get any vegetables she wanted to cook. She always gave me a detailed list of what she had bought and how much it cost.

Jade Market

Near Nanyang, there was a mountain—some called it a hill—named Dushan (du' shahn) where jade was mined. We had a jade market in Nanyang where the pieces of jade were carved into beautiful sculptures. You could buy these sculptures pre-made or have them made to order. The jade from this mountain came in many colors—dark green, light green, white, brown, black, and some blue, red, and purple. We were told that the more colors a sculpture had in it, the more valuable it was. Over the years, I learned to tell where in China different types of jade came from by its color. We were told that the best jade came from Burma, but the jade from Nanyang was considered a good-quality jade. The hardness of jade was one of the criteria of judging the quality of this stone. Traditionally, the Chinese have prized jade above all other stones and metals. There is a Chinese saying that goes "Gold has value, but jade is invaluable." It is said to be the most noble of all gems. The Chinese believe it possesses the five essential virtues of compassion, modesty, courage, justice, and wisdom along with the other virtues of benevolence, knowledge, righteousness, virtuosity, purity, endurance, ingenuousness, morality, and music. In ancient times, kings were often buried in "suits" made of jade, and jade articles have been found in the tombs of high officials. Many young girls put a round solid jade bangle bracelet on their wrist, which they are never supposed to take off, and as they grow, it becomes impossible to do so.

Unfortunately, the jade from this mountain is playing out, so because it is becoming less plentiful, Nanyang jade is also becoming more valuable. We were given several sculptures during our stay in China, and I have displayed them all in our home.

Animals in Nanyang

Little dogs were everywhere, rummaging around looking for anything edible, most of them as dusty and dirty as the streets. I suppose they probably had homes but just wandered about during the daytime since I never saw any at night. They were very street smart and could cross the busy streets better than I could. I even watched two of them get to the middle of a street, assess the traffic situation as unwise to cross and return to the side of the street from which they had started. Then they waited until it was clear before proceeding to cross successfully. Most of the dogs that were pets were little pug-nosed dogs such as Pekingese, as that seemed to be the preferred breed. Some were excessively pampered with a red dot placed on their foreheads. Linda says a dot such as that meant the dog was dearly loved. Occasionally, I also saw this dot on some of the small children. The owners of many of the dogs would take them with them when they went on errands. Many times, they would put them in their bicycle baskets and the dogs reacted happily, much like dogs do here when they get to ride in a car or truck.

It was not common for cats to roam freely. Most that I saw were on rope leashes that were tied to something in the shops where they spent the days with their owners. They also had the dirty, dusty fur that was inevitable in the polluted air that permeated Nanyang. Xiao Hang, however, had an extremely randy male cat that was forever leaving home for weeks at a time in order to pursue his business of fathering innumerable litters of kittens. Somehow, Xiao Hang's family usually wound up with these kittens until they managed to find homes for them. I think the whole family was predisposed to a love for animals as they always had at least one dog and sometimes several cats.

The cows were ever present and were a docile bunch. Those used for milk were usually black and white and were "parked" on the street corners for accessibility. The ones that were slaughtered were a red color. I was told the red cows were the "famous Nanyang cows." I once saw a man leading one of these red cows down a street. He suddenly stopped and seemed to have a one-sided conversation with the cow. I don't know what the cow did to deserve that lecture, but it was so funny to watch him talking so seriously to the cow and the cow appearing to listen to every word. To feed so many people, you had to have a huge meat supply; and scores of cows and other animals were coming into town on a daily basis for this purpose.

The donkeys were beasts of burden and were worked hard. They pulled carts loaded with lumber, bricks, charcoal, and such. I never saw one mistreated, but I used to wonder if they ever got a day of rest. The Chinese themselves didn't seem to really have one unless it was a holiday, so I guess if their owners worked every day, so did the donkeys. Donkeys were also food sources, and there were restaurants that specialized in donkey meat.

Chickens roamed freely in empty lots and in all areas except the marketplaces—where they were caged or tied by their legs until they were sold or slaughtered. We would see bicycles loaded with chickens tied to handlebars by ropes around their legs hanging head down. I don't know how far they traveled that way, but it must not have done them much damage because that was the way almost all of them were brought into and carted all around the city. Because of the numerous chickens, eggs were in bountiful supply at all times. Most Chinese people eat lots of eggs that are either fried, scrambled, boiled in water, or those that are boiled in tea—a popular snack food in China.

And then there were the goats—small herds of them living in the city. They gave me much entertainment with their "lofty attitude." It seemed they knew everything that was going on everywhere and sat in indignant judgment of us all. When they were taken to graze in the empty lots, they would cross the streets with dignity and an assumed assurance that the vehicles would not dare hit them. They never ceased to amuse and entertain me with their superior disposition. They provided many services to the city—other than being slaughtered and eaten on a daily basis, they were also a milk supply. And they served as much needed garbage disposals throughout the city as they ate their way through the vegetables and other edibles thrown into the streets by the residents of the city.

There were sheep in Nanyang also, but I never saw them in small herds as I did the goats. I usually saw them in pairs or just one tied up outside a restaurant. I don't know where they were kept, but possibly, it was just outside the city. In the outdoor markets, I sometimes saw meat on a table with the head of a sheep or other animal below it to identify the meat.

Hospitals and Medical Care

Most Chinese people prefer the traditional medicines, which have been used for centuries, over the more modern manufactured medicines. The traditional medicines include herbal treatments, acupuncture, dietary choices, and various types of massages. They depend upon these cures for everything from a headache to malfunctions of major body organs. In today's world, many people in China may use a combination of the traditional medicines and western pharmaceuticals.

In Nanyang, we had several hospitals, and we used to visit friends who were hospitalized for various reasons. My first visit to one of these hospitals was one of utter disbelief at the unsanitary conditions found there. I wondered how anyone could enter one of these dark, dirty places of "healing" and come out alive. Upon entering the hospital, there were the inevitable globs of spit and trash all over the floors. The rooms were dingy and dark, the sheets were gray as were the doctors' "white" coats, the pillows were made of straw, the mattresses were boards with about an inch of padding, and the smell of "eau de urine" permeated the air. Relatives would come to take care of the personal needs of the patients since nurses only gave injections and changed bandages. As there was no cafeteria on the premises, the relatives would also come to cook meals for the patients in the hallways using round charcoal bricks. I suppose the smoke from the burning charcoal could account for the gray sheets and the dinginess of the walls. Of course, I was looking at things from the perspective of what we in America have learned to expect of hospitals and sanitization measures. To the people of Nanyang, these conditions were normal.

When Scott was diagnosed with TB (a common disease in developing countries), this gave everyone at NGLE a scare. We were all tested in a local clinic, which was as dismal as all the other health-care facilities in town; however, we were relieved to find that clean, disposable needles were used. The results showed that nine people in the office building tested positive, but no one was termed infectious. Thankfully, Ralph and I were negative. Many people in the office wanted Ralph to fire Scott—even those who had tested positive—and I'm sure he was definitely very afraid of losing his job. I said to one of those in favor of firing him, "You don't fire people because they are sick," which was met with much disagreement. Ralph, of course, didn't fire Scott, and we even went to see him a couple of times in the dreary hospital where he was being treated. After several weeks, Scott was declared healthy once again and was released. Having survived tuberculosis and the hospital experience, he returned to work, where at first his coworkers were leery of him. Eventually, though, things returned to normal, and he was accepted back into the fold.

Upon my getting a cold or feeling somewhat sick, everyone asked if I wanted to go get an injection. I always answered no because I had medicine at home I could take. It was not uncommon to see

116 Jean M. Life

people walking around town holding a bag up high that was filled with a liquid medicine which was attached to a tube with a needle going into their arm. They had gone to get an injection and either they didn't want to stay for the bag to empty its contents or they had been released to administer the medication themselves. I used to pray that I would survive my stay in China without needing medical care in one of those hospitals.

Beauty Shops

Beauty shops were all over the place in Nanyang, some operating out on the streets and some inside the little shops. The only question I had was which were the cleanest? Upon the advice of a friend, I went to the shop of her choice to get a haircut. The young guy working that day had dyed his hair red and was dressed in the "uniform" of many kids in the U.S. his age—spiked hair, tight pants, and tee shirt. He was from South China, and I was his very first American customer. The shop looked clean enough by Nanyang standards, and so I was willing to proceed with my haircut.

He took me to a shop chair and indicated he wanted me to sit there. Then to my surprise, he took some shampoo and began working it into my dry hair, applying the shampoo several times until he had worked up a massive amount of lather. He continued this for several minutes and then began thumping my head and massaging my temples. This was only one type of massage to be had in China, and I wasn't enjoying it. The worst part was yet to come—he had one of those long fingernails on his little finger that many people there have, which seemed to be used as a tool for cleaning out whatever orifice is in need of it. He stuck that fingernail into my ears and dug around a little. Eeeeww! I thought about bolting out of there right then, but I didn't, and soon he leaned the chair back to the sink and began rinsing all that lather out of my hair.

The next step was to go to his station where he began cutting my hair. I don't know if the comb he used was sterilized or not, but my guess is it was not. In all the time I lived in China and no matter where I got my hair cut, I never saw them use a solution for cleaning their combs. Anyway, I got a fairly decent cut—just like almost all the Chinese women my age had. I have to admit, though, the cut looked better on them than on me. So my first foray into the beauty world of Nanyang had been accomplished, and I lived to tell the tale.

My next visit to this shop was not so satisfactory. After the usual dry-hair shampooing and rinsing, I let them convince me to get a hot-oil treatment. Since I had never had one before, I had no idea what to expect. When it was over, I realized they were going to leave the oil in my hair. My hair looked like a greasy wet rag, but they said I was beautiful and took pictures to display in their shop album—the first American to be in the album and an ugly one at that. I got in the car with Linda, and Mr. Bai turned around to look at me. He immediately burst out laughing, and I would say he laughed with good reason. As soon as I got home, I washed my hair—I had to shampoo three times to get all the oil out. That was my first and last hot oil treatment in China, or anywhere else for that matter.

Nanyang, city and river on a fairly clear day

Nanyang, two-wheeled carts used for
carrying heavy loads

Nanyang, cat guarding liquor and beer supply in a shop

Nanyang, large outdoor market called center market

Nanyang, center market (2)

Nanyang, center market (3)

Nanyang, center market (4)

Nanyang, center market (5)

Nanyang, center market (6)

Nanyang, center market (7)

Nanyang, fruit and vegetable market

Treating Xiao Hang (on right) and her sister to
their first trip to Beijing by first-class train cabins

Nanyang, Bonnie exiting a yellow taxi

A Cleaning Up of Nanyang

There were several mayors and vice mayors of Nanyang during our stay. We frequently had dinners with them due to Ralph's position in the city and the province. As we do here with our politicians, everyone complained about them and often with justification. The usual opinions were they either "did nothing" or "did the wrong things."

Eventually, a mayor was sent to Nanyang who began a campaign to modernize and clean up the city. The people did not like him because he was forcing change, and change comes hard. He pushed and pulled the populace into a cleaner and more modern existence by changing the way things had always been done. Trash cans started appearing on the streets—an object normally avoided like the plague, as the people were accustomed to throwing trash and garbage on the streets instead. A camera was installed at one intersection that took pictures of people who ran red lights, and also a huge sign was erected that posted the license plate numbers of the offenders. Policemen were stationed all along the main streets to make sure that motorcyclists wore helmets and drivers obeyed all the new traffic regulations. Barriers were put up to designate lanes for bicycles only to use. Traffic and pedestrians began waiting for lights to change before they proceeded on their way. As gratifying as it was for us westerners to see an end to the chaos, this was the way it was being done on the main streets only.

Elsewhere, everything remained the normal free-for-all, as everyone went in all directions with no orderly manner of procedure.

The mayor also made a great effort in trying to get the street vendors off the sidewalks and into shops or in alleyways. This was not very successful though, because as soon as one street became vendor-free, people began setting up business again on a different street with their mobile carts full of produce, meat, or other wares.

I also heard that plans were in the making to rid the city of the yellow taxis, and this eventually became a reality. Smaller green cars soon replaced the minivans. These newer taxis were very clean but smaller in size. They would only hold five or six people each, whereas the minivans would hold as many as could be crammed into one. The newer taxis cost a little more, but I thought the increase in price was well worth the comfort they afforded.

The mayor also began a major cleanup of the street along the river, which included a renovation of the Jade Market. The most resistance he got was when he wanted to demolish the homes of people who had lived near the river for ages. Angry as the people were at this, they did lose their homes and had to move to newer apartments. This is the pattern in all of China—when government decides it is going to do something, the people have no say in the matter, giving question to the name of "The *People's* Republic of China." In the end, it was definitely an improvement in the appearance of the city, as it got rid of some of the older, more unattractive buildings.

I think this entire cleanup was mostly done in preparation of the Jade and Traditional Medicine festivals that were to be held in Nanyang that summer. The closer it got to holding these festivals, which were being held at the same time, the more excitement was running through the city. The students called this event "One Meeting, Two Festivals." The students at NIT and the Teachers' College (also known as the Normal School) were involved with organizing and performing in a show that was going to include not only the local population but famous singing and performing stars from other parts of China. I don't think the students had much choice in whether they participated or not, but as it turned out, it was quite an extravaganza, and we, along with the other foreigners in the city, were given royal treatment with a dinner beforehand and great seats at the show. I had to laugh at Roy Wilson, from London, who said we Nanyang westerners were most likely being used as the "useful idiots" for the spectacle. Also in attendance were some people from Thailand who were in town on business and were seated behind us and a white-haired foreigner accompanied by his wife and baby who was said to be the Russian ambassador. Whether he was actually the ambassador or not is questionable, since Nanyang was definitely not a major city that would attract such a dignitary. At any rate, they were escorted to favored-status seats by the city officials. The city was at its best in appearance, and the performances exceeded expectations. It was quite a coup for a small city such as Nanyang, and I'm sure it gave the city and the politicians the all-important "good face."

School System

Chinese students attend school 270 days a year, with each school day running from 7:30 AM to about 5:30 PM. They do get a two—to three-hour break in the middle, and if they live in a town or city, they return home for that time. If the school is fairly far from the students' homes, they will walk to and from school even if it is a distance of several miles. Some may live at the school in dormitories, especially if they are attending a private boarding school.

The educational system encompasses preschool, kindergarten, primary, secondary, junior high, senior high, vocational, technical, and agricultural schools, along with the regular colleges and universities. While there is a mandatory nine-year education for all children in China, in the rural areas, sometimes only the brightest children are sent to school at all. Many of these village children do not continue their education beyond elementary or middle school. Advancing their education in the colleges and universities to the next level depends on the scores of the many tests they are given throughout their college life. Only the best and brightest are allowed to continue. Our young cook, Xiao Hang, had two years of college in Xian, but she did not test well enough to further her education. Her sister did not have any college at all and was termed "just a worker" by Xiao Hang.

The government has total control of the educational system. There is a Communist Party secretary at each school, and I made sure my foreign teacher friends knew this so that they would be wary of criticizing the government and its policies and also not proselytizing with their religious beliefs.

There is total discipline in the schools. Sometimes the students sit at their desks with their arms folded on top of the desk, and if they want to raise their hands, they must do so by leaving their elbows on the desktop. The teachers often have sixty or more students in their class, and they cannot afford to allow things to get out of control. Hitting or slapping students in the face was not uncommon, and demeaning a student who was behaving badly was a method used frequently. Colleges use the "shame board" to help maintain discipline by using humiliation to punish students. These boards are placed in prominent places so that fellow students and the teachers can see the names of those who committed an infraction of the rules. These methods to maintain discipline have always been used, and they don't seem to know any other way to handle misbehavior. Although we westerners find these methods rather harsh, I did talk to one young man who had been to college in the U.S. He was critical of the teachers he had here because he said that they were not strict enough. I guess it's all in what you are used to.

Teachers are given great respect in China—almost to the point of the teachers having more power over the student than parents. Of course, the parents realize the unrelenting competition in every aspect of life in China and want their child to be pushed to the limit so they can be "first in the class." The position of "first" is all-important to the Chinese way of life. With so many people, only the best in whatever they do will succeed. Unfortunately, corruption is a way of life for the Chinese people and is even found in the school system. Bribing teachers with money or gifts often works quite well in getting children accepted into certain schools and how much attention the children receive. There are horror stories of teachers actually mistreating or else ignoring the children whose parents did not give bribes.

Memorization is the teaching method used most. A teacher can tell a child what he/she must study that night (which usually means "memorize" the material) and the student will do exactly that, no matter how much memorization is required, staying up all night if necessary. A parent may tell the child to go to sleep and the child may agree, but if he has not mastered the memorization and is a motivated student, he will get up after his parents have gone to sleep to study. Sometimes the teacher may have given the wrong book or material to study and the test is given on something entirely different that what was studied. This can happen to a whole college class, and I knew of one such instance where it did. It makes one wonder if the wrong material was purposely given so that only the very best students will qualify for further college study. This is frustrating to the western mind, as the unfairness of such a system is totally opposite to our way of thinking.

Each class has a monitor, whose job is to keep everyone in the class in line. They are like the "boss of the class" and may even be in charge of helping to keep the classroom neat and as clean as possible. I have seen some who are very good at the job and are admired by their fellow students. I have also seen some who are overzealous and some who were not well-suited to being a monitor. One girl especially was very uncomfortable in her monitoring position. She would tell me she didn't know how to be in charge of the class and asked what she could do to assert herself. These kids thought I had all the answers to everything! I told her to make herself appear to be confident and then that would convince the other students that she knew what she was doing and they would follow her leadership. However, she was unable to follow this advice as her nature was very gentle. This same girl asked me to telephone her at her home over the Spring Festival holidays. I did so, although she wasn't at home when I called. When she returned to college, she excitedly told me that she received the message that I had called. By her reaction, I reasoned that it must have given her great status that a foreigner had thought her important enough to telephone her. Sometimes it takes so little effort to make someone happy.

All students must meet for early morning exercises each day. About once a week, they also raise the flag, sing patriotic songs, and hear a lecture before classes. Boarding schools have classes every day of the week, with evening classes also being held, as well as Sunday morning classes; but they usually do not have any on Sunday afternoons. They get a four—or five-day break at the end of the month. Public schools have pretty much the same schedule as a boarding school but do not have classes on Sunday or night classes. About the time students reach middle school, their "free time" is usually occupied by being tutored in their studies or by music lessons or other constructive activity such as training in the martial arts. The parents are eager to push them to the limit to be ahead of the others. One reason for this is that the more successful the child becomes, the better life the parents will have in their old age. One friend who had a middle-school son asked me what she should do about her son wanting to play video games. I advised her to allow him about a half hour a day to play the games and give him some rest from his studies and musical practice. She was very unsure of this advice, and I doubt she followed it lest another student get ahead of him at school or in his music lessons.

Given the fact that there are so few jobs for so many people, many children in the villages don't go to school at all since they would still be doing the same type of work as they would if money had been spent on any education. Young girls are often sent to a factory far from home to do menial labor at low wages. We saw this when we visited a silk rug factory not too far from Nanyang. Several small girls sat among the older girls and women at the looms tying the knots which made the rugs. The price of the rugs depended on how many knots were used in the rug, so small fingers were needed to get between the rows of the silk threads. I heard there was a village near Nanyang where these rugs were made in homes and could be bought very cheaply. The silk rugs made in such places were bought by people all over the world—some were in the markets in Nanyang that sold them, some were marked for shipment to the Middle East and marked as "Persian rugs." I saw a European man buying them in Nanyang at the hotel. I was given one of these rugs as a gift, and while I do love it, I often think of the children or poor people who worked so hard for so little benefit in order for me to enjoy its beauty in my home.

Freshman college students must report to college about two weeks after the upperclassmen have begun their classes. The freshmen will be assigned to a group of fellow students with a soldier from the People's Liberation Army as their leader. They do a form of basic training for two to three weeks, then most return home to celebrate the week-long celebration of the National Day holiday, which falls on October 1—that is, they will do so if they are fortunate enough to be able to purchase a ticket for train or bus travel. After this holiday, they will return to the college and begin their studies and their campus life.

Because parents have poured so much hard-earned money into the whole process of giving their children an education, the pressure for the students to succeed is enormous. I heard that students would sometimes commit suicide because of this pressure and their inability to perform as desired. Two instances I personally knew of concerning this pressure and the money worries that go with it are as follows:

One of my favorite students named Erica, who regularly attended my classes and often came to our apartment to visit, was suddenly absent. I asked some of the other students about her but was met with, "We'll talk about that later." I asked repeatedly about Erica, but I could never get them to tell me where she was. Then one day, another girl student named Vicky was visiting me in our apartment, and I asked once again about Erica. She finally said, "Erica died." I was shocked and asked what happened. She hesitated a moment before saying, "She went to the bathroom, lost her breath, and died." That was all I could get her to say. It is typical of the Chinese not to want to tell you bad news, and I think the students were trying to protect me from being sad. I did later find out that Erica's mother had died and her father had remarried. According to the students who were telling me this, the stepsiblings were very intelligent and were succeeding at their educations more so than Erica. I wondered if this was more than Erica could bear, and she may have taken her own life because of the shame she felt. This is something I will never know for sure, but I do know how serious she was about her education.

Another student I had come to like very much told me about how hard his parents were working in order to pay for his education. His name was Jerry, and he had a dream to go to New Zealand to study. Ralph and I offered to lend him the money, but after a few weeks, he became silent about New Zealand. I finally asked him if he still hoped to go there. He said he couldn't go because his mother was very sick and he had to take care of her. He then asked us if we would lend him the money we had offered him to go to New Zealand in order for his mother to have an operation. We agreed to do this, and he was very grateful but also humble in accepting it—it was the first time I ever saw anyone actually wring their hands. We told him we knew he would try to pay the money back, but if in the end he could not do so, we hoped he would help someone else sometime later in his life. A few weeks later, he told me his mother had become ill because she had stopped taking her medicine. She hadn't bought her medicine because she wanted to use the money for his education. He said that she was doing well now since they insisted she buy the needed medications. Soon afterward, Ralph and I returned to the U.S. for good, and we lost track of him. Unfortunately, Jerry was one of the students who failed to pass the next test necessary for him to continue college and had to leave school to find a job. He contacted Bonnie when he couldn't reach us and told her he had been trying to get back to Nanyang to return the money to us but he couldn't leave his job at the time. So it is my hope that he used the money wisely and will indeed pay this favor forward at some point in his life.

College students are constantly busy. During my time there, they used the phrase "24/7" all the time to describe their plight of nonstop study and duties. They would often doze off in class from their perpetual mental and/or physical exhaustion. Few American students could handle the stress these kids deal with. Chinese students were amazed at the schedule of American schools—school bus transportation, the shorter day at school, no rest time after lunch, band or sports after school (either practice or games), students with jobs after school, others who go home to study or to their various classes (music, karate, gymnastics, dance, etc.), and that students actually have cars to drive. They were appalled to learn that some teenagers in the U.S. have babies while they are in school and unmarried. They asked, "Why would they do that when they have so much to do?" Although many had some college education, there were often not enough jobs for even these kids, and sometimes they found questionable employment in remote areas of the country without guarantee of pay. Since money concerns were constantly a part of their lives, the question they asked me most was, "Could I find a job in America?"

In our poor province, there was a boy who tested so well on his math scores that he was admitted to the highest ranked university in Beijing. Sadly, though, his family was too poor to pay the tuition costs. Our friend Eric from Taiwan learned of this situation and sent word to the boy's family to come to see him. The father and son rode their bicycles the whole way from their village to Nanyang, which was many hours away from their home. When they met with Eric, he informed them that his own son and daughter would not have to worry about the cost of their education as he could pay for theirs. Then he told them he wanted to help this talented young man with his education and would pay the tuition for him if the boy's family could pay for other costs. The boy and his father gratefully accepted Eric's offer. This young man had the dream of a lifetime come true all because of the kindness of a stranger. I often wonder what became of him and if he still keeps in touch with Eric.

Religion

*F*ollowing the revolution in 1949, when the atheist Communist Party came to power, all religions were looked upon as backward and were banned. All places of worship of all religions were closed, destroyed, or used for secular purposes. But when Mao's repressive Cultural Revolution ended in the late 1970s, a more tolerant attitude toward religion emerged. It seemed many Chinese turned back to religion to have something to believe in when the "cradle to grave" system failed. However, most of the college-aged kids I met in China did not have any religious beliefs because they said they "can't see the god." Of course, they had not had any religious training their whole lives. It could also have to do with their parents growing up during the Cultural Revolution when all religions were banned. Their parents probably had no religious beliefs either to pass on to the children.

As long as the Communist government can monitor each religious group and keep an eye on them, there is religious freedom in China. The house churches you sometimes read about in the news are mostly in Henan Province, particularly Nanyang County, and are deemed illegal by the government because they meet in secret. The name "house churches" comes from the fact that they meet in homes since they cannot own property due to being illegal. If found, they are persecuted severely by government officials who use cruel and inhumane means of punishment such as long prison sentences, forced labor, beatings, starvation, electrical shocks, etc. The house churches refuse to belong to the "legal" Christian churches organized by the Three-Self Patriotic Movement, which can be and are monitored by the government. The legal churches might also be members of the China Christian Council. I never knew of any house churches while living in Nanyang, but I am sure that was most likely because of the secrecy of their meetings.

The religions now recognized by the government in China are Buddhism, Taoism, Islam, Judaism, and Christianity (both Catholicism and Protestantism.)

Ancestor Worship

Before other religions began to emerge, most of the ancient Chinese believed in ancestor worship. They did not believe that the dead became like gods but believed that there was an afterlife much like the earthly life where the dead family members could influence the life of the living. They would put items such as food, fake paper money, clothes, shoes, and other necessities into the coffins not only to assure the ancestors a comfortable existence in the afterlife but also to keep their goodwill.

After the funeral, they usually continued the offerings on home altars. These offerings consisted of things necessary to provide the ancestors with a good start in the next life—wine, spirit money, fruits and vegetables and other favorite foods, but no meat because that was associated with killing. They would do this and bow before the altar for forty-nine days, after which time this ancestor was worshipped along with all the other family ancestors. This form of "worship" was done to honor the ancestors and to ask the ancestors to continue to look after their well-being. Mostly, though, it was done out of filial piety.

It was believed that the ancestors then dwelt in commemorative tablets made of wood. Incense was burned before these tablets every day with the food offerings given two times a month. Many Chinese still continue some or all of these practices.

Confucianism

Confucianism began in the fifth century BCE and came from the teachings of a sage and social philosopher named Confucius. He taught ethical, moral, and social values. Confucianism was actually a philosophy on how society should live and was not considered a religion until after the death of Confucius. I found it interesting that one of the quotes of Confucius was this: "*What you do not want others to do to you, do not do to others*"—very similar to the Golden Rule Jesus taught.

Confucianism has had a major influence on the Chinese people and was made the official state culture during the Han Dynasty, which ruled from 206 BCE to 220 CE. It remained the official social and political system until it was rejected in 1912 when the Republic of China came to power. It was again rejected when the People's Republic of China began its rule. However, it is now becoming popular again. Confucianism has not only influenced the culture and history of China but also that of all of East Asia.

Taoism

Taoism (most often pronounced Daoism) appeared about the same time as Confucianism and also had an influence on all of East Asia. Tao (or Dao) means "path" or "way." Taoism was a philosophy that emphasized nature and taught harmony with nature and other people. Taoists believe in living a simple life and calmly meditating on all things concerned with the universe. This is where the yin-yang symbol comes from, which represents the balance of opposites in the universe. Compassion, moderation, and humility are called the three jewels of the Tao. During the four and a half years we lived in China, we only toured one Taoist temple and I met only one person who was an active believer in Taoism. However, the emphasis Taoism placed on health and longevity is still a big part of modern Chinese thought.

Buddhism

Monks from India brought Buddhism to China in the first century BCE, and both the Confucians and the Taoists opposed this religious movement. It was not until the late fifth century and the early sixth century CE that the form of Buddhism known as Mahayana took hold. Eventually, Buddhism became integrated with the beliefs of Confucianism and Taoism and contributed greatly to the culture and thinking of the Chinese people. Buddhism is mainly known for its belief in reincarnation.

When it came to visiting Buddhist temples, we became "templed out" after the first three and came to the realization that once we had seen about a half dozen of them, we had pretty much seen them all. The temples were often located on top of a mountain that sometimes meant we not only had to climb the mountain, but also the numerous steps of the temple.

Probably the most famous of these temples to those of us in the western world is the Shaolin Temple in our province of Henan. It is located near Zhengzhou, which is the capital of the province. The Shaolin Temple is also a monastery. There the monks teach martial arts, including Kung Fu, which they pronounce as Gong Fu. We went to this temple when our daughter Amanda was visiting us after her graduation from college, and we saw several of the monks and the young boys who were studying there. We also were fortunate to see a martial arts demonstration. However, when Amanda tried to take a picture of some of the monks dressed in their yellow robes, she was told photos were not allowed—although they were being filmed for a television documentary at the same time. She wasn't interfering with the filming and wasn't even anywhere near them. So I guess it depends on who's doing the photographing . . . go figure.

During our travels throughout China, visiting a Buddhist temple was usually included in the agenda. The routine was the same—the believers would burn incense and bow and pray to the statues. Each Buddha had its own "specialty," such as fertility, healing, prosperity, etc. We usually traveled with at least three people who would practice this worshipful ritual, and thus spent much time observing the statues and the praying to the Buddha we were viewing. Once, after a long day of sightseeing, I was anxious to get back to the hotel to get some rest before dinner. Much to my disappointment, I had to forget my longed-for rest as I soon learned that we were going to visit yet another temple. It was a lovely, sunny day, and since we were not in a city with polluted air, I decided that I would prefer to sit on the steps outside of the temple than join the group going inside. Ralph went on with the others, only to return about five minutes later with a Muslim friend who was traveling with us. Neither of us could verbally communicate very well, but we knew certain words that sufficed. We also found each other amusing. He and Ralph sat down on the steps beside me, and he smiled and said, "Same God," pointing to him and me. I smiled back and answered, "Yes." I guess he thought I didn't go in the temple because of religious reasons, but it was mainly because I had done this routine so many times that I was frankly bored with it.

Islam

The Muslims came to China by way of the Silk Road to engage in trade. The Silk Road actually consisted of several trade routes joining China to other parts of Asia and the Mediterranean area. It was not officially called the Silk Road until the nineteenth century when a German by the name of von Richthofen used the term. The Muslims arrived about twenty years after the death of Muhammad and have been there for centuries. Over the years, they generally assimilated into the Chinese culture. In our city, most of the Muslims are typically Chinese in appearance and dress. Some of the men wear the small white caps, but never did I see the women wearing the type of clothing Muslim women elsewhere wear. The

Muslims we knew were not any different than our other Chinese friends, and I never saw them practice their religion.

Muslims did much of the butchering of animals in Nanyang, with the exception of pigs, although some of my friends said they knew of Muslims who will eat pork but call it mutton. They are known to be good cooks, and in Xian, where the Terra Cotta Soldiers were discovered, there is a Muslim section where many tourists go to eat.

Although Muslims are found in many areas of China, most of them live in the northwest and southwest provinces. Our province of Henan in central China also has a large Muslim population. In recent years, there has been some unrest in the Xinjiang Province near Afghanistan. The Muslims there want independence from China, but I feel certain this will never happen if you take into account

1. the recent "liberation of Tibet" which China claims to be their province;
2. China's desire to reclaim Taiwan which they also claim is their province.

Christianity

It is believed that Christianity first came to China in the seventh century. The pope sent the Franciscans in 1294. The Jesuits arrived during the Ming Dynasty (1368-1644). Russian Orthodoxy first came in 1715 and the Protestants arrived in 1807. Today, the Christians are divided into two groups: Catholic and Protestant. I have never heard of any other denominational name. As stated before, the house churches that you hear about are persecuted since they meet in secret without government approval. The Henan Province where we lived is where most of those churches are. And yes, the persecution of these Christians is severe.

Soon after we came to Nanyang, Linda, our translator, told me she was a Christian. Then she went on to tell me how she had become a Christian. She had gone to Singapore to learn western nursing methods. While she was there, she heard the Christian songs, and she became a Christian because these songs kept her mother's ghost from sitting on her chest at night. She said this really scared her, so I asked if her mother hurt her when she was alive. "Of course not!" she replied. I told her that her mother wouldn't hurt her after her death either. "Well, I'm scared of the ghost!" she said. I was ignorant at that time of the Chinese belief that after death, the soul of a person can visit the living and "sit on their chest." Later, I asked her about some Christian theology, but she didn't seem to know any. She said she had refused to be baptized because she didn't understand what it was all about. This leads me to believe that the church leaders must have been more interested in the number of baptisms than in teaching the meaning of Christianity. Her husband had given her a gold pendant with the image of Jesus on it, but she also bowed to statues of Buddha and burned incense to them whenever we toured a Buddhist temple. I guess she was covering all her bases religion-wise, so I decided to leave her Christianity between her and God. I also decided to live my faith quietly and not to be accused of proselytizing, which could result in being kicked out of China or put in a Chinese prison, God forbid!

She wanted to know if I would like to go to church one Sunday, and I said I definitely would. So on the arranged Sunday morning that summer, we left in a taxi about 9:30 AM and soon arrived at the church. After getting out of the taxi, we had to walk through a path lined with beggars, all with major deformities but most without either arms or legs or even both. Linda quickly pulled me through them and said she didn't know why they were there. I tried to explain how Christianity teaches charity, but that didn't cut any ice with her at the time. The huge church was located in a walled-in courtyard and was packed with people. Services had begun at 7:30 AM and would go on all day. There were no seats left, but a man graciously got up and offered us his place. We squeezed into the pew and immediately started sweltering in the oppressive heat. We were surrounded by a sea of Chinese worshipers all dressed simply in black, brown, or navy. I sat there in my bright green dress and white heels, feeling very conspicuous and way overdressed. I could not understand a single thing about what was going on.

A hymn was soon sung, but since there were no hymnbooks, a leader sang a line of the hymn with the people repeating the words afterward. Then a man began reading out of a book that I assume was a Bible. Linda said he was telling a story. After a while of sitting in the intense heat, Linda said, "Let's go find the pastor." I readily agreed.

We went upstairs and eventually found the pastor in a small room by himself. With Linda doing the translating, he told me his story and the story of the church:

> Years ago, when he was a young man, his wife and mother-in-law tried to get him to become a Christian. He resisted for quite a while but finally agreed to go to the church with them. Once there, he became agitated and angry and could not understand anything about this religion. He left and went to another building, but a voice came to him and said, "Go back to the church." He obeyed the voice, and this time, he said it all became clear to him and he understood everything. At the time, he had tuberculosis but was healed of this disease through prayer. He went on to become a pastor in 1982 and tried valiantly to get the doors of the church opened. The Communist Party official in charge of this refused every time he was asked. Then one day, the official came to the pastor and said his wife had cancer and asked if the pastor would pray for her. Of course, the pastor agreed to do so, and the man's wife was healed through this prayer. The official then agreed to allow the church to open its doors. Since then, the pastor said they had had many amazing healings in the church. As of the day we were there, the church had a membership of six thousand and supported an old folks home and also a home for children, which

I assumed was an orphanage. A church in Norway was helping to fund this Chinese church, and he showed us pictures of the Norwegians. He said they send people to Nanyang once a year to visit. Then, abruptly, Linda said it was time to go. As we were leaving, we put money in a box by the sanctuary door and walked through the beggars again. This time, though, we both gave them money.

I later heard that there was a Catholic church outside the city, but I think this was a Protestant church because the cross in the front was plain and not a crucifix. That was my one and only church experience the entire four and a half years we lived in China.

Judaism

There is also some Judaism in China. The first Jews came to China in small groups during the Tang Dynasty sometime between the seventh and tenth century. The largest group settled in "our" Henan Province in the city of Kaifeng. There was a Jewish Temple there once, but it was destroyed by a flood. What is left is now part of a hospital. Many more came in the twentieth century during World War II because they were trying to escape the Holocaust and the revolution in Russia. This time, they mostly settled in Shanghai and Hong Kong, where they still live. There is now a Jewish community also in Beijing. As far as I know, I never met any Jewish people while we lived in China.

Falun Gong

The Falun Gong was publically introduced in China in 1992 by its leader Li Hongzhi. Other than practicing tai chi, I honestly can't tell you what the beliefs of this religion are because to me it sounds mostly like a combination of the early Chinese religions. Therefore, the most succinct way I think to do this is to quote the leading Falun Gong scholar David Ownby, who sees Falun Gong as primarily "concerned with moral purpose and the ultimate meaning of life and death." Li Hongzhi moved to the U.S. in 1998, but the movement continued to grow in China.

In 1999 over ten thousand members of the Falun Gong appeared at the Communist Party residence compound in Tianjin to protest the media criticism of their movement. It was perceived as a potential threat to the Communist Party, and so soon the government's crackdown on the Falun Gong began in earnest. Stories of torture of some members of the Falun Gong began circulating. Newspaper articles appeared on a regular basis of Falun Gong members who had been accused of terrible actions against the state, reporting that some members had even set themselves on fire—horrific to the average Chinese person who immediately thought this was a strange and dangerous religion. There were also articles in the newspaper about those who had "seen the light" and had renounced their belief in this movement. I don't know how much government "help" they had received to reach this state of enlightenment, but even our Chinese friends seemed to find it all predictable and were somewhat amused at the recantations. However, I heard that those who refused to recant were severely tortured.

From the media hype, Li Hongzhi sounded familiarly like some religious leaders in the U.S. as there were reports of believers sending him money for healings and such. I eventually told some of my friends, "I don't understand what all the fuss is about. We have religious leaders like this in my country and if you send them money, it's your own business." Oh, they jumped on that statement in a hurry telling me, "You don't understand, in China's long history, many governments have been overthrown by religious movements." (I wish I had kept track of how many times I heard the phrase "in China's long history.") Anyway, I kept quiet after that and watched it all play out in the press. Eventually, the government must have been successful enough in quieting the supposed threat of the Falun Gong as the media coverage lessened considerably and soon I heard no more about it.

Cultural Differences

Having come from a country that has only a few hundred years of written history, it was sometimes difficult to relate to a country that has a five-thousand-year history. While we are more used to changes in our culture, the current Chinese culture has developed over many centuries. The behaviors are ingrained, and these are not easily changed. This applies to the foods they eat, the way they think, the way business is done, and the way they treat other members of their society. It is difficult to describe the Chinese as a people, but the best description I can give you is that of author David Bonavia who so eloquently wrote, "They are admirable, infuriating, humorous, priggish, modest, overweening, mendacious, loyal, mercenary, ethereal, sadistic, and tender. They are quite unlike anybody else. They are the Chinese."

Circles: They operate in circles, which are comprised of family and friends. They will do almost anything for those in their circles but are not too concerned about the welfare of those outside their circles. I assume this is because there are so many Chinese people—and there always has been—they have developed the system of taking care of those nearest and dearest to them. We, on the other hand, have been greatly influenced by Judeo-Christian beliefs, which have taught us to help out those in need whether we know them or not. Soon after arriving in China, I was witness to this behavior of not being aware of the needs of others outside of people's circles. One Sunday afternoon, we were on a sightseeing trip with several of Ralph's coworkers. We had gone to a lake near Nanyang that was in the countryside. As we were enjoying the peaceful scenery, I saw a woman carrying a huge bundle of sticks on her back. She was bent nearly double from the weight of her burden and seemed to be having some difficulty carrying such a load. As she walked down the pathway to what I assumed was her home in a village, I apparently was the only one in our group who saw her. I commented on her situation and was met by the comment, "She's just poor!" Obviously, that was none of their concern.

Another firsthand example of this occurred one day as I was walking to Ralph's office for lunch. When I reached my favorite street for outdoor shopping, I happened to see a tricycle cart overturn. The elderly woman who had been riding the tricycle was trying to set it up upright again. Without even thinking, I immediately ran to help her as I am sure most of you reading this would have done. As I reached for her cart, she looked up and saw perhaps the first foreign face she had seen in her lifetime. Not only was she startled, but I think I frightened her terribly! I just smiled at her to show I meant no harm, helped her get her cart upright,and then went on my way. Now, mind you, there were hundreds of other people around who apparently didn't even see her.

Another instance of learning the way circles operated was when we had our first dinner party. I had bought some ground beef on a trip to Beijing and had brought it back to Nanyang to make hamburgers. I wanted to cook an American meal for a young boy who came to practice his English every Saturday to show him part of our culture. I invited Linda to be there since his English wasn't very good at this time—my Chinese being nonexistent. We had also invited Eric to join us. I had enough meat for each of us to have one hamburger. When Linda arrived, we discovered she had brought a coworker named Miss. Feng with her. Since Miss Feng worked for NGLE, she qualified as part of our circle and, according to Chinese etiquette, was welcome to come along. I quietly slipped into the

kitchen to hastily take enough meat out of the existing burgers
to create another one. Along with the hamburgers, the menu
included deviled eggs, baked beans, French fries, and a sweet/
sour cabbage salad. After Ms. Feng saw the food, she immediately
called her fiancé known as Blue Tiger to come and join us. Their
relationship included him in our ever widening circle also. There
went the hamburger that I had been so looking forward to eating!
He arrived quickly, and everyone sat down to their first American
meal. We told them the plate of tomatoes, onions, lettuce, catsup,
mustard, and mayonnaise could be added to the burgers if they so
desired and thus began their adventure of dining American style.
They had great fun and wolfed the food down eagerly. No one
enjoys eating more than the Chinese—if it's something they like.
And so our first dinner party in China with a small portion of our
circle was a roaring success and most likely gave them a great story
to tell their friends.

"Nothing is as it appears in China": This was the best advice we
were given before and after arriving in China. We quickly learned
that this was true. In all dealings, including business and social,
their behaviors are the result of cultural dictates which are in most
instances exact opposites of what people in the western world
consider normal or proper. Westerners must have patience and
knowledge of this cultural difference to interact with the Chinese at
just about any level. They will use a "round about" way of behaving
that westerners in our directness find exhausting and unacceptable.
If, for example, you ask for something that they cannot or will
not be able to do, they may say that they will consider it instead
of just saying no, which would be against their cultural etiquette.
We, on the other hand, would immediately say no to something
we could not or would not fulfill. This goes along with what we
were told about their telling you what you want to hear. We were
advised to phrase our questions so that they could not be answered
with a yes or no. Instead of asking, "Is this the way to the market?"
to which they would reply yes, whether it was actually the way or

not, we should ask it this way, "Can you show me the way to the market?" Another example of "nothing is as it appears in China" is the manner in which they present themselves to others. For instance, after searching all of China for the perfect voice to sing the song at the opening ceremonies at the 2008 Beijing Summer Olympics, they decided that the little girl was not pretty enough for the cameras. So a little girl of adequate beauty was found to lip-sync the song. While westerners found this unfair, humiliating for the child, and abhorrently dishonest, changing the girls for the cameras was a perfect solution for the Chinese. They were on the world stage, and the best foot was going to be put forward. I can only hope and assume that the family of the little girl who actually sang the song was most likely rewarded handsomely.

Giving and Receiving: One of the first things I noticed in our cultural differences was the practice of using both hands in the giving and receiving of items. For instance, when you check into your hotel, the person at the counter will use both hands to receive your passport and credit card/money. Likewise, they will give these items back to you using both hands. This also pertains to anything given or received in all areas of China—business cards, teacups, paper, pens, chopsticks, etc. They seem to appreciate it when we do the same.

Business cards: If you do not have any with you when you arrive in China, it is wise to inquire about having some made for you. It is a social and business necessity for doing almost any business in China, and the Chinese seem to value them very much. When you receive a business card, take a moment or two to carefully look it over to show proper respect to the giver before putting it in your pocket or purse.

Pushing and Shoving: This is a characteristic that westerners find very offensive. For the Chinese, on the other hand, it is a way of life. With so many people in China, they are encouraged to try to be the first in line since many times only the first succeed in getting a seat, a place on a bus, boat, or airplane, etc. To them, it is just a way of getting through the crowds. In Beijing, I used to hear westerners from all English-speaking countries complain about the way the Chinese put their forearm in front of them to push through the mass of shoppers. They are not doing this to be rude—it is just a way to contend with the constant crowded conditions there. I could never learn to do this, though, as I had been so thoroughly indoctrinated in being polite. I think Linda would get frustrated at my hesitance to follow closely behind her as she forged a path through the crowds.

Affection: Two women or two girls walking down the street arm in arm or holding hands is a common sight; two men or young boys with their arms about each other's shoulders is also common. This is merely their way of showing fondness for a dear friend or family member. Although, affection is common between members of the same sex, it is not so with those of the opposite sex—even a friendly hug is frowned upon. Once, after our friend Eddie and I had finished modeling for the brochure at the new five-star hotel, we shared a brief hug before I went back to our apartment and he returned to the university. Ms. Ge (guh), who was a teacher at the university, was with us. She was so startled at this innocent expression of public affection that she covered her mouth to suppress her gasping sounds of shock. We explained that in our culture, this was permissible between friends, but for her, this was definitely improper behavior, and I can only imagine the story she would tell about this breach of proper conduct.

Bargaining: An essential skill to acquire in China is learning how to bargain. At first, this was an art form I had trouble learning, but learn it I did. Of course, anyone with a foreign face is going to pay more for things than a Chinese person, but to do most shopping in China, one needs to learn the process of bargaining. If you are in a "free market," where bargaining is expected, you should know that the first asking price is much too high. If you can't speak the language, don't worry—they have a calculator on which they will enter their price and ask you to enter your counter offer. I always started at about a third of the first asking price and worked up from that price. The process goes as such: You ask how much, and they will give you a price in Chinese money. Don't let their insistence of "No, I lose money" affect you. If you stay firm, you will be able to get the items for a lower price. Keep this process up until you agree on a price. If you walk away without agreeing to pay their price, they will usually call you back for more bargaining. If they don't, it means you have insulted them or they really were going to "lose money." Once I learned to speak the words for the number increments, I could bargain not only for myself but would go with friends to jade markets and help them. In the bigger cities, the sales people all speak enough English to do business, and that makes shopping there easier.

Three phrases will help you get through the throngs of insistent people who are trying to sell you their merchandise as you tour at the famous sites or shop at a major market such as the Hongqiao:

> can can (con con) which means "just looking," bu yao (boo' yow) which means "don't want," tai gui le (ty gway' luh) which means "too expensive."

One day, I heard an American accent in the Hongqiao Market and could tell the lady was very angry at the vendors. She was telling her friends, "If they touch me one more time, I'm going to hit them." I walked around the corner, saw she had balled up her fist, so I told her the sales girls didn't mean any harm. They were just doing as they had been told to do. This didn't do much good at calming her down though. I then told her to say "can can" to them. She immediately wanted to know what that meant, and I said it means you are just looking. I left soon after that, so I don't know if anyone got hit that day or not. These market places are not for the timid or the ones with short fuses. They can be overwhelming at first, but if you just relax and have fun with the bargaining, you will have a great time.

One thing I would not bargain for was food. The people were so poor in Nanyang and the food was so cheap, I felt I was already getting a good bargain. This did not set well with Linda or Scott, as it was culturally not acceptable to just pay the first price. In the government-owned businesses and in the newer supermarkets, there was no bargaining. The prices marked were the actual costs. Just like home!

Birth dates: Determining birth dates are interestingly different from the way westerners count age. Babies in China are considered to be one year old at birth since they start counting birth at conception instead of date of birth.

Criticism: One thing that was difficult for me to deal with our entire time in China was their eagerness to criticize each other. I found this characteristic evident first in the schools where the teachers were quick to be critical of students, often telling them that they would never succeed. Then I found it to be used among coworkers, friends, and family members where they would be judgmental of appearance, clothing, or behavior. On the family level, a parent would often make it well known that one child was preferred over another if they were fortunate enough to have had children before the one-child policy was enforced. Often, it was a broad criticism of the peasants, sometimes by the very people who had just escaped the village life. It always seemed to be hurtful rather than constructive criticism and it seemed to encompass all social levels. Once you are considered a member of their "circle of friends," you may also be told such things as "you need to lose weight" or "your hair doesn't look good" or "you are too old to wear that color." (I never learned at what age "too old" was, but I think somewhere in early middle age was the cut-off age for wearing brightly colored clothing.) It is as if the concept of "If you can't say something good about someone, don't say anything at all" has never been introduced to them.

Logic: Chinese vs. Western logic is totally different. I always tell people going to China to check their logic at the airport and pick it back up on their return home. Upon entering China, everything you have considered normal is turned upside down. Most of this stems from their age-old belief in collectivism and our belief in individualism. Collective societies work together for the harmony and good of the whole society or workplace and have more control of the people, the press, and the economy. Individualistic societies value honesty, privacy, working for personal gain, and limited government control of their lives. With these two societal differences, there are usually two opposite approaches to almost everything. Trying to get the Chinese to see a different way of doing things is almost impossible. Their answer to any objection to their course of action is "But it's the Chinese way!" After a year or so, I gave up on any attempt at trying to offer other courses of action and just fell into line. As our friend Eddie said, "Just submit. It's easier."

Smoking: More tobacco is produced and consumed in China than any other country in the world. There seem to be hundreds of brands. You cannot escape cigarette smoke anywhere in China, as it is a habit that has become part of the culture. They smoke everywhere—before, during, and after meals, in elevators and under the No Smoking signs. I think they could smoke in their sleep. Once, when Bonnie and I had traveled to Beijing by train, we were riding the elevator down to the hotel lobby and one of the men riding down with us lit up a cigarette. Bonnie, being the most avid advocate of anti-smoking, quickly pointed to the well-placed sign that said No Smoking. Well, there was no trash can or ashtray on the elevator, so he dropped the cigarette on the carpet and ground it out with his shoe, leaving a burn mark in the carpet.

The carpet not being in his living space was of no consequence to him.

While currently more men smoke, it is now becoming popular for young girls to take up the habit. I didn't personally know of any of our women friends who smoked, but I was often offered cigarettes at dinners we attended. I hope I didn't offend them when I refused because a refusal to accept their gift can be interpreted as rudeness. Being the first to offer a cigarette to a guest and light it for them is considered good manners and a way of showing friendship. Many doctors and other healthcare workers smoke and receive them as gifts of gratitude from patients. Cigarettes are used as gifts at weddings, New Year's gifts, bribes to government officials, business gifts, and even given at funerals. Although there is an effort being made to curb smoking, it is not very successful. Smoking is not only a physical addiction for the Chinese people but has also become a culturally social addiction as well.

Work Day: Work day schedules are also different. Our eight-to-five schedule is totally alien to them. Traditionally, the Chinese like to come to work fairly early and break for a hot lunch at noon with a long nap following. After their nap, they return to work around 3:00 PM and then work until 6:00 PM or later into the evening. In order to get the employees to work "western hours," NGLE agreed to pay for their lunches, which worked fairly well. However, Ralph said whenever he called a meeting immediately after lunch, at least one person would nod off and sleep for most of the meeting.

Wardrobes: We have different clothes for different occasions, but this is a new concept for the Chinese. Where we lived, they don't usually have as much clothing as we westerners do, so depending on the extent of their wardrobe, they tend to either wear what they have or what they want to wear, never even thinking that their clothes may be inappropriate for the occasion. For instance, I would often see men building a wall or other structure in a white dress shirt and dress pants. This was probably the only suit of clothing they owned. I did find this a refreshing freedom from the "fashion Nazis" of our world, but I can't seem to change my own cultural indoctrination on this one.

The Chinese all tend to dress pretty much alike in the colors and styles of their clothes and hair. Young girls have more fashion freedom than middle-aged women and like to wear the latest styles and bright colors. Middle-aged women tend to dress pretty much alike in dark colors and the same style tops, pants, and shoes. Men and older boys also wear the same style of clothing and shoes (always black). I think they buy only one belt to last a lifetime. The belts must come in a universal size to be able to adjust according to girth because on the younger, thinner men, the belt often wrapped their waist one and a half times. I think they are more comfortable in some type of "uniformity," and I still saw some village men wearing the "Mao suits."

They also have no problem wearing the same clothes for several days. Linda soon picked up on our American penchant to wear something different each day and began to do likewise. She was questioned why she did this by a coworker, and she replied that she liked to feel and smell clean. The other person said he wore the same clothes for several days and asked her if he smelled bad. I don't know how she answered him, but I never smelled anyone in the office who had a body odor. Some of the Chinese, who go to the West for work or an education, learn to dress as we do, although the younger generation is learning this through reading, watching movies, or working with westerners. When we were traveling, I sometimes saw Chinese teenagers dressed like American kids and would often ask them if they were from the U.S. Usually, they were from Taiwan, and when we met Eric's daughter and son, we found they were very westernized in their clothing, ideas, and in their attitude about cleanliness and such.

Bathing: Due to non-heated homes, people in Nanyang tended not to bathe often in the winter. Some of the university students I knew who were from South China said that they were used to taking daily baths and could not get used to some of their friends going so long between showers. Of course, the showers at the universities were not heated, making it difficult for anyone to bathe much in the winter. The rule in Ralph's office was that the employees had to bathe once a week and were allowed to use the showers at the office to do so. On weekends, they would bring their whole family with soap and towels for their weekly bath. When I first arrived, going to the office on Sundays gave me a good opportunity to meet the families of the employees. Glenn Davis, who was one of the project engineers, was once invited to the home of one of the employees. He said they did have a bathtub in the bathroom, but it was totally filled up with their "stuff." Guess they found it was more useful as a storage unit.

Efficiency: In our quest for efficiency, we find multitasking works well in getting things done. We try to accomplish as many things as possible in one trip out of the home or office. Not so for the Chinese. It seems that the "one thing at a time" system works better. They don't see the necessity of first calling ahead to see if the person they want to see is in. A teacher once said she had heard that we Americans make appointments when we want to see someone. I told her "Yes, this is true," and tried to explain about appointment books, scheduling ahead, etc. She just shook her head and said, "I wouldn't like that!"

If we have children, we tend to keep them home with us no matter how busy we are. Quite different for the Chinese, though. If their parents are not living with them or at least nearby, they often "send the child away" to the grandparents or other relatives or friends if they are "studying" or have a "busy job" since they can't do those things and take care of a child—the only one they have. Of course, traditionally and in our part of China, the grandparents retire and do take care of the small children while both parents work outside the home or are furthering their education. I once tried to explain to my students at the university about fathers in the U.S. sometimes staying home with the children while the wives go to work. It was such an unbelievable shock to them to hear such a thing, I didn't bring that up again.

Along with our bent for efficiency comes a sense of urgency. We tend to get impatient when things don't go according to plan. After all, we are on a schedule most of the time. Unlike us, the Chinese are content to work on a slower timetable and have an ability to take disappointments more easily. The only things I have seen a sense of urgency about are eating and sleeping. They just don't seem to function very well if they don't eat or sleep at the proper times.

Face: Saving face is extremely important to the Chinese. It is not only a measure of the esteem in which others hold them but also their own self esteem. "Face" can also mean the way a person presents himself to society, such as honorably or shamelessly. The Chinese do almost anything to keep from losing face, which is a much more serious matter than just being embarrassed or ridiculed. Losing face can be a shameful reflection on the family. A loss of face can also result from a person not meeting the expectations of family or friends in becoming successful. A loss of face can be so disastrous that people, both young and old, have committed suicide.

Compliments: It is very difficult to compliment the Chinese verbally. If you say they are pretty/handsome, very intelligent (don't tell them they are smart—to them this means sly), or have some other desirable attribute, they will insist that this is not so. Do not be offended when your compliment is consistently met with a no or not at all, etc.; accepting the compliment would be considered poor etiquette on their part. I have heard that they do not give compliments freely either, but I found this to be untrue. Both my friend Bonnie and I were told frequently how "beautiful" we were. Neither of us believing this to be true, we denied the truth of this many times saying, "No, I'm not," only to be met with, "Yes, you are!" Finally, we just got tired of the ongoing process and reverted back to the western practice of saying thank you to put an end to it.

Gifting: Giving and receiving gifts is an essential part of doing business with the Chinese. We gave such things as pens, coin sets, bourbon, wine, candy, books on the U.S., Ohio State shirts, and anything we could find that was made in the USA. Before the year 2000 arrived, I cross-stitched a dragon and had it framed for Mr. Li, who was head of Henan Power Bureau. I presented it to him and his wife at a dinner we attended in Zhengzhou at the onset of the year 2000, the Year of the Dragon. His wife said no one had ever made them anything like this before and seemed very appreciative. If you are touring and want to give things to the children you meet, I would suggest coins, notebooks, pencils, or anything that would be easy to pack. On a tour, you most likely won't be meeting an adult that you would feel you should give a gift, although some people become very fond of their tour guides and would like to present him/her with a gift of appreciation. In this case, I think a good-quality pen, a box of candy, or a nice bottle of wine would be appropriate. There are shops in many of the larger cities that carry some western food, drinks, and other items. The hotel concierge should be able to help you in finding one.

For wedding gifts, the appropriate thing to give is money in red envelopes. Three, six, eight, and nine are lucky numbers for the Chinese, and yuan in increments of these numbers (such as three hundred yuan) are favorable. There will be a table near the entrance of the banquet room where you will hand the envelopes to the people at the table with "the book." The amount given by each guest will be written in the book. This is the record for reciprocating the gift at the weddings of the guests and their family members.

At the Chinese New Year celebrations, children usually receive small red envelopes called hong bao (hong' bow) with money inside. Bags of assorted candies can also be given to children at this time.

Where we lived, the Chinese do not usually wrap the things they give. They just put the gift items in a paper bag with handles. Since it was difficult to find wrapping paper where we lived, we gave our gifts in the paper bags also. Most products sold in China used in gifting have bags with the name on the outside identifying the contents of the bag.

When you present a gift to the Chinese, they will thank you and then put it aside without even looking at it. In their culture, for them to do otherwise would indicate greediness. Later, they will open it and may even re-gift it to someone else. I always thought this was partly because they do not have the space to keep all the gifts they receive and also because it gives them a way to keep the gift-giving custom without a lot of expense. I had an experience with this once after I had helped a teacher win a contest by giving her ideas and visual aids on how to prepare a lesson on the way Americans celebrate Christmas. To show her appreciation, she asked me to lunch one day. Upon her arrival, she also had a gift in hand—a bottle of French brandy. She proudly told me someone had given that to her husband, but he didn't like it, so she decided to give it to me. By that time, I had lived there long enough to accept the gift with only an inward smile at how different our cultures are in this respect.

Once, we were invited to a birthday dinner for a young girl who had given herself the English name of Apple, since her face had an apple-type shape. She was the student of two of my friends from the U.S., who were her teachers, Bonnie and Michael Zargarov. Some friends of Bonnie were visiting her at that time, so they were invited also. Apple's mother and father both had their own businesses, but lived separately and barely spoke to each other the entire evening. I believe they stayed married in name only until Apple completed high school and had successfully become a student in Canada. We all took gifts (Ralph and I took a set of uncirculated coins) and placed them on a side table. Then we ate dinner and listened to Apple play a traditional Chinese musical instrument. All this while the gifts lay unopened on the side table.

Soon after Apple's performance was over, Bonnie's friends, who were visiting, began encouraging her to open her birthday gifts. Apple was in a quandary as to what to do but finally acquiesced and began opening her presents. I felt so sorry for her as she began the process since I knew she was going against everything she had been taught about proper behavior when receiving gifts. But open them she did and was sufficiently appreciative of everything she received. Ironically, as difficult as it is for them to open gifts in the presence of others, they exhibit much pleasure in watching westerners open the things they give us and enjoy the reactions of gratitude and pleasure we show.

Spitting: This is one custom the Chinese practice I never got used to. They consider it unhealthy to have the phlegm in their bodies, so men, women, and children alike hock and spit it out with much gusto, sharing it with the world. Since we heard it all the time in Nanyang, we used to laughingly say it was their "mating call." We had to watch where we stepped because big globs of it were all over the streets and floors of buildings, including hospitals. The rule in Ralph's office was that they were not allowed to spit on the floors—they had to use the trash cans for that. Seldom did I hear much spitting noises in the office. However, much to my dismay, at the university I would often hear the hocking sounds and see a student spitting on the floor. Added to the spitting was also the one-finger-against-the-nostril nose-blowing technique. Done noisily and enthusiastically by the general population, it also added to the mess we tried to avoid.

Names: In all of China, the family name is spoken first with the given name(s) following. For example: Scott's name is Wu Changping, so he would be Wu or Mr. Wu and not Mr. Changping.

It was amusing to us when we would be welcomed as visitors with signs reading "Welcome Mr. Ralph and Mrs. Jean." This was the "Chinese way" of name use. Many of the younger Chinese will choose a western name if dealing with foreigners. Sometimes they would ask us to give them an English name and would always want to know the meaning of the name we suggested. I told them we usually don't give a name to our children because of what it means but whether we like the name or not. Well, they weren't having any of that. So the next time I came back to the States, I bought a book of baby names with the meanings of the names, and this worked very well.

Of course, if they chose their own names, we would sometimes find those very unusual or amusing. For instance, the names "Slug" and "Beaver" were chosen because they were very industrious animals. "Pitt" was chosen in honor of Brad Pitt and "Blues" was chosen because he liked blues music. And then there were two best friends who called themselves "Flame" and "Water"—names that I suppose were chosen because they are strong elements of nature. One boy called himself "Grass," for which I suppose he had his own reasons. Another chose the name "General," which I thought was an obvious choice, but the reasons one student called himself "Apathy" and another named himself "Bone" remain a mystery. The most humorous name I thought was "Chewing Gum," chosen because he said his Chinese name sounded like those words in English. Once you got used to calling them these names, it became natural to do so, but I must admit it was not easy to call a grown man "Chewing Gum" at first, and over time it was shortened to "C.G."

Government: Of course, everyone knows China is a communist country. What I didn't know until moving there is that not everyone is a Communist. You can't just join the Communist Party like we can instantly become a Republican, Democrat, Libertarian, Independent, or whatever we wish. You must be asked to join the party in China and those who are members of the party have the best jobs and the best homes. Hence, they are the ones who have the most money—they are the elite at the top of the heap with the peasants at the bottom. Forget about equality in communism. From what I saw, that doesn't happen. To me, this system is very much like their ruling systems of the past—strong government in complete control with those at the top getting all the best benefits, the bribing of those who can grant favors, heavy-handed law enforcement, and corruption at all levels.

When the Chinese government had a change of leadership in 2002, I went to the Internet to see who the new party leaders were going to be. I thought it would be nice to give this information to Xiao Hang so she could take it to her parents. Little did I know this was not going to be an easy task to accomplish. First, I went to a Web site with this information—it was nothing much, just a picture and a short bio (name, education, home province, etc.) on each leader. No state secrets were revealed that I could see. I was about halfway through printing out this information when the site was suddenly shut down, so I quickly went to another news source and had barely finished when this site also shut down. I thought that was odd, but I gave the pages to Xiao Hang who was cooking supper at the time. I told her to give them to her father so he could show his friends what their new leaders looked like. Her reaction of total fear stunned me as she immediately asked, "Who wrote this?" I showed her the man's name who happened to be Mr. McDonald. She insistently asked me, "Where is he from?" I replied I imagined he was from America or Great Britain due to his name. She was very agitated and said, "Chinese people cannot know this!" I was taken aback, to say the least, because there was nothing in the information that was harmful, disrespectful, or critical of the leaders or government. However, she did take the papers home, and I suppose under cover of darkness, she secretly translated it into Chinese for her family. As far as I know, that was as close as I ever came to breaking Chinese law—thank heaven, because I didn't want to spend any time in a Chinese prison.

Crime and Punishment: The teachings of Confucius have affected the very psyche of the Chinese people. He believed that everyone should work for the good of all resulting in happiness for all. Whereas, we stress the importance of individual worth and esteem, the Chinese do not place much emphasis on individuality. They believe that everyone should exhibit proper behavior, think alike, and, of course, obey the laws of the government which makes for a better society as a whole. Anyone disrupting the harmony of society by behaving badly is therefore subject to a severe penalty. Capital punishment is alive and well in China and is seen as a logical way to deal with murder and other offenses to society. This is usually carried out by means of a bullet to the back of the head or firing squads, mostly because it is the cheapest method of execution. I have heard that, now, lethal injections are used and that there are mobile units called "death vans" that travel to the towns where executions are scheduled to be carried out by this method.

The students at the university would question me about shootings in the U.S. They seemed to think practically everyone in America ran around with guns killing people and shooting up neighborhoods. They were horrified by this. I told them that this occurred mainly in inner cities and was done mostly by gang members. Since they saw this violent behavior in movies, on the news, and read about it in newspapers, I could understand their thinking on this. The whole time we lived in China, I saw guns only in the hands of the guards at the embassies and once as a military unit was routinely marching down the street in Beijing. But just because they didn't have guns did not mean they didn't commit murder and mayhem in their own society. Their weapons consisted of knives, poison, and explosives, and they managed quite well to commit murder and destruction with these instruments.

One case in point was a mass poisoning incident in Nanyang not too long after we arrived. One Saturday morning, our phone began ringing quite early with several students and friends warning us not to go to the local supermarkets that day. They went on to tell me that some rice or other dry grains had been poisoned in one of the larger supermarkets. These products at that time were displayed in open barrels or containers, making it very easy to use poison in such a way. Everyone thought it was a competitor who had done this in order to gain more business at their own establishment. But it only took a couple of days before it was discovered that a lone man had done the poisoning because he "wanted to kill his wife and worthless son." He was arrested and most likely put to death soon after, as that seemed to be the way justice for murder was handled. Many people got sick from the poison and a few died. I never did find out if the wife and son were among the victims. To me, this man was as much of a mass murderer as a man with a gun in the U. S.

Explosives were mainly used on trains or were targeted at other highly populated places, so it eventually became necessary for our baggage and any liquids to be examined when traveling on all public transportation. Usually, whoever was responsible for this mass killing was discovered in a very short time and met his/her death soon thereafter.

One final note on capital crime in China: Occasionally, we would hear of a bridge or building that had collapsed, killing and injuring many people. It usually turned out that someone had cut construction costs or had taken bribes to allow the builders to cut the costs and/or the quality of the work. These people also were usually put to death quickly.

At the time we arrived in China, the major crime was theft. We were told at our cross-cultural class in Chicago that in the case we were robbed and knew how to identify the thief, we should only report them to the police if we were willing to see them put to death for their crime. We eventually did fall victim to a robbery one night after living in Nanyang about two and a half years. This was mostly due to our misconception that since our apartment was on the second floor, we had no need of the bars covering the windows of almost all the other apartments in our complex. Plus, we had guards at the gate and a wall surrounding us so, we felt quite safe. But wrong we were in believing that these safeguards were enough to protect us. The thieves in their tenacity and agility evidently climbed over the walls and used the bars on the window below to boost themselves up to the porch of our apartment. There they gained entry through the windows and then came into the apartment by the door leading to the kitchen. Although the things they stole were on a dresser not ten feet from our bed, we slept right through the whole thing. It's probably best that we were asleep since otherwise this story could have a different ending. When Ralph got up to go to work, he discovered that his wallet was gone but then found it discarded on the porch. The money was missing as were two "Rolex" watches and our mobile phone. The watches were fakes and the mobile phone, I'm sure, was mistaken for a cell phone (which was later found discarded in the bushes outside). All they actually got for their efforts was the equivalent of $200 worth of money and merchandise.

When Madam Zhang, the manager at the power plant, found out about the robbery, she immediately got the police department involved. They came and made a big deal of taking fingerprints and gathering information, all of which produced no results. There were probably countless robberies all over Nanyang that same night, and unless the thieves were caught in the act, I doubt any of them were ever prosecuted. Soon thereafter, we had bars installed on the windows of all three of the apartments owned by AEP to prevent this from ever happening again.

Our translator, Linda, also became a victim of the rampant robbery in the city. She was robbed of her purse as she rode her scooter home from work one day. This method of purse snatching involved another scooter riding up beside someone with a purse, snatching it, and quickly disappearing into the traffic. The problem with Linda's purse getting taken is that she had it on cross-body style, and when they grabbed her purse, they upset her scooter and dragged her for several feet before she could manage to break the strap. She was pretty badly scratched and bruised and missed several days of work due to her injuries. These men were never caught, and this type of robbery went on.

One day, I saw a young boy running from an angry woman chasing him with a brick. He escaped into the crowded streets before she could catch him. I suppose he had stolen something from her and she was going to exact her own type of justice with that brick if she caught him.

A Better Way: The Chinese people usually have a better way of doing things other than the way proposed to them. A prime example of this was when we bent over backward to help a young man come to the U.S. to study. We sent a letter stating that he would be living with us, a picture of our home, and our income tax statement to the U.S. embassy in Beijing—all requirements for his coming to the States to study. On his end, he was to (1) provide a guarantee that he would actually be a student and not working in the U.S., (2) be able to pay for the education either by his own funds or scholarships, and (3) be able to convince the visa officers that he would return to China upon completion of his studies. We waited to hear the news that he had been granted permission to come here but were surprised to receive an email from this young man that he had been rejected. He admitted he had not followed the guidelines on the procedures he should follow and said he "thought he had a better way to do it." We were told that the U.S. embassy in Beijing received about seven hundred applications a day to come to the U.S. in 2003 and were very strict about granting visas. This was due to the fact that many of them get here and then disappear into society and never return to China.

Begging: The only people I gave money to were the severely maimed adults and old people in Nanyang who were begging. Linda told me that if old people were begging, it meant that they had no one to take care of them in their old age. Soon after I arrived in Nanyang, Linda and I were shopping in a department store one day and a young man, whom I assumed was a Buddhist monk or a religious man of some sect, started trying to talk to me. I had no idea what he wanted of me, but Linda quickly appeared beside me, shielding me from him. She was talking to him in a loud, angry voice as I stood there confusedly. Soon he left us alone, but Linda was still angry and said, "He's a young healthy man; he can go work for the money he wants and not beg from others!"

The people of Nanyang trained their children, especially sons, to be careful of strangers because children were often stolen and then trained to beg to earn money for their "owners." Sometimes, these children were maimed to encourage people to give more money to them. One day, as I was walking down the street, two young boys who should have been in school ran up to me and asked for money. I told them "mayo" which is "don't have" in Chinese because I had already made the tough decision to refuse to give money to children. My reasoning was that if this system worked, then more children would fall prey to these horrible people.

We were told by a Beijing resident that begging was a big business there and in the other larger cities. She also said it was well organized; so well organized that lunch would be brought to them so they wouldn't have to leave their station. They would put on old clothes, make themselves appear dirty and frail and pitifully hold out their cups as people, especially foreigners, walked by. They stationed themselves near busy places that tourists liked to frequent. They could also be very persistent and annoying. During the celebration of a major holiday, the beggars were "sent away" to give the city a better image.

I knew someone who had seen a woman digging food scraps out of a trash can in the city of Shenzhen. He had made up his mind to give money to this woman until one day he saw her arrive at her station with trash can in hand, put some scraps into the trash can, and begin eating the scraps as people passed her by. Most Chinese people are very hard workers, so they have no use for such laziness and hold this type of people in contempt.

Money: Money is extremely important to the Chinese. It is the means to provide for the family and can buy them the desired things such as jobs, homes, good food, cars, entry into the best schools if the grades aren't good enough, and even diplomas. My observation of priority went as such: money = education = job = money, resulting in family success. We say that the "love of money is the root of all evil," and I have never seen this to be more true than in China, as there is corruption in business and government at all levels. Soon after we arrived in China, someone asked me if I could change one thing, what would it be? I know they were expecting me to say the living conditions or the food, but I answered, "The way business is done." I have known of people who took huge risks to make more money, risks that could land them in jail or result in a death sentence, and often did. There were several people working at the power plant who were accused of corrupt business practices. They either went to jail or fled the province to escape prosecution. I did, however, find a bit of humor in this whole sad process. One of the men who was involved in this corruption went into hiding and could not be found. However, his wife came to the power plant in an attempt to collect his wages. I don't know if she was brave, desperate, or crazy, but she evidently thought she had a chance to get the money.

But all said and done, I do admire their amazing ability to make money if given the chance to do so. I also admire their ability to live on very little and save almost everything they make. In our city, there were many men who came from the countryside with their two-wheeled, hand-pulled carts to earn a living hauling heavy items. The carts were not only their means of earning a living but also their "homes." They lived on the streets, sleeping on the carts in all kinds of weather, with quilts as their only protection against the elements. They would seek the cover of recessed doorways or sleep under bridges, etc., during rainy or snowy conditions. They worked for almost nothing, lived on almost nothing, and sent almost everything they made back to the family in the village.

I became friendly with one of these men who lived on the corner near our apartment where a small supermarket was located. He was very interested in me, probably because I was the first foreigner he had ever seen. He would follow me into the store and stare at me as I shopped. This didn't scare me at all, as by now I was used to all the staring. One day, as I was leaving the market with him following closely behind, I turned around and said bye-bye and waved to him. He immediately began smiling and answered bye-bye with a wave to me. Every time I went to that market, he would begin smiling as soon as he saw me and wave and say bye-bye, and I would answer in kind. Upon leaving, we played out the same scenario. I think I provided him a little pleasure and a story to tell his friends and family about the foreign woman and the English words he knew. I called him "Bye Bye" which is the same sound as the Chinese word "bai."

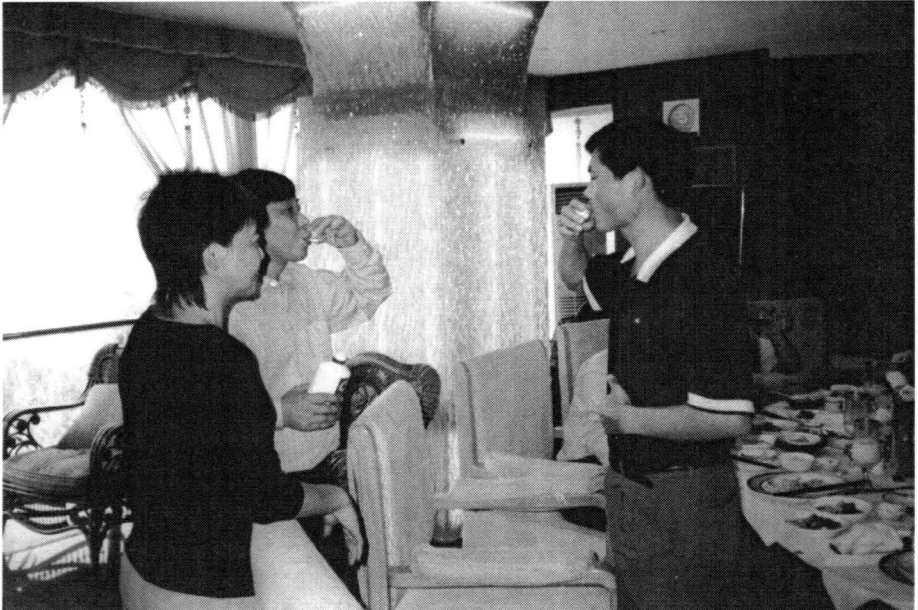

Our driver, Mr. Bai (on right), being toasted with rocket
fuel at a dinner

Foods and Dining

Provinces are very important to the Chinese people, and they are very proud of their own particular province, much like we Americans feel about our own states. Each province has its own characteristics, dialects, and foods. There are about four different styles of Chinese food. For instance, Sichuan (most Chinese people we knew pronounced this as "sit'ron" not "sesh'wan") and Hunan Provinces are known for spicy foods and is called the *Sichuan/Hunan style.* Beijing is known for *the Peking style,* which includes Peking duck, noodles, dumplings, and breads. The *Shanghai style* includes meats cooked much like stews in a sweet, brown sauce, and seafood dishes. Guangzhou in the Guangdong Province is famous for the *Cantonese style* food, which includes much seafood and steamed and stir-fried foods lightly seasoned with the traditional spices. The Cantonese also are known for deep fried, steamed, and braised dishes. In the U.S., most Chinese restaurants serve Cantonese style food because of the early immigration of people from this part of China. Our Henan Province along with the other northern provinces had several different kinds of delicious noodles and jiosa (jow'zuh), a dumpling that is made with many different fillings such as meats or vegetables (these are called pot stickers in the U.S.). The ones made with meat were a traditional Chinese New Year's dish. We also had steamed buns and fried breads. We did have rice—lots of it, and there were differing opinions among the people on which was better, rice or noodles. My vote goes to the noodles. I still miss them.

One of the first things I learned about eating when we moved to Nanyang was that we could be quite full after eating a lavish banquet meal but then were asked what kind of food we wanted to be served. I learned that noodles, rice, dumplings, or breads were called "the food"; everything else was just dishes. You finished off the meal with "the food" before a platter of fresh fruit was brought to the table as a dessert and which was the indication the meal was over. We might get a cookie with our meal, but that would be served with the other dishes. Sweets were not used as dessert items. The thing I liked about their cookies and cakes was they were about a third as sweet as the ones we have in the U.S. We usually only had cake when we celebrated Ralph's birthday, and I don't remember having it any other time, although I would see them in the windows at the bakeries. Birthday parties and cakes with candles were new to the Chinese, and only the more wealthy people celebrated birthdays this way. I asked Scott one day how he celebrated his birthday when he was small and living in the village. He said with pride and a smile, "My mother gave me a whole egg!" I just smiled because I could think of nothing to say after that.

The main concern about food in China seemed to be that the fresher the food, the better—closely followed by how the food would affect the body heat. Anything consumed by the Chinese has to do with how it affects "the body heat." This is a part of the traditional medicine lore and therefore was gospel to them. I was wary of the meat sold by the street vendors as I wasn't sure just how fresh those chunks of meat laid out on a metal table or hanging on the hooks really were. Also, in the summer, flies were all over any meat that was not covered with a piece of cloth. When we first arrived, Scott found out who was butchering a cow one day and took me to that vendor quickly. They had a hunk of beef lying on a metal table, and I just used my hands to show how big a piece I wanted. They then cut that size piece for me and put into a plastic bag. I took it home, recut it into meal-sized portions, and froze it. I was very pleased with my purchase—until I tried to cook it, that is. I had managed to locate two crock pots in Nanyang on my Saturday shopping trips. They were on sale because Linda said no one liked to cook in that manner. They like to cook quickly in a wok, and this just didn't suit the traditional style or taste of the Chinese. Well, I got one of those crock pots out of the cabinet and cooked some of the beef. It cooked all day but was so tough after many hours of cooking that we couldn't chew it. So I shredded it and made barbeque. That didn't work either because even after cooking some more in the slow cooker, it was still as tough as shoe leather. I just gave up and threw it away. At any rate, the beef we ate at the hotel and at business dinners was very tender and edible, so perhaps they used MSG. I never tried to cook the local beef again, but during our travels, I could sometimes find westernized supermarkets and would bring some beef and other foodstuffs back to Nanyang. I also sent boxes of food to our address in China while I was back home visiting. Either way was expensive, so I had to decide how important it was to do either. I went with doing both because it was worth the expense to eat "our" food occasionally, and it was a special treat for our western friends in Nanyang too.

The food served in American Chinese restaurants is different from real Chinese food. The first immigrants from China must have adapted their foods to our tastes, just as pizza and other western foods have been adapted to suit the Chinese tastes. McDonald's and KFC, however, taste pretty much the same as it does here in the States, and the Chinese love dining at these establishments. Hence, they are beginning to gain weight as they eat more fast food, watch TV, sit in front of their computers, and ride in cars more.

As we traveled in China, we got to sample many of the different styles of cooking and the delicacies of several of the provinces. While we enjoyed many of those foods, we were always glad to get back to Henan, and especially Nanyang, and get the soup noodles and other typical foods of the area.

Don't even think of serving a lunch consisting of a cold sandwich, some chips, and a cold drink to a Chinese person. When some of the people who worked with Ralph visited an AEP power plant in the U.S., this type of box lunch was served. They found this rather appalling, and Mr. Guo, an older gentleman, was still talking about this, making faces and shaking his head about it when we left China several years later. The Chinese believe they have the best food in the world and expect everyone else to think so too. However, they have no problem showing disgust and dislike for foods other cultures like but that they find distasteful.

Chinese people do not drink anything cold such as a soft drink with ice in it. They drink soft drinks and beer at room temperature. Hot tea and even plain hot water are their usual beverages of choice. Hot water is especially recommended when you are sick, and at first I would drink it only if served to me. After a year or so, I found that hot water actually did make me feel better when I was cold, had a cold, or was just not feeling up to par. Even after coming back to the U.S., I still drink hot water when I am cold or not feeling well.

Milk is not a popular drink for the Chinese, nor is cheese a popular food. We were told that milk was associated with the barbarians who kept herds of animals for milk production. Thus, the Chinese shunned milk and products made from it. Sometimes we would see a baby with a "band" of baldness going around their head. According to a friend, this was due to a lack of calcium.

I found I liked much of the foods in China, but it was mainly the wheat noodles, rice, fruits, and vegetables. The only vegetable, or maybe you would call it a fruit, I did not like was bitter melon. It was so bitter that I just could not eat it even though I was encouraged to do so because it was good for the body heat. But there were hardly any other fruits or vegetables that I didn't like. One dish that was served in Nanyang that everyone who came from the U.S. loved was scrambled eggs with tomatoes. I don't know what they did to those two ingredients that made them taste so good, but if that dish were served, we were all over it like white on rice.

Potatoes are eaten frequently, and I could always find plenty at the local street markets, but they are not as popular in China as they are in western countries. Many times we would be served French fries because they had learned this was a favorite food among Americans. But instead of catsup and salt to go with them, they were often served with sugar and a sweet white sauce. Linda once asked me why we liked "those things" so much, and I told her that potatoes were to us like rice and noodles were to the Chinese.

There are differences in spice usage in our cultures, also. Soon after we first arrived, I would sometimes invite our Chinese friends over for a meal. On these occasions, I often served baked apples with sugar and cinnamon, but they were rarely ever eaten. Finally, I was told that they do not like cinnamon on apples—it was a spice used on meat instead. Likewise, there was a huge difference in seasoning popcorn—we like it with salt, and they like it with sugar.

The Chinese seem to like their meats bony, gristly, chewy, slimy, and fatty, and I had great difficulty with these textures. There is a crab they really like that we called a "hairy crab." To most of us westerners, these crabs were very difficult to eat because there was very little crab and lots of shell on these creatures. But the Chinese could eat these with no trouble at all, putting them in their mouths and extracting whatever meat there was and then spitting the shell back onto their plates. This skill pertained to anything with bones or shells. I was amazed at this talent and used to wonder if they had a device in their mouths that we don't possess.

The first of what I called "shock foods" served to us was fried scorpions. I managed to close my mind of any thought and just ate one. Actually, there was no taste to it really. It was just a little bit of crunchy fried food. The second shock food was rooster comb, and no way was I even going to attempt that one. It wasn't fried, and I figured I would not be able to handle the texture. I pretended to taste it and put it into my mouth (barely), but I didn't bite into it. I just put it back on my plate.

Once we were served a bowl of "chicken knees," or at least that's what our host at the dinner called them. We were told that it took a hundred chickens to make the bowl of "knees" on the table. They looked like small tasty pieces of deep fried chicken, so I took one and began to chew. It turned out that it was nothing but gristle. I thought I must have just found a bad piece, and so I tried another "knee," but it was the same as the first. I decided then that I would leave these delicacies to others at the table. No chicken I have ever seen has had knees, so I am assuming it was the part of the leg where the foot meets the leg.

Speaking of chicken, they prefer to eat the parts that move, such as the legs, thighs, heads, and feet. They advised us not to eat the breasts of chickens, which they called chicken chests. They said they were only good for "developing" your chest. But they also ate ox penis, so it does make one wonder about the reasoning on this. In case you are wondering, I ate plenty of the "chests" but always passed on the ox appendage and would have even if I had had something it would have helped develop. A word to the wise on ordering chicken: anything that says "chopped chicken" usually means just that—they just chop the chicken up with the cleaver, bones and all.

There is a chicken with white feathers that has black meat that is considered a delicacy, but I never heard it called by a name. It was usually served in a soup. I actually found the taste was quite good, but I found the appearance a little disconcerting at first.

The "tea eggs" were a favorite snack food and could be taken on hikes and trips much as we take our granola-type bars. I found them to be delicious! This is a recipe for them, but I think the spices vary in different parts of China:

Tea eggs are made by boiling the eggs in a black tea for about five minutes, then tapping them with the back of a spoon to make cracks in the shell, returning them to the pan of black tea to which soy sauce and salt, and even cinnamon or star anise has been added, then bringing the tea solution and eggs back to a boil and simmering the eggs for one to three hours. Turn the heat off and let the eggs sit in the solution for a while. When peeling them, they should have the marbled effect where the tea liquid has seeped into the cracks of the shell. They can be eaten warm or cold.

Donkey was eaten in our province, and there were restaurants that were known for their donkey meat. I don't believe I was ever served donkey and would have had a hard time eating it if I had. Once I told a friend that donkeys were sometimes kept as pets in the U.S., and she was not only amazed at the very thought, but I think disgusted at this as well. I really don't think she believed me. Donkeys in China are work animals and sources of food.

Fat pork was exactly that—a slab of fat. To the Chinese, it is a highly prized piece of meat, and they would consume it with great gusto and joy. They were surprised that we would refuse to eat it and would say, "Mao said fat makes you beautiful." I replied that I would have to remain ugly if this were so. I told them our doctors had been telling us for many years of the dangers of eating too much animal fat. I later came to understand that in the rural villages, the fat of the pig was considered the best part to eat. That may have had to do with the extreme poverty in those villages and the heat it added to the body.

Dog is eaten in most of China, but I was told it was only eaten in Nanyang in the winter because it gave the all-important heat to the body. Certain breeds are raised for consumption with a black dog being considered best and a brown dog second to best. I once saw a dog being butchered in the street as we rode through the city. It made me almost throw up. Xiao Hang told us that when she was small her little dog ran out into the street and was killed. Her mother went out and retrieved the dead body and cooked it for supper. She said she couldn't eat it, though.

Since anything that breathes, moves, or even exists is a food source, I'm sure cat is also eaten, but as far as I know, I was never served this and did not hear of anyone eating cat in Nanyang.

Fish and eels are often served at meals. These items will usually be brought to the table in a plastic bag for approval to show that they are still alive and, therefore, fresh. The fish is normally steamed and served whole in some kind of sauce. To eat, you use your chopsticks and take out a piece of the fish and put it on your plate. If you wanted some of the sauce, you would usually have a spoon for dipping some out. I have seen children almost fight to eat the fish eyes. Eels were normally fried but were also fixed numerous other ways.

Snakes, my greatest fear in the world, were consumed at a great rate. We would sometimes enter restaurants with cage upon cage filled with snakes. Once we were in one of the "pick your own dinner items" restaurants in Beijing, and I saw a vat of small live snakes. Then I saw a chef put his hand in the vat and just pull out a handful of snakes. I thought I would pass out! We went to a restaurant once in Shenzhen that was known for their snake specialties. Every part of the snake was served in some way, and the men even mixed the "rocket fuel" with snake blood to toast each other. I tried to take a bite of a piece of the reptile in a soup, but just couldn't do it. So my meal that night was rice and broccoli, with Eric and his wife joining me in this choice. On another evening, we were having a very pleasant dinner in Nanyang and in came two chefs holding up long snakes for our approval before cooking them. My fear just took over, and I ran to a corner of the room to "hide." Mr. Guo told the chefs to take the snakes out immediately. I have no idea if they were served that evening or not, but I didn't eat anything the rest of the dinner if I wasn't sure what it was.

One other bit of information about snake consumption: there is a wine that is made with (dead) snakes in it. This wine is displayed in some of the restaurants in huge jars containing snakes, herbs, and other ingredients that look like long twigs. I never saw anyone drink it, but I heard that one man who worked with Ralph drank it at lunch. It is supposed to have medicinal powers—but only for the men. We called it Chinese Viagra.

We were served many unusual items—unusual to westerners, but normal to the Chinese. Some of the unusual foods we were served included:

- silk worms in their various stages of development;
- pigs' ears;
- jellyfish;
- small birds cooked whole;
- baby bee soup (bee larvae), which actually tasted pretty good;
- turtle and turtle soup;
- camel and camel's "paw";
- shrimp with heads intact;
- shrimp battered and cooked with the shell on (considered a good source of calcium);
- deer tendon;
- cow stomach; and
- the inevitable plate of chicken feet at almost every dinner.

I managed to live there four and a half years without ever eating a chicken foot or head, whole cooked birds, or any reproductive part of any animal. If something is put on your plate for you that you just can't eat, try moving it around a little, sometimes put it to your mouth and then back on your plate, or use things like discarded shells and bones to partially cover it up. Once those small plates get full of things you aren't going to eat, one of the young serving girls around the table will remove that plate for a clean one. If you're in a home, it is more difficult not to eat what is served.

Lobster was served several times, but it was usually chopped up into what resembled a gelatinous mass and served raw. They gave us a wasabi sauce to dip it in, which would "cook" the lobster. I hated it!

I suppose I should include table manners in talking about dining customs. I must remind you that this is what we did and/or were told in Nanyang. Do not begin eating until the proper toasting is done, or until you see others at the table doing so. It is okay to bring bowls up to your mouth to eat; actually, it makes it easier to get food such as noodles or rice into the mouth using chopsticks. It is also considered correct to make as much noise as you wish in eating, such as slurping your soup noodles. Not only does this noise show enjoyment of the food, but the slurping also helps to cool the noodles in the hot broth as you eat them. No one who worked with Ralph liked to sit next to me at dinners because I didn't make eating noises and did not slurp my noodles. When they asked me why I didn't, I told them, "If I did that, Ralph's mother would ask me to leave the table." I figured that they would accept that explanation since traditionally mothers-in-law in China are the bosses of the daughters-in-law and very critical of their behavior. It must have worked since no one ever asked me that again.

Noise is preferred over quiet while dining; hence, we were sometimes "treated" to Chinese opera as we ate. The Chinese love this music, but to western ears it resembles loud screeching. There is at least one noodle restaurant in Beijing where you are greeted loudly by the staff upon entering. Then they use the dishes to clack together when serving your food. Most restaurants in China have a happy clientele who vociferously consume large amounts of food while talking and laughing loudly.

Spitting inedible things such as bones or shells out onto your plate is acceptable, and I did learn to do this since I didn't know of any other way to get them out of my mouth without using my fingers. Body noises such as burping or passing gas are tolerated too as well as spitting on the floor during a meal. If wine is opened, they will most likely throw the paper and foil around the bottle on the floor. We were also told not to stand chopsticks upright into a bowl of rice as this resembles the sticks of incense burned at a death. And finally, after the meal, you may use a toothpick to clean your teeth, but you should always cover your mouth with your other hand while doing this.

Eating communally out of dishes was a new concept to us and to everyone else who came to China for the first time. The term eating communally means you use your chopsticks to take out portions of the dishes on the table to put on your small plate. Do not use your chopsticks to dig around in the dishes to find what you want, just take what is available and within easy reach. If you cannot pick up something with the chopsticks, there is usually a large spoon available to use for taking out your portion. At business dinners or banquets, we usually ate at round tables with a lazy Susan turntable to make the dishes available to all. Also, in the center of the banquet table in Nanyang was an exquisitely carved sculpture made out of some large vegetable. This was only for decoration, and as soon as the food came out, the sculpture was removed. At home, we had a small rectangular table and would pass dishes that were out of reach. Many times we were given an individual bowl of rice, and we would put the food from the communal dishes on the rice to eat as desired.

The inevitable toasting at banquets and business dinners also has its own etiquette. By providing too much food and drink on these occasions, they are showing their great hospitality. Usually, Moutai or some other brand of the "firewater" is used, but sometimes a red wine or beer is used. A reminder of the toasting procedure goes as follows: after the first toast is made by the host, you begin eating the cold dishes on the table. A little while later, the host makes the second toast, and you continue eating as hot dishes are added. Then comes the third toast made by the host whereby you continue eating and prepare to toast and be toasted continually thereafter by all present until the dinner is over. There is a game that is sometimes played where two people use their fingers to represent the numbers from one to ten. If you put up the wrong number, you lose and must drink whatever alcoholic beverage is being used—it reminded me somewhat of "rock, paper, scissors." I never did figure out the rules of this game, but I did learn how to do the numbers with my fingers. I just put up whatever number I felt like, then let them tell me if I won or lost, which meant I either drank or watched them drink. Usually, you leave the dinners feeling either pretty tipsy or else quite drunk. It didn't matter how drunk you got; it only mattered that you had had a good time. The only way a person could get out of the drinking was to tell them you were on medication, or you couldn't drink for health reasons. I got used to the drinking after a while and could hold my own at these dinners. After all, I had begun my reputation for handling the drinking at my first banquet upon my arrival in Zhengzhou. I also learned some ways to pretend I was drinking the brew, but if I was caught using green tea or water in my little cup, they would pour it out and give me the real stuff. I actually lived there long enough and drank enough of the different brands of the rocket fuel to find out there were certain brands I preferred over others. Whether this was a good or bad thing is debatable.

One thing to remember is that if you are asked if you would like to have white wine at the dinner, they do not mean Pinot Grigio or Chardonnay. White wine is the literal translation of baijiu (by' joe), which is the rocket fuel. I only made the mistake of agreeing to toast with beer once and brandy one other time. Although I thought I was choosing a less potent beverage and envisioned leisurely sipping the brandy in the tiny cups used for baijiu, water glasses were used for beer, and wine glasses are used for brandy. The toasting methods remained the same—bottoms up, or as they say "ganbei," to the full contents of the glasses many times throughout the dinner. I think maybe it is best to stick to the baijiu.

NGLE Dinner—Zhao Yao, Eric, and Zhou Jin

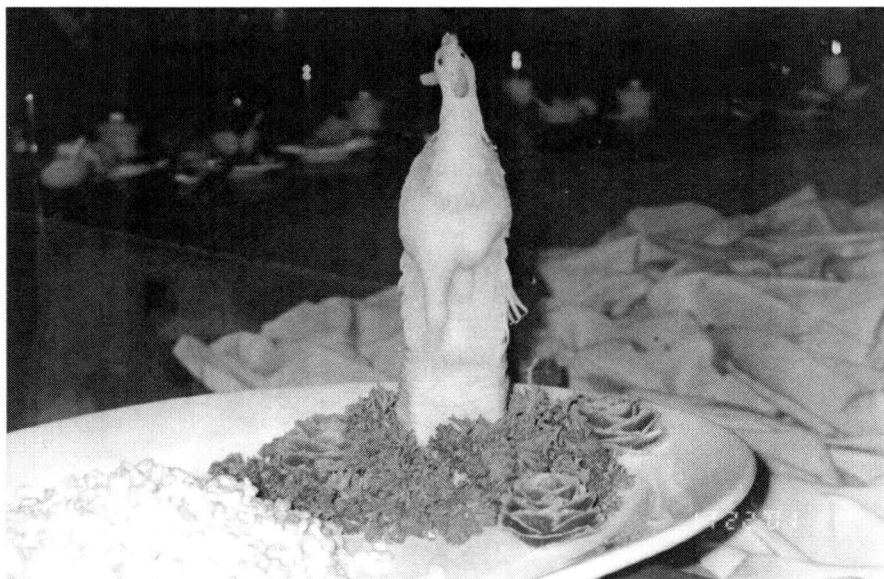

Vegetable Sculpture on Table before a Dinner

Nanyang—Ladies Selling Noodles and Fried Bread on
Street near Hotel

Pouring Tea with Long-Spout Tea Kettle

International Incidents

First Incident

During our first spring in China in May of 1999, Ralph and Eric had to attend a meeting in Beijing with Bernard Hu, who worked as an agent for AEP in the Beijing office. Glenn Davis who was an AEP engineer involved with the joint venture project also came for the meeting. Ralph and I, along with several employees of NGLE, were on a plane headed for Beijing when one of the accountants showed us a newspaper with the news of the U.S. bombing of the Chinese Embassy in Belgrade, Yugoslavia. Of course, it was all in Chinese, so we didn't know the details and only saw the picture in the newspaper. Upon landing, it became quite clear that things were in turmoil in the city. Kathy Wang from the AEP office had been sent to pick us up and was able to tell us what was going on. Traffic was a real mess, even for Beijing, and it took about twice as long to arrive at the AEP office. We stayed there for a while and then headed to the Great Wall Sheraton Hotel to check in.

Once we got to the hotel, we could watch Fox News and CNN and see how the media was handling the reporting of the protests in Beijing. Of course, the cameras were all at the U.S. Embassy where mainly college students were vigorously protesting the U.S. and the bombing. They were saying things like they "would never eat McDonald's or KFC again"—good news to our ears since you could hardly get a seat in either of these restaurants because of all the Chinese who love these American fast foods. We were staying at a five-star hotel, and since no one was menacing us at all, we felt completely safe. That night (morning for Columbus), the AEP office in Columbus called and told us to "get out of there" and go to the AEP office in Singapore. We tried to convince them that we were fine, but all they could see was what was on TV so, of course, they thought we were in imminent danger.

So Ralph, Glenn, Bernard et al. had their meeting the next morning, while I did a little shopping in a mall across the street from the office. No one paid me a bit of attention. But as soon as the meeting was over, we raced back to the hotel to get our luggage, sped to the airport, and managed to make our hastily arranged flight to Singapore.

We had a nice little vacation in Singapore where I got to meet Don Boyd who was Ralph's boss, all those who worked in that office, and Mike Dancison from the Columbus office who was soon to become a very good friend.

For those of you who have never been to Singapore, it is a beautiful, clean, small city-state, although very hot and humid since it is so near the equator. It is called a "fine city" because there are hefty fines for breaking any of the many laws they use to keep it clean and well-ordered. These laws are strictly enforced so remember to obey them if you don't want to pay these fines, many of them in the thousands of dollars. Some of the laws are no littering, no jaywalking, no spitting, no chewing gum (don't even try to "smuggle" it into the country), and no smoking inside a building or anywhere there is a "no smoking" sign posted. Besides these laws, there was the one that required flushing the toilet after use since not doing so is also against the law.

The population of Singapore is mostly made up of Chinese, Malaysians, Indians, and Caucasians. The students have to be able to speak two languages, and most choose to study their ethnic language plus a foreign language. As you could guess, the variety of foods was very diverse, but at the time we were craving western food. We were treated to dining at the famous Raffles Hotel where we indulged in a delicious and sumptuous buffet and an elegant dining experience.

We returned to Beijing as soon as the protests were over, which lasted three days. The students were back in the classrooms—and also back in the McDonald's and KFCs that are all over China. We went back to Nanyang and discovered that all the students at the university and Ralph's coworkers were told not to ask us about this incident since we had nothing to do with it and could not help it.

Second Incident

In March of 2001, there was another cause for concern. An American "spy plane" crashed with a Chinese fighter jet over the South China Sea near the island province of Hainan (hi nahn'). The fighter jet split in two and fell into the ocean, resulting in the death of the pilot. The American plane made an emergency landing at a Chinese air base on Hainan Island, which China said was illegal, and the crew of the plane was taken into custody by Chinese officials. The American government said this incident was the fault of the aggressive actions of the pilot of the Chinese fighter; the Chinese said the American spy plane was in Chinese airspace. The crew was finally released in April of 2001, but China kept the plane until July when it was disassembled and returned to the U.S. During the time of the landing of the plane and the time it was returned to the U.S., the Chinese had had sufficient time to thoroughly examine the plane and its technology. Of course, the U.S. had to pay for not only the dismantling and shipping of the airplane back to the States but also for the food and lodging of the crew while they were held captive. What a country!

During this incident, we stayed in Nanyang, and again it was a subject not discussed much in our presence. Only one student at a private school where I had gone during this time questioned me about it, and I might add belligerently too. He said, "I saw on CNN where the U.S. said that it was China's fault for the crash of the planes!" I answered calmly, "Well, you will believe what your government tells you, and I will believe what my government tells me—and neither of us will ever know the truth." He didn't say anything after that. Besides, I don't know how he saw anything on CNN since at that time it was supposedly only available in the best hotels—and then only when there was nothing critical of or sensitive to the Chinese government. When something was thought to be anti-Chinese government, the TV became snowy, and CNN became "unavailable."

We did get another trip to Singapore in May of 2000. Don Boyd thought it might be best if we left China during the May Day holiday since there was a possibility of demonstrations of the 1999 Embassy bombing incident. Never to turn down a trip to Singapore, we gladly accepted his invitation and had another lovely visit with our friends there.

Yangtze River Tour

In the spring of 2000, Ralph's parents and sister Mary came to China on a tour that included a cruise on the Yangtze (yahnt' zee) River. We decided to meet their tour group in the city of Wuhan (woo' hahn), which is the capital city of the Hubei (hoo bay') Province and about six hours south of Nanyang. It is also called "China's Oven" because of the intense heat and humidity in the summer months.

Mr. Bai drove us and Eric to Wuhan because Eric was going to visit some relatives who lived there. We had lunch while we were waiting for everyone on the tour to arrive and then met them at the airport. We all toured the city of Wuhan and then had dinner together. Ralph and I began eating communally as usual out of the dishes that had been placed on the table. Mary told us that only those at our table would have been able to handle that style of eating. We noticed that everyone else just filled their plates instead of eating in the Chinese manner. Not wanting to offend anyone, we began to do likewise.

After dinner we boarded the yacht with the tour group and began our interesting and leisurely cruise on the Yangtze westward toward Chongqing (chong ching') in the Sichuan (people we knew pronounced this as sit'ron) Province. Along with the Yellow River in the north, it is one of the most important rivers in China and also the longest. While the northern part of China considers the Yellow River the source of their civilization, there is a debate with southern China that it is the Yangtze where it began.

After settling into our rooms, we began socializing with the people in our group and familiarizing ourselves with the ship. At breakfast the next morning, which was normal buffet-style Chinese food, we were almost trampled by another group of Americans. We thought they must have been famished because they certainly were in a hurry to get to the food, which we discovered was really not worth that behavior. They continued to push ahead of everyone at every meal, so we soon learned to sit and wait until they had filled their plates before approaching the buffet. We were to discover that these particular people were a church group—who later told us all about how great their church was, how large a membership they had, about their pizza ovens and the many young people who came to their pizza evenings, and finally about how many Chinese students came to their church. I had had several Chinese people who had studied in the U.S. tell us that they went to churches to practice their English. I figured this was the attraction for the students to this particular church, but I didn't burst the group's bubble about their thinking it was because of their brand of religion.

The crew of the yacht provided nightly programs for us, which usually involved us as the participants in the games or in dancing. The cruise also included demonstrations of the Chinese skill in painting scenery inside small bottles, which in olden times had been used to hold snuff and opium. Of course, pearl vendors were set up with a good supply of China's pearls to sell to the passengers. But mostly, we just enjoyed the passing scenery that was definitely different from the flatlands of Nanyang. However, Ralph actually saw a dead body floating by us one day, which was not an enjoyable sight but was a reminder of how polluted this river was said to be.

The Yangtze is a dangerous river when it floods, but the huge dam they were building to control the river floods was very controversial. Once the dam was completed, the river waters would cover many towns and historical artifacts that could be found along the river. Much farmland was also going to be lost. Many of the farmers whose ancestors had farmed the land along the river for many past generations were carrying the soil by bucketfuls to the top of the hillsides where the new homes were being built.

We stopped at some small towns along the river to tour the sights they had to offer. The one that I remember most was the show we saw with children who performed amazing acrobatic feats such as you would see in a circus. They seemed so young to be able to be so accomplished in their performances. But as we traveled on up the gorges, we saw young boys run straight up the side of a mountain without any apparent effort, so possibly it is an inborn ability and the acrobatic tricks come easily to them.

We also traveled by boat up the Three Gorges of the Yangtze and saw the famous hanging coffins of the ancient people called the Bo. It boggled the mind to see those coffins on ledges and in caves in the cliffs so high above the river and ground. It made us wonder at the skill the ancients possessed to be able to get the coffins to their resting places.

We stopped at the site of the new dam that was then under construction, and I must say Ralph was in engineer heaven. It was a monumental project, and he could have stayed there all day. Unlike his interest in the building of the project, I enjoyed seeing the displayed replica of what the completed project would look like when finished.

On the fifth day, we landed at Chongqing, ending our cruise of this gigantic river. We toured the city and the Stillwell Museum in honor of General Joseph Stillwell who had given the Chinese training and help during WWII against the Japanese. One American man in our group who had been stationed in China during that time with General Stillwell returned to the town where he had lived. He reported back to us that it still looked the same and had not changed at all over the years since he was there. After touring the city and several historical places, Ruth, Granville, and Mary went on with the others to finish their tour. Ralph and I headed to a local hotel to await our flight back to Nanyang. We ordered hamburgers for lunch in the dining room, causing some Americans in another tour group on their way to the usual Chinese buffet to exclaim in loud voices, "We want what they're having!"

It had been a wonderful time spent with family and getting to see a part of China that we had not visited before. Soon we were back in Nanyang with our friends there, and our time on the Yangtze was another pleasant memory we added to all the others we were accumulating.

Yangtze River Tour

Yangtze River Tour—Three Gorges

Yangtze River Tour—Three Gorges (2)

Yangtze River Tour—Three Gorges (3)

Yangtze River Tour—Three Gorges Waving at Chinese
People on a Taxi Boat (continued below)

Yangtze River Tour—Building the Dam

Yangtze River Tour—Building the Dam (2)

Yangtze River Tour—Replica of the Completed Dam

Yangtze River Tour—Old Village on Left to be Covered
by River—New Village on Right at Top of Hill

Other Foreigners in Nanyang

When we first arrived in Nanyang, there were only two other foreigners actually living in Nanyang—a pair of British teachers who taught at the Teachers' College, which was also called the Normal School. They were members of the VSO in the UK, a volunteer organization that sends teachers and other volunteers to developing countries. We made many attempts to contact them, but either they weren't interested in meeting us, or they weren't told about us and our desire to meet them. Soon they left as they had completed their assignment in Nanyang, and two more teachers arrived to replace them—Maria Linnemann and Roy Wilson. Maria is an accomplished musician and a guitar composer and gave concerts in Nanyang with Roy accompanying her vocally. Unfortunately, we were never able to hear any of their performances. Roy is gifted with immense teaching talents and especially enjoys teaching students from other countries of the world. Roy and Maria were very willing to not only meet us but also joined in our socializing with other foreigners who eventually came to Nanyang.

I was responsible for the first full-time foreign teacher to come to Nanyang Institute of Technology, "my" university. He was currently from Australia but was born in Scotland and had previously taught in Wales. I had met him in the airport in Beijing when I was waiting on my flight back to Nanyang. He had come to China to "make money" and was hoping to find a teaching job in

Zhengzhou, which was our provincial capital. Then he informed me he was also going there to meet a girl "pen pal." I told him if things didn't work out in Zhengzhou, NIT was looking for a full-time English teacher. To make a long story short, he wound up in Nanyang with the "pen pal/girlfriend" in tow. He was fifty-seven years old at the time, and she was very young, I am guessing about twenty years old. They lived together in an apartment at the school, and he always insisted they were going to have a big Catholic wedding at the Catholic Church just outside of Nanyang, but that never happened. Finally, the school demanded that they marry, and so they had a small, quickly arranged wedding. They came to visit often, and sometimes I invited them to eat with us. They ate so ravenously that I wondered how much food they had at home since by now I knew how "thrifty" this man was. He was quite proud of himself and thought himself quite handsome—a view not shared by others. He would tell anyone he saw how good he was at just about everything from teaching, to music, to tennis, and so on. He talked me into team teaching once, and I didn't understand a thing he was saying, so I'm sure the students didn't either. Whenever he called on them to stand and read, they would visibly shake, so I wondered how he treated them on a regular basis. This paragon of the teaching profession could not even explain Christianity to his own wife. He taught for a year and a half at the university and was insulted that the school didn't hire him for the following year. But by then, I think he had burned all his bridges there, and everyone, including his students, was glad to see him go. Besides, at that time, the school was learning how to use the Internet to contact teachers who wanted to teach English in China.

Next to arrive was our friend Bonnie Turner from Cross Lanes, West Virginia, and Michael Zargarov from Houston, Texas, both of whom came to teach at NIT. Heather and John Pickworth from New Zealand and Alicia Guy from Seattle came to teach at a private school. Of course, they were more than willing to socialize with us and thus began my brunches, Sunday dinners, and dinners in restaurants. Eric always joined us and did the ordering of food items when we went to restaurants. Being from Taiwan and having traveled the world, he was more familiar with western tastes in food.

Michael had taught in other countries and had come to NIT after teaching in Shanghai. The following year, he decided it was time to go home to Houston, leaving his days of teaching in China behind—and also the dreaded baijiu, which he called "Dragon Spit." Bonnie signed on for another year, and more people came to teach at NIT. They included Bonnie's brother Eddie from San Francisco, Gail from Canada, and Akiko from Japan. Heather and John Pickworth returned from New Zealand and Alicia Guy from Seattle to teach at the private school once again. David Yarwood arrived from Toronto, Canada, to teach there also. Carl Slaughter from Kentucky came to teach at the Teacher's College with Maria and Roy. We had a very nice group of western people now and the socializing continued with Eric as our chauffeur and translator. This was the year I managed to have an American Thanksgiving celebration in the apartment where Helen Sun stayed when she was working in Nanyang. It was down the hallway from our apartment. We set up tables and chairs there, and I did the cooking in our apartment. No turkey could be found, although Mr. Guo from NGLE and Eric made heroic efforts to find one. Instead, I bought chicken "chests" at the new supermarket and cooked them in the crock pots with onion, celery, and apple slices. Then I cut them like slices of turkey breasts, made stuffing, salads, vegetable dishes, deviled eggs, mashed potatoes and gravy, rolls, and dessert. I did all this with a toaster oven, a two-burner stovetop, and two crock pots. Alicia, Heather, and John arrived early to help with the food preparations. Alicia asked if we had any football games on tape, and we did indeed have the previous year's Super Bowl game our friend Dr. David Rice had made and sent. So it not only smelled like Thanksgiving Day but also sounded like it with the game playing in the background. Bonnie and Eddie arrived with a big bowl of glazed cooked carrots, followed by Carl with a bag of fruit in hand, and everyone else showed up soon after. Those celebrating their first American Thanksgiving were Heather, John, David and his visitor and friend Dara, and Eric and his wife Zhou (Jo). So it was up to Alicia, Carl, Bonnie, Eddie, Ralph, and me to show them how to celebrate in style. First we gathered around the table with sheets serving as tablecloths, lit candles, and centerpieces Alicia had made—very festive! We all held hands, and each person told us the thing they were most thankful for that day. Then we began filling our plates and continued to have a lovely Thanksgiving celebration.

During our last year, more people came to Nanyang as teachers at the various schools. Akiko left the same year as did Alicia and Roy when their contracts expired. Since we were closer to Alicia and Roy, it was very difficult to say goodbye to them. Bill Blackwood from Great Britain and Brandon Stoltenkamp from South Africa came to teach at the teachers' college, and soon after Sandra Bagnall and Michael arrived from Great Britain to teach there also. Bill and Carl completed their contracts that summer and left for other parts of the world to teach. NIT hired Dave from the UK and a husband and wife couple named Francois and Aline—he from Sweden and she from the Seychelles Islands off East Africa. Another man from the UK also came to teach at NIT, but he was not interested in socializing with anyone but a fellow Brit. I found him to be arrogant and rude and soon knew he was in China for all the wrong reasons. He had an immense ego and incessantly bragged about his very own "wonderfulness." After he told everyone what a genius he was and how he had invented a system of teaching English to anyone in three week's time, we waited to see this miracle develop. Well, it didn't happen—ever. He was grossly impatient with the students and would send them from the classroom if they didn't answer his questions quickly enough. He eventually moved a young Chinese girlfriend in with him and had a very vocal and heated argument with the school officials because of that. I am sorry to say he won out and kept the young girl with him. I was very happy that he was not an American because he would definitely have been an "ugly" one.

On some Sunday evenings, we foreigners would meet at our apartment and then go out to a restaurant for dinner, giving the locals a novel treat for the eyes. We would literally stop traffic as they would just stop and stare at us. To accommodate them, we would position ourselves in a group for those who wanted to take pictures or just get a good look. I have to admit we were quite a sight as we comprised a local "United Nations" of all sizes, colors, and nationalities. Most of the people who came there to teach or work behaved very well and acted like good ambassadors of their own country, but there were the few who were disappointments to the entire human race.

Foreign Teachers' Tour of Pushan Power Plant

Chinglish

"Chinglish" is the term to describe English wording often mixed with the Chinese literal translations. You will see signs written in Chinglish all over China. These signs are usually amusing to English-speaking westerners because they often make no sense, or the translation is inappropriately sexual in content. Some are totally hilarious because of the way the literal translation of the Chinese character turns into English. I would think that it would be fairly easy to find some native English speaker or someone who is familiar with the English language to discuss the actual translation before making these signs, especially in Beijing and the larger cities. It seems as if there is a rush to print them without any thought to the correctness or the actual meanings, some of which have no meaning in English at all. Beijing tried to stop Chinglish before the 2008 Olympics, but I don't think they were totally successful

If everyone in charge of signage had been as earnest as one of my students, there would not have been so many signs done with bad spelling, bad grammar, not to mention funny translations. This student at the university who was very serious about any task assigned to him actually called me for information on the signage for which he was responsible. He had been put in charge of the signs for the restrooms at the university. He wanted to know what words he should use for the female and male WCs (this stands for water closets, which was the common name for restrooms all over China). I told him either "women or ladies" and "men or gentlemen" would be appropriate. "But," he asked very seriously, "which is better?" I told him I would use Women and Men, but that it really did not matter at all which he used. I did not add that it especially would not matter at the university where there were very few westerners. We had learned from the engineers who had worked on the joint venture project that the difference in the Chinese characters for the men's and women's WCs was as such: the character that had a cross mark at the bottom resembled a woman crossing her legs, and thus, that was how we knew which one was the women's toilet. This worked quite well for me when there was no one around to ask, and I passed this bit of knowledge on to all the western women I knew.

I suppose that due to our movies and the constant usage of the "F" word, they think everyone in the western world uses this word freely. The "F" bomb is used on the Chinglish signs quite a bit—although it is usually shockingly absurd but always funny. Another word they must have picked up from our movies is the "S" word. They don't know that this word is offensive in polite conversation, so they used it quite often. One girl told us how many times her dog "s**t" on a particular walk. Some would tell us when they found mouse "s**t" on their kitchen counter.

At the airport in Zhengzhou, which was the capital of our province, there was the sign for those just disembarking from a plane that read "Arrials" (Arrivals); there was one near the Hongqiao Market in Beijing that read "Ticture Woild" (Picture World); there was a warning sign at a park outside Beijing that read "Don't Step on the Baby Grass"; another on a wall near a new building in Beijing that said, "You are in the mountains now. Love and hug each other"; but my favorite was on the back of the front seat in a taxi that warned "Don't forget to take your thing." We got a huge laugh out of that one.

More examples of Chinglish seen throughout China:

On a supermarket:	"Very Suspicious Supermarket"
Outside a toilet:	"Deformed Man Toilet" (toilet for the handicapped)
Outside a toilet:	"*Pubic* Toilet"
On a *can* of water:	"Bottled Water"
Hospital in Beijing:	"Dongda Hospital for Anus and Intestine Disease"
In an airport:	"Smorking Room" (smoking room)
On a wall:	"No Climbing—In Case of Thunderstorm"
In an airport:	"We Take Your Bags and Send Them to All Directions"
In a terminal:	"For Restrooms—Go Back toward Your Behind"
In a restaurant:	"The Shrimp F**ks the Cabbage"
In an airport:	"Civilized Airport"
In a drycleaners:	"Please Drop Your Trousers Here for Best Results"
On an ATM:	"Cash Recycling Machine"
In a supermarket:	"Private Vegetables"
Name of a restaurant:	"Faggot"
Name of a restaurant:	"Assman Restaurant"
Directions to a park:	"Racist Park" (a park for China's ethnic minorities)
Seen often:	"Slip Carefully" (warning to watch for slippery conditions)
Items on menu:	"Husband and Wife Lung Slice"
Item on menu:	"Deep-fried and Look Like Squirrel"
Item on menu:	"Saliva Chicken"
At a fish pond:	"Please Do Not Feed the Fishes with Your Private."

Next to an escalator: "Please Keep Your Legs"
In a toilet: "Mang Out after Shit"
Ad for dentist: "Teeth Extracted by Latest Methodists"

The funniest story I heard about oral Chinglish went like this: a Chinese man was hosting a dinner, and the guest of honor was a man from Great Britain. The host decided to use English in toasting his guests—but he should have stuck to the Chinese word *ganbei*! which means "bottoms up." Instead, he enthusiastically shouted, "Up your bottoms!" The Brit did not miss a beat—he replied in like fashion, "Up yours too!"

小草有生命　脚下请留情
Little grass has life,
Please watch your step.

Chinglish Sign

Celebrity

Since Ralph and I were some of the few westerners in Henan Province at the time, and Ralph had an important job with the joint venture project, we were often photographed for the newspapers and interviewed on the TV stations. This was all new to both of us, although Ralph had had a few TV interviews while he was manager of the Kammer/Mitchell power plants near Wheeling, West Virginia. I, however, was a complete novice at this and had to learn "by the baptism of the fire." Our friends in Nanyang would often tell us when they had seen us on local TV, or when they read an interview with us in the newspaper. I quickly learned to phrase positive and complimentary comments for the newspapers, hoping that they translated it as I said it. Since I never received any negative feedback, I always assumed that they did. I also found out how staged the filmed events could be with the cameras rolling since we were told what to do and sometimes how to do them. I guess you could say we were big fish in a small pond in Nanyang.

One time we were asked to allow the provincial media to include us in a documentary about foreigners who lived in our province who were contributing to the economy and educational process. Of course, we said yes, not realizing that this would take several days to accomplish. First they went to the power plant and did a segment on Ralph. Then they came to do my segment. They took me to the local points of interest where I walked around exhibiting a great deal of interest in the historically famous places. Then they came to our apartment to document how we lived inside our home. They took the cameras everywhere in the apartment and even to the kitchen to film Xiao Hang as she cooked our dinner. After this, they strongly encouraged us to stage a "welcome home from work kiss" as Ralph went out the door only to come back in as if he had just arrived from work. This part of the interview went on for quite some time. The final segment was to film me volunteering at the university (NIT). As usual, the students for this filming were chosen and were not actually all my students. But by now, this did not surprise me. I had prepared what I would do for the cameras and began by writing things on the board for them to practice saying. I then interacted with the students in helping with their pronunciation of English words. After this segment was finished, I told them that my friends Bonnie Turner and Michael Zargarov were foreign teachers at the university who had chosen to come to Nanyang to teach. They quickly sent for them to come to be filmed with me. As we were lined up and smiling for the camera, Bonnie's brother Eddie Leffew arrived for a visit with Bonnie. After landing in Beijing, he had completed the long train trip to Nanyang and had just arrived at NIT. We told him to come on over and stand with us as the cameras rolled. With amazement on his face and in his voice, he asked me, "Is it like this every day?" I replied, "Sometimes it is!" Finally, after a tour of the campus with the cameras following us and telling us when to stop and look at something, etc., the interview was over. We were told this documentary was going to be televised nationally and possibly internationally. We never actually saw it televised while we lived in China; however, many people told us they had seen the documentary. Not long after it was filmed, Bernard Hu saw it on TV in the city of Shenzhen where he had an apartment. Perhaps if it ever goes international, we may someday turn on our television and actually get to see ourselves performing for the cameras.

Richard, our Chinese friend, who had come to Nanyang from Beijing to open a foreign language school asked me to be vice president of his school. I told him I really didn't want to take on any more jobs due to our traveling so much, but he convinced me all he really wanted to do was include my name on the paperwork and his business cards to make it look like he had foreigners involved. I agreed to do this for him all the while thinking, "Business as usual in China." Anyway, I really didn't have to do anything except appear for interviews with the newspapers and TV stations when necessary. Once when someone—most likely a competitor—spray painted over his sign at the doorway of his school, I was called upon to talk to the press. Of course, I said all the politically correct things about how I didn't understand anyone from Nanyang doing such a terrible thing since I had always found the people there to be good and kind. I received calls from Richard who operated the school and other friends telling me that they had see me on TV, and that I had done a good job saying the right things to the press.

The "celebrity status" continued into our daily life as we went about doing mundane, everyday things. Whenever I would go shopping, I was scrutinized by those on the streets, especially if they had never seen a foreigner before. Women my age didn't wear blue jeans or tennis shoes in Nanyang at that time, and I would be looked up and down whenever I wore clothes that were different from the "uniform" considered proper for middle-aged women—dark tops, pants, and shoes. Once Linda, who was thirty years old at the time, wore a beautiful fuchsia-colored suit to a dinner and looked so pretty in it; however, she was chastised by one of the other employees of NGLE that she was too old to wear that color. Nothing I could say could convince her to wear that suit again. I suppose those who consider themselves the fashion police exist everywhere. At any rate, I dressed as I wished and let them look. Sometimes I would be stopped by a woman who was a street vendor whom I passed frequently on my way to and from the supermarket. She would look me over, and if I met her approval, she would give me a thumbs-up. If I didn't meet her approval, she would say something that I took to be advice or criticism. Thankfully, I usually passed muster with her. Even after living there

several years, I would still hear someone say "lao wai" (foreigner)
loud enough for me to hear. I don't think this was a particularly
complimentary term, although Linda said it was not offensive.
As usual, if I answered back with "Meguo ren" (American) they
displayed some embarrassment that I had understood what they
said. It was always interesting what would happen when I was out
and about, but by the second year I was more comfortable with all
the attention.

Once when Ralph's family—his mother Ruth, father Granville,
sister Mary, and brother Dennis—had come to Nanyang to visit,
I took them on a walk through the streets since I wanted to show
them another glimpse of the "real" China. We stopped at a vegetable
vendor I frequented regularly, and a tiny elderly woman came up
to me, took my face in her hands, looked into my eyes, and felt
my face. I just let her look since by then I knew that she meant
no harm and was just curious. She had lived long enough to not
only see a foreigner but to also touch one. Then I gave her a hug,
and we left to continue our walk through Nanyang. On we went
until we came to Meixi Lu (may she loo'), my favorite shopping
street. It was a Saturday and was packed with people. Suddenly,
out of the huge mass of people, I heard my name "Jean! Teacher!
Jean!" It was one of my NIT students who had the English name of
Sunshine—a very appropriate choice of names in this instance as
her face reminded me of a ray of sunshine. I introduced her and
her boyfriend to the family, and they were quite impressed that
I was actually recognized by someone in such a large crowd. We
also went to the Jade Market to see the sculptures being carved
and those on display. Then we went to Center Market, which was a
large outdoor market that sold everything from herbs, medicines,
dishware, cookware, and food items including live animals, meat,
vegetables, fish, eels, bugs, and snakes. I think it was one of their
most memorable China experiences, and I think it gave the
people of Nanyang a memorable experience also to see us in a
family group. Ralph and I were told several times by our Chinese
friends that they had been told things about Americans that they

found were not true after meeting us—things such as we throw our children out of the house when they are eighteen, and we don't take care of our old people. I think they saw through us that Americans truly do value and care about family members of all ages.

Because I was a foreigner, it was assumed that I knew much about everything, especially by the students. I would receive visits and phone calls from students and adults I knew asking advice about anything from their job, what to do about their child, and even their love life. Sometimes I would get a call from "someone who knew someone who knew me." These were usually students who were in a quandary over a girlfriend/boyfriend love situation. Since I didn't have a clue to whom I was talking or anything about them, I told them they should talk things over with their mother. But they quickly pointed out that their mother was not educated and could not help them—by this they meant that their mothers would tell them to follow Chinese tradition. In a society where tradition plays a major part in their lives, the answers to most things in life have already been decided. Other times, I would receive a call from a student who just wanted to practice his/her English or perhaps sing me a song over the phone. I never knew what would happen when the phone rang or how quickly I would have to think to give the proper answer to their questions or dilemmas.

Some days I didn't leave the apartment since I just didn't want to have to deal with all the attention. Other days, I had great fun with it. But I have to admit that when we got back to the States, the anonymity I instantly achieved at home was very welcomed.

Meeting with High-Ranking Communist Party
Official in Nanyang

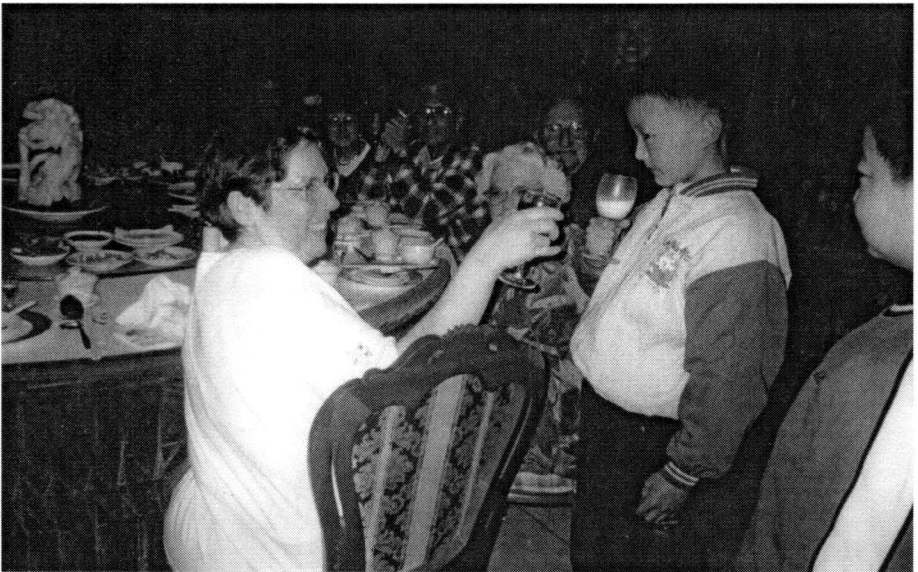

Ralph's Family Visit—The Kids Toasting Mary at a
NGLE Dinner Given in Their Honor

Ralph's Family's Visit in Nanyang—Parents and Scott
at Center Market

Ralph's Family's Visit—At Ding's Jewelry Shop in
Hongqiao Market, Beijing

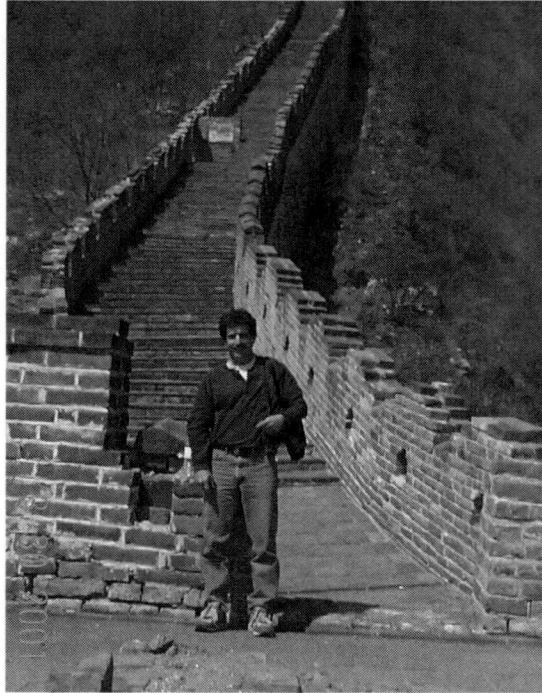

Ralph's Family's Visit—Dennis at Mutianyu

Ralph's Family's Visit—Helen, Granville, Ruth, Dennis,
Jean Ralph, Mary at Mutianyu

Ralph's Family's Visit—Mary and Jean Resting
before a Steep Climb

Ralph's Family's Visit—At Drum Tower in Xian

Ralph's Family's Visit—Touring the Shopping on Meixi
Lu in Nanyang (Continued below)

Ralph's Family's Visit—Xian—Painted Ceiling in
Ancient Building

Ralph's Family's Visit—Xian City Square

Ralph's Family's Visit—At Forbidden City

Visitors from the Home Office

Whenever anyone from the U.S. came to Nanyang, it was cause for great excitement, especially during that first year. We were starved for our own culture and really looked forward to visits from home. Other than Bonnie's visit that first year and our daughter Amanda coming for a month, no other American woman had visited since the first month of moving to Nanyang when Frosty Cunningham's wife Retha had come for a few days. Frosty had completed his work with the project, and they first toured much of China before making Retha's first and Frosty's final visit to Nanyang. Most of the visits were from American Electric Power's home office in Columbus. Glenn Davis was our most frequent visitor, and Frank Van Pelt would come occasionally. They were engineers who had worked on the joint venture project. Before we came to Nanyang, Frank had met and married Serena, a local girl who had been a translator for NGLE. Besides the work he had come to do, he also had in-laws in Nanyang to visit.

On one visit Glenn and Frank made, they brought Cindy Frye from their AEP office in Columbus. She came to organize the NGLE company files at Ralph's office. She got the usual initiation into Nanyang culture by being stared at, riding in the shotgun seat while being driven through the teeming city, having the full banquet treatment complete with the toasting customs, and then visiting "The Hole" (the karaoke bar) under the hotel for dancing afterward. Cindy had gorgeous white hair, and one Chinese woman in an outdoor market on Meixi Lu asked if she could touch her hair.

When we went to Beijing before she left China, we went to the famous Hong Qiao market to shop. During the taxi ride to the market, Cindy sat in the front seat with the taxi driver who could barely drive for looking at Cindy in her low-cut blouse and shorts. Those of us in the back seat made no effort to contain our enjoyment of the situation. When we got out of the taxi, Glenn told Cindy to bend over fairly low to pay the driver and give him a better look at her cleavage. I think we could have gotten that ride for free, but the cost was surely worth all the laughter we got out of his reaction. He didn't even count the money because he was too busy looking at Cindy's chest. He was still sitting there looking at her as we walked away laughing and is probably still talking about his experience with the lovely white-haired lady from the U.S.—that is, if the cat doesn't still have his tongue.

Dennis Lantzy, who was Glenn and Frank's boss, would also come over for important events in the course of the project. We enjoyed these visits immensely, especially when their wives Debbie Davis and Karen Lantzy came with them. It was quite a treat for me to have other women from my own culture to talk with. Eventually, Mike Dancison, whom we had met in Singapore, and his wife Marge joined the Lantzys, and Glenn Davis and also came for a visit. We had so much fun with them, even though Marge had a difficult time walking through Center Market and seeing the animals for sale, especially the dogs. I also had had difficulty with the animal situation when I first arrived, and still did at times, but by then I had learned to keep myself from thinking about this too much.

On one visit, the Lantzys made to Nanyang, they brought their daughter Denise and son Tim. They were given the extreme version of a Nanyang visit and were great sports about the drinking games, the food, and even a karaoke girl hired for Tim named Bing Bing. She persistently pursued Tim the whole evening, but to no avail. He refrained from succumbing to her charms the whole evening.

The kids said it was the best vacation their parents had ever given them.

No matter who came to visit, after about two days in Nanyang, I could see their desire to get away from all Nanyang had to offer and go to cleaner and more prosperous places. They were also desperately hoping to say goodbye to the extremely hard beds at the hotel where they stayed. If there was a board meeting or other meetings in Beijing, Shenzhen, or Hong Kong, we would leave Nanyang for those cities and stay in five-star hotels. I would be amused when upon arrival in these hotels, the wives said things such as "It's so clean" or "It's so pretty"—things I myself had said whenever I got to such places in those early days. Bernard Hu saw to it that we didn't have to stay in Nanyang too long at a time and would schedule meetings in Beijing and other cities—and for this, I will be forever grateful. I did love the people of Nanyang and over the years had learned to cope with the conditions there quite well, but I have to admit it was nice to get away occasionally.

Jean with Karen, Marge, Mike, and Scott on
Walk-Over Bridge in Nanyang

Mike and Marge—Ski Lift to Top of Great Wall at
Mutianyu

Mike and Marge Climbing Mutianyu

Marge Toasting Mr. Guo at Her First Dinner

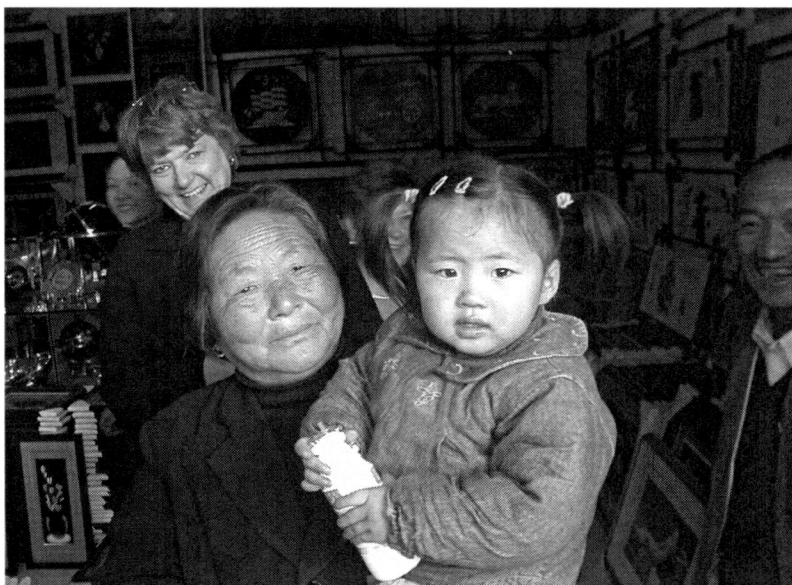

Marge Enjoying the Grandmother with Granddaughter

The Hole—A Visit after Dinner for Mike and Marge

The Hole—Dancing

The Hole—Dancing around Linda

The Hole—Marge Singing Karaoke

The Hole—Ralph and Mike Just Couldn't
Keep Up the Pace

Everyone Toasting Mike on His First Visit to Nanyang

Celebrating American Festivals

After being in a foreign country for several months where the culture is vastly different from our own, we found we missed our "festivals" and the customs that went with celebrating them. When our first Fourth of July in Nanyang rolled around, we were treated to a dinner by Ralph's coworkers to honor this festival and help us celebrate. We were touched by their thoughtfulness and appreciated it very much, but the thought did enter my mind that never in my wildest dreams had I ever imagined that one day we would be celebrating our Independence Day with a roomful of Chinese people, several of whom were Communists. However, these were our friends, and we had a very pleasant time eating together and toasting each other with Moutai.

The following year, we decided we should be the ones to host the dinner. We invited them to join us once again in celebrating this momentous day for Americans. Ralph also said that since it was our holiday, the toasting should be done with American liquor—bourbon to be exact. Eric drove us to the restaurant, and we prominently displayed the bourbon on the table. In walked our Chinese friends, and we saw the inevitable "purse" under Mr. Kang's arm that was used to carry money, cell phones, and any other important accessories. We knew then that we were not going to be paying for that dinner, but we were still going to insist that they drink our "firewater" for the occasion. We first poured a little in the glasses, and Ralph made the first toast. As usual, the toast

ended with "ganbei!" (bottoms up). Well, you have never seen
such faces—even worse than the ones made by Americans when
we first tasted Chinese rocket fuel! It got to the point where I felt
sorry for them and suggested mixing the bourbon with some Coca
Cola or Sprite. Unfortunately, that didn't help them deal with it
either, but we're thinking "what's good for the goose is good for
the gander." The bourbon continued to be consumed, and in spite
of the grimacing faces, everyone survived their ordeal.

Thanksgiving was another of our festivals they celebrated with
us every year. They would take us to a nice restaurant and order a
lavish meal, always trying to incorporate foods similar to what we
would eat. One year we had the hollowed-out shell of an orange
stuffed with a creamy orange and sweet potato mixture—delicious!
One year we had fried chicken legs. It was the effort to please
us that meant the most. Then after dinner, we went to a karaoke
bar for dancing. Mao had liked ballroom dancing, so that was an
activity everyone enjoyed. All went well until the year I accidentally
got kicked in the ankle by the heel of a girl's shoe. It was such a
sharp kick that I went down quickly, instinctively putting out my
hand to break the fall. I guess I was so well fortified by the rocket
fuel we had consumed at dinner that I didn't immediately realize
I was actually hurt. I got up, declared I was okay, and danced three
more dances before I began feeling the pain. By the time we got
back to our apartment, my wrist and ankle were throbbing and
hurting. I took some Advil, and Ralph made me some ice packs.
I finally went to sleep. The next morning, I knew I had to face
one of my worst fears—go see a local doctor. We went to the #1
Hospital (every organization and school is assigned a number),
and I was able to see a doctor almost immediately. Of course, I
may have been put at the head of the line since I was a foreigner.
They felt my wrist and took X-rays and then told me I needed to
have an operation. Ralph and I both said "No!" to that, so they
countered with the fact that I had broken bones in my wrist and
hand, and they would have to set them. I reasoned that the doctors
in Nanyang were trained mostly in traditional Chinese medicine,

and that bone setting was traditional medicine at its most basic, so I agreed to allow them to do it. They told me it would be very painful. I replied that I didn't have a choice and would just have to endure the pain.

They took me into a room with a hospital table and very little else. Linda went with me since she had been a nurse prior to being a translator. Ralph and Eric waited in the hallway. Suddenly, several other doctors appeared, and they put a needle into the middle of the back of my hand. This, they said, was a painkiller. Well, as far as killing pain went, I could just as well have taken aspirin. A time of agony soon followed as three doctors held my hand and pushed the bones around to get them back into place—oh, how that hurt! Then with the three doctors pulling on my hand and the three doctors behind my shoulder, they pushed and pulled my arm and manipulated the bones in my wrist and hand until I thought I could no longer stand the pain. But I was determined they were not going to see an American cry or scream and began to do childbirth breathing exercises to try to get my mind off the tortuous procedure. It didn't work, but it did give me an outlet for getting through the excruciating pain. The doctors kept looking at me as I continued the breathing exercises. Finally, they were satisfied with their work and made a cast for my wrist and hand.

It was about lunchtime by then, so as was the custom, we invited the head doctor to have lunch with us. As we were sitting at the table, the doctor told Linda that Chinese women my age would have been screaming with the pain, but I was better educated and had a better system. I wanted to inform him that education had nothing to do with it—it was just sheer determination and a show of American strength—but I let it go. The whole time we lived there I would hear Scott or even women say they would like to fight an American. I never understood why, unless they just wanted to see how strong Americans really were.

I refused to stay at the hospital, but they had assigned me a bed anyway. I had to go sit on that bed with the gray sheets and straw pillow the following week, while they examined my wrist and hand, with all of them smoking cigarettes as they bent over my wrist. The doctors determined that a bone had moved so they needed to reset it. The repeat of the procedure was as agonizing as it was the first time, if not more so. But I breathed and breathed once again, and finally they were finished. Again I endured their pulling and pushing and did not cry out in pain—it was close, but I managed to keep my resolve.

I went home and returned to the hospital the following week to sit on "my bed" for the examination. They said another bone had moved, and they would have to set it once more. That was it for me and bone setting in China. I told Ralph, "I'm going home to have it fixed." We asked for the X-rays of my wrist and hand that were taken at the #1 Hospital in Nanyang but were told that documents such as that could not leave the country. You would have thought I had asked for state documents! Using all her persuasive powers and money to boot, Linda was finally able to get them to let me have them. We had to give our word along with the money that they would be returned.

It was nearing Christmas, and Ralph couldn't leave yet, so I went back to the States without him. Sarah notified Dr. Lahue my family doctor in Columbus, Ohio, and he arranged an appointment for me with an orthopedic surgeon. The doctor looked at the X-rays taken in China and the X-rays he had taken. He said I definitely needed surgery. So a few days later, I had the surgery—quite a bit more than was anticipated since my doctor said none of the X-rays showed just how much damage there actually was. I wound up with two surgeries instead of one—my hand and wrist were opened up to reposition bones and add titanium, and it was determined that they also needed to take a bone graft from my hip to complete the process. I woke up in the recovery room to find Ralph had arrived while I was still in surgery, and he and Sarah were sitting by my bed. I also discovered I had a metal contraption on my arm—with pins screwed into my arm and hand. I certainly wasn't counting on this!

We went to Sarah and Pat's as soon as I was released that same night, and sometime in the middle of the night, I knew I was going to live. We stayed a few days there before leaving to visit and spend Christmas with our families in Virginia.

After Christmas, Ralph had to return to Nanyang to get necessary work done before the board meeting in Australia. I stayed in Columbus with Sarah and Patrick while I healed and went to occupational therapy several times before heading back to China. My friend Linda Vineyard made sure I got to my therapy sessions since driving in the city was not easy for me at this time. I returned to China just in time to join Ralph et al. on the trip to Melbourne for the board meeting. Once the board meeting had concluded, we were able to do some sightseeing, my favorite being the spectacular scenery along the southern coastline called the Great Ocean Road. This is the coastline to the Southern Ocean, which lies between Southern Australia and Antarctica. We were told this was a very dangerous ocean due to the glaciers, winds, ocean currents, and freezing waters. We enjoyed the restaurants, the shopping, and touring Melbourne. We also enjoyed the friendliness of the Australian people. There was only one person who was rude and frankly an ass. It was a taxi driver who became extremely angry that I only had large bills with me and he had to go to the bank to get change, which in my opinion was his job to have in the first place.

Then we traveled to Sydney where we did get to see the world famous opera house—as that is the first question everyone always asks—although no shows were being held there at the time. Sydney was pretty and interesting, but I found the friendliness and homey feeling of Melbourne more to my liking. We ate lots of delicious fresh seafood while there, but I can't say I cared much for the octopus.

After our sojourn in Australia, we flew back to China and the routine of Nanyang where my wrist and hand healed as well as they were ever going to. I returned the X-rays to the #1 Hospital, and life in China went on. Linda never told me if she got her money back or not but I certainly hope she did.

Surgery in Beijing

About a month before Amanda and Nick's wedding in August, 2001, Ralph and I went to Beijing for him to attend to some business with Bernard Hu and for me to catch my flight home to help with the final phases of wedding plans. I went to the Hongqiao Market to buy some jewelry when suddenly I began feeling sick. My lower left abdomen was hurting like crazy, and I became extremely nauseous. I sat on a stool in Ding's shop and rested my head on her countertop. Soon Ralph and Bernard came to pick me up, and I told them I was so sick I had to go back to the hotel. Bernard had his driver, Mr. Guo, pick us up and rush us to the hotel. I was in great pain by then, and I think poor Mr. Guo was afraid I was dying because he kept looking back at me as I was lying down in the back seat grimacing with pain. After getting to our hotel room and lying on the bed for about a half hour, I realized this problem was not going to go away. Ralph called the front desk to inquire about calling a doctor, and they informed us they would contact the clinic near the hotel and have a doctor sent to us. In a short time, a doctor from the Sino-Japanese Hospital arrived. After examining my abdomen, he told me I had a strangulated hernia and must have surgery. I replied that I was going home to America the next day and would have the surgery there. He quickly and urgently stated, "You don't understand. You have to have surgery immediately, or you could die!" *Oh!* Well, that certainly wasn't an option I wanted to consider, so I agreed to have the surgery done there in Beijing at the Sino-Japanese Hospital.

Upon arrival at the hospital, I was soon put on a cart and wheeled into a stark, bare, utilitarian room. Ralph waited there with me, while Bernard took care of getting all the paperwork done to admit me to the hospital. This included leaving his passport with them until the bill was paid—a practice we had found was "business as usual" in China since many people leave and don't pay. I do have to admit the hospital was clean, unlike the ones in Nanyang. So there I waited until they came to wheel me into the operating room.

When I entered the OR, I felt I had been transported back to the technology and medications of the '50s and '60s in the U.S. They gave me a spinal and then prepared to give me ether. The last thing they told me before putting the ether mask over my face was, "Don't worry . . . when you wake up it will all be over," and I drifted off into oblivion. Well, they were half right—I woke up, but it wasn't over. I laid there and thought, "They must be almost done, and since I'm not in any real pain, I'll just wait a few minutes." Well, that didn't work out too well as the pressure I did feel was becoming very uncomfortable. So I announced that I was awake. One doctor said, "You feel pain?" I didn't know how much longer this would go on, or if I would soon actually feel a great deal of pain, so I replied, "Yes!" Immediately, the ether mask was placed over my face, and I greedily inhaled as much of it as I could and slipped into oblivion once again. This remedy proved to be a two-edged sword—I was not aware of the operation process anymore, but when I did wake up, I was deathly sick from the ether. I was back in my room waking up, throwing up, and disoriented. I eventually discovered I was also completely naked with only a sheet covering me.

Since nurses in China only change bandages and give medication and injections, personal care usually falls to family members or friends to provide food, assistance to the bathroom, etc. Stephanie, who worked for Bernard in the Beijing AEP office, came to spend the night with me. It must have been a horrible night for her. There I was in a dark room, lying naked under a sheet, hooked up to a catheter and a feeding IV, and holding a bag of sand over my incision as I was instructed to do. For some reason, I became obsessed with what time it was. I must have wakened Stephanie ten times during the night to ask the time. I thought that night would never end, and she must have also, but eventually dawn did arrive. With dawn, Stephanie was released from her watch, and Ralph came to spend the day with me. I was informed I couldn't eat anything by mouth until I passed gas—and who knew when that would be since at that time in my life this was not a regular activity—so I wasn't even getting meals to look forward to.

Linda, Ralph's translator, arrived by train that evening. She would spend nights with me, and Ralph would spend days. Since Linda had knowledge of western nursing procedures, she knew how to turn me and assist me with bathing and such. I was kinder to Linda during that night than I was to Stephanie the night before and didn't bother her with keeping an account of the hours.

With the next day came many visitors bearing flowers—at this time, most of the visitors were from Beijing. While I appreciated the visits very much, I still wasn't feeling very well, and I wasn't up to conversation yet. And I was still naked under the sheet. However, I had spied what appeared to be a pair of hospital pajamas on the window sill. I longed for those pajamas, wondering if I had to remain naked, or if eventually they would allow me to wear them.

On the third day, I finally passed gas, much to my delight, and they took out the catheter and IV and said I could have real food. I asked Linda to inquire if I could put on the pajamas still on the window sill. They said, "Yes!" and I got into those as quickly as possible. Ralph came to relieve Linda, and I told him I wanted some real food; so he went downstairs and purchased a huge bowl of soup noodles, which I inhaled gratefully. They were so good! What a day! Pajamas and noodles! Life was looking better.

I was beginning to get antsy about leaving the hospital but was informed that I had to stay a full seven days according to Chinese custom. They believe the body heals better if it has complete rest—much unlike our belief that the body heals better if we move around and make it heal. Now mind you, this type of surgery would have most likely been outpatient surgery here in the U.S., but you know the old saying: "When in Rome—"

The next day, Linda walked me to the bathroom for my first shower in quite a while. It was heavenly. Then Ralph came and so did many visitors, this time mostly from Nanyang. The many bouquets of flowers were too abundant for the size of the room, so I had most of them sent to other patients. I was beginning to feel so much better, and I really wanted to leave the hospital, but no way was that going to happen until I had completed a full seven days' stay and the doctors thought I was healthy enough to survive on my own.

Ralph had to get back to Nanyang and catch up on missed work, and that left Linda and me at the hospital. Linda began coming days and then visiting with her friends in Beijing in the evenings. The hospital staff also began coming to visit me to practice their English. So the days went on until the required seven days were completed, and I was released. Linda and I checked into the hotel, and I waited a few more days until Ralph got back to Beijing, and we could catch a flight to Columbus.

Another Wedding and Honeymoon

*F*inally, we were on the way home for the wedding. Thank goodness, Nick was such a big help in getting wedding preparations done. Amanda also had our families and Nick's family there to talk things over with and advise her. By the time I arrived, most of the details had been taken care of.

Ralph stayed in Columbus to get some work done at the AEP office, while Sarah and I drove to Elkton, Virginia, to meet with Amanda, Nick's mother Cheryl, and sister Lindsey in choosing the bridesmaids' dresses. I was also there in time to see the wedding gown and to give my opinions on the veil and jewelry. I was able to attend Amanda's bridal shower and travel to Hampton, Virginia, for the bachelor/bachelorette parties and meet Nick's extended family there. A couple of days before the wedding date, Ralph, Sarah, and Pat drove from Columbus, and the festivities began at the Elkton Presbyterian Church. When Amanda began walking down the aisle, Nick teared up, which made several friends comment, "I knew he was a good guy when he cried at the sight of Amanda coming down the aisle." It was another beautiful wedding and lovely reception, and then we were ready for "our" honeymoon in China.

Two days later, we were on our way back to China with Amanda and Nick as well as Sarah and her best friend Holly Longmore, definitely making this a real "group honeymoon." In Beijing, we all checked into the five-star hotel called the Great Wall Sheraton, and I think they were all rather impressed with how nice it was. While in Beijing, we did some shopping at the Hongqiao Market and the Silk Road Shopping Street, and, of course, they got to meet Ding and bought some jewelry from her. We toured Tiananmen Square, the Forbidden City, and the Great Wall at the Mutianyu site, my favorite place to experience this great historical achievement. I think it gives one more of an idea of how life was for those living on and manning the wall so long ago. You get to see the countryside between Beijing and the wall, and you can walk for miles along the top of it. It is a little further from Beijing than Badaling or JuYongGuan Pass, which is where most tour groups are taken, but I think it is well worth the extra time. We had perfect weather and, of course, we stopped at the same McDonald's for a taste of home as we had on Sarah and Pat's honeymoon on our way back to the hotel.

Then it was on to Nanyang to experience the "real China." Our friends were anxious to see Amanda again, meet her new husband, and meet Sarah and Holly as well. Our friends who worked with Ralph hosted the first of many banquets for them—it was called their wedding banquet. The dinner was held at the Nanyang Hotel so we were driven there by Eric and Mr. Bai. As the girls emerged from the cars, our friends were surprised and delighted to see the girls wearing the traditional Chinese dresses they had purchased in Beijing. They were given the usual royal treatment with a lovely dinner of tasty and unusual foods and much toasting to the newly married couple.

In the following days, they were invited to more banquets and given lavish gifts not only from Ralph's company (NGLE) but from the insurance company (PICC) and people from the city government. They were so impressed with Nick's size (six feet three inches and a muscular build) that he found himself challenged to several arm-wrestling contests with some of the people who worked at the power plant—including the lady plant manager. At least it kept her from picking me up, swinging me around, and then patting my butt as she often did. Nick handily won every time, and I think they admired him all the more. Several of these friends had said many times they wanted to fight an American, and this was most likely the closest they were going to get to that wish.

I took the "kids" to the Jade Market and on walks to see the street life of our city, which I think was their favorite part of the visit. The most amusing thing to them was being stared at—especially by three older men who had been doing some manual labor. The men could not stop staring, and we became quite amused at their interest. After several minutes, Holly got her camera ready to take their picture, but they gestured for her to wait—these gentlemen then proceeded to put on their shirts on this hot September day before having their picture taken—although one did leave his pants unzipped, which gave us another great laugh. None of them except Amanda had ever before had this type of close scrutiny, and although it was a bit unnerving, they also thought it was extremely funny. One thing they noticed quickly about the Chinese was their manner of speaking loudly and energetically when talking together. Sarah asked me if they were angry at each other, and I told her, "No, they're just having a good time."

After a few days in Nanyang, we went by car to Xian to see the Terra Cotta Warriors who were created to guard the tomb of China's first emperor Qin Shi Huangdi (chin shur whang dee). Traveling by car instead of flying gave everyone a chance to see the countryside and pass through several villages. With Mr. Bai driving, Sarah, Holly, and me in a car and Eric driving a van with Amanda, Nick, and Ralph, we left Nanyang for yet another adventure. Mr. Bai led the way driving in his usual aggressive manner through the flatlands and the winding roads on the mountains—which were perilously close to the edge of the mountain and totally void of guard rails. This was a terrifying experience for Holly. I don't think Sarah was any too keen on this matter either, but she didn't comment. Holly asked me, "How can you just sit there so calmly?" I told her I had lived there long enough to learn that you just relax and let the driver do his job. Although Amanda had gotten used to the more erratic driving methods in China when she visited us earlier upon her graduation from college, she and Nick were both thankful that Eric's style of driving was of a calmer nature during the trip. As for there being no guard rails on the mountain roads, China does not go to the extremes on safety measures like we in the U.S. do. I suppose they feel people should be smart enough to realize the dangers of going too close to the edge of a mountainside or a hole in the street. Even if they did get too close and got hurt or died, they couldn't sue anyone. Besides that, the thinking seemed to be that there are enough Chinese to replace any that die. Nevertheless, we did arrive safely in Xian—much to Holly and Sarah's relief.

We went to our five-star hotel (not quite as grand as the five-star hotels in Beijing, but very nice) and checked in. Then we went to see those amazing Terra Cotta Warriors. Each one has a different face and was originally painted very colorfully by the artist. The craftsmen and artists worked very hard to create the magnificent warriors. But they were rewarded in a most cruel fashion. After Emperor Qin died, these artisans were buried alive so they could not tell the location of the emperor's tomb. After his death, the people he ruled delivered a measure of revenge for his cruelty. They broke into the chambers of the warriors guarding his tomb and set it on fire, causing the timbers to burn and fall onto the terra cotta warriors. That is why they are broken into pieces and have to be painstakingly restored today. Although many lives were lost by those who created this massive tribute to the cruel Emperor Qin (chin), the first emperor of a united China, it is indeed an impressive accomplishment. I could never get enough of this ancient marvel and went there as often as possible to see them.

The next day, we flew back to Beijing and began preparing for all the "honeymooners" to return to America. We did more Hongqiao shopping, toured the Summer Palace, Tiananmen Square, the Forbidden City, and visited our friend Helen who worked for NGLE at her home in Beijing. Holly had a friend in

Beijing, and she was able to spend a day with him touring the Temple of Heaven.

One of the most memorable things we did was go to the restaurant called Afante (ah fun tay'). This was a favorite place for tourists and locals alike. The food and entertainment was supposedly from the Xinjiang (shin jee yahng') Province in northwestern China. This province shares borders with Kazakhstan, Kyrgyzstan, Tajikistan, Afghanistan, Pakistan, India, Russia, and Mongolia and has one of the largest Muslim populations in China. The Muslim people living in the Xinjiang Province are called the Uyghur (wee' gur) ethnic group, and they have been trying to gain their independence from China in recent years. The food was definitely different here than at other restaurants offering Chinese fare as they served shish-kabobs and other mideastern food. We were accompanied by a group of people who worked for Bernard Hu at the AEP Beijing office. Once seated, we chose our food courses and had a great time visiting together. After eating a wonderful dinner, we watched a whole roasted goat pass by us on its way to another table. Of course, Nick got up and followed to get a picture of this unusual sight.

Then the show began. It was performed by the people from the Xinjiang province—two men and a woman belly dancer. It was definitely mideastern music, and the performers were a cross of Chinese/mideastern in appearance. The female dancer always called on tourists from the western countries to come up and dance with her and try to do some mideastern dance maneuvers and acrobatic tricks, which if the person was a good sport, provided many laughs for the audience. Then immediately after the show was over, all the long tables in the center of the restaurant were cleared off and rock and roll music began blaring loudly from the sound system. The routine was that everyone jumped up on the tables and began dancing to their hearts' content until they were just too tired to continue. Our only problem that night was that the long well-built tables were full, so Ralph began dancing on a smaller table, which evidently was not made for dancing, and it promptly dumped him onto the floor. He suffered a long scrape on his leg from the fall, and we decided that maybe we had had enough dancing and brought the evening to a close. We went back to the hotel with more good memories of this group honeymoon in China.

The night before they were all to leave, we met with a couple of my former students—Blues and Vicky—at an outside restaurant on Bar Street on the night of September 11 (China is twelve hours ahead of the U.S.). As we were sitting there chatting and enjoying our visit, Ralph got a call from Eric who was in Nanyang. Eric said his wife in Taipei, Taiwan, had called with the news of a plane flying into one of the World Trade Center towers in New York. We were shocked but thought it had to be some kind of freak accident. Ralph's cell phone rang again a short time later. It was Eric once more with news of the second tower being hit by another plane. A passerby who was a dazed fellow American confirmed the news we had just heard. By now we were stunned and shaken to the core. Blues and Vicky tried to comfort us by saying, "It is all right. Don't worry." But worried we were and decided we needed to get back to the hotel to see what Fox News and CNN were reporting. Our worst fears were soon realized, and we stayed glued to the TV watching the horror. We also wondered how this would affect the airline flights.

The next day, we went to the U.S. Embassy to see about trying to get Nick home as his chief had told him to get back as soon as possible. The fence around the embassy was filled with flowers that had been placed there by those sympathizing with America. Unfortunately, we had no luck in getting a flight for Nick or any of the others because we were told no planes were coming in, and none were going out. We got a taxi back to the hotel and glued ourselves once again to the TV.

After spending the rest of the morning in the hotel seeing the same tragic events played over and over, I told them we needed a break from it all. We decided to go to the Summer Palace for the remainder of the day since it was in a parklike setting and might take some of the stress away. We went to the western-style supermarket across the street and bought bread, peanut butter, and jelly to make sandwiches for a picnic on the lake at the palace. Our taxi driver that day could not speak English but held up a newspaper with a picture of one of the planes flying into a tower and sympathetically said "bu hao" (boo' how) meaning "not good." The following day, we went to the Hongqiao Market to browse all the merchandise and make final purchases. We did whatever we could to keep ourselves busy and away from the events playing over and over on TV.

After a couple of days, Ralph had to get back to Nanyang and to work, so I went with him, taking all the dirty clothes to launder and bring back to Beijing since we didn't know how long the cancellation of the flights would last. As expected, everyone in the U.S. was frantic with worry about the situation and just wanted them back home ASAP.

I returned to Beijing with clean clothes to find that the kids had discovered much about Beijing that we didn't even know. They had found a TGI Fridays and an Outback Steakhouse near the hotel and had bought popcorn at the supermarket and had gotten the kitchen staff to pop it for them. Oh, the resilience of youth! But the most amazing news was that they had also been able to book flights home for all of them on the following day.

That night, Nick took his "harem" up to the first-class lounge in the hotel. Their honeymoon suite qualified them to have access to this lounge. When we all walked in, the young man who was in charge of admittance to this resplendent room became very agitated—I don't know if it was because of their ages or Nick's size, which must have seemed gigantic to his small stature. Also, since young Russian women came to China to work as prostitutes, I wonder if his thoughts were wildly going in this direction (although I don't know where I would have fit into that scenario). I have seen some of these "working girls" refused food and beverage service in the lobby bar, so who knows what was going on in this young man's head. He asked if he could help us, and Nick said "No, we just want to get something to drink." Very nervously, he asked to see Nick's proof of room number. Poor guy! He was almost shaking, but upon seeing our credentials, he quickly allowed us entrance and saw that we were served immediately.

The next day, we got up before dawn to get them to the airport and ready for their flights back home. It was hard leaving them there, but they were anxious to get checked in for their flights and back to all the worried loved ones and their jobs in the States. I had decided to stay in Beijing until I knew they made it safely home. I was afraid they would have to turn around and come back, so I went to the hotel to wait apprehensively for their phone calls. Thankfully, the calls came in that night with the good news they had all arrived safely home.

The following day, I went back to Nanyang and commiserated with Bonnie and Eddie who were the only other Americans there at the time. They had been able to see the events on the local news stations but could not understand what was being said. We had the Internet, though, and most of our knowledge of what was going on came from that source. Although we kept up with things in the U.S., I always felt we missed out on sharing this terrible part of our history with our homeland.

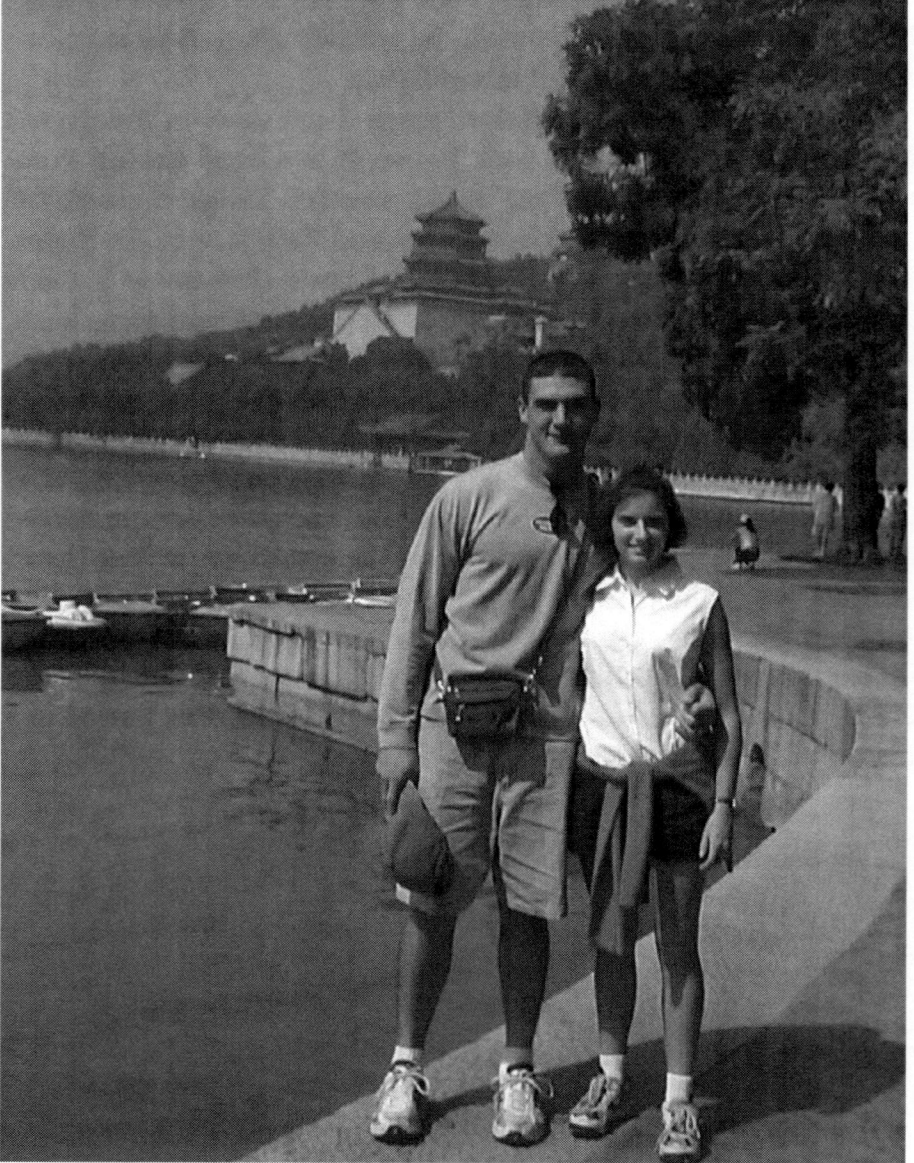

#2 Honeymoon—Amanda and Nick at Summer Palace
Lake in Beijing

#2 Honeymoon—Dinner at Helen's Apartment in Beijing

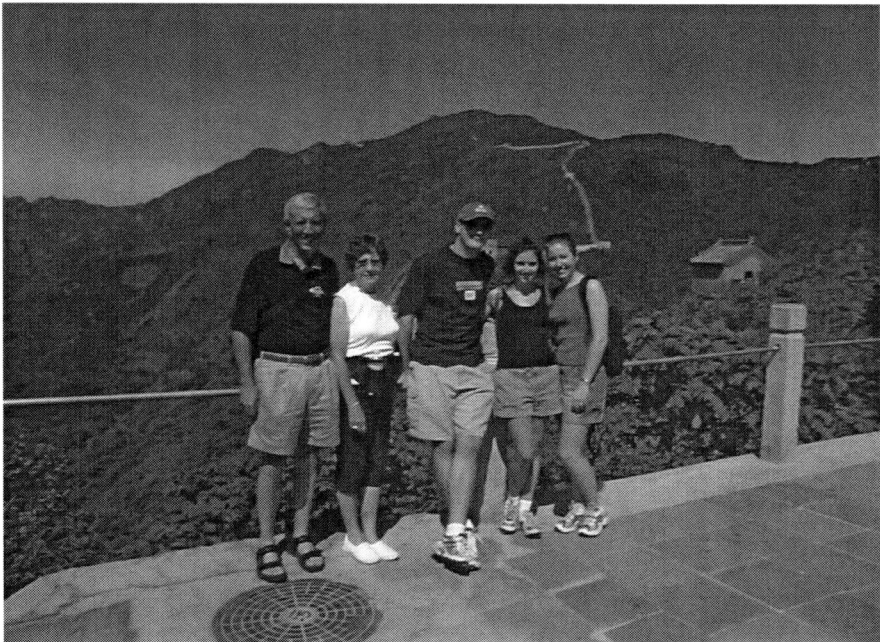

#2 Honeymoon—At Great Wall—Mutianyu Site

#2 Honeymoon—Amanda and Nick in a Tower Window—Mutianyu Site

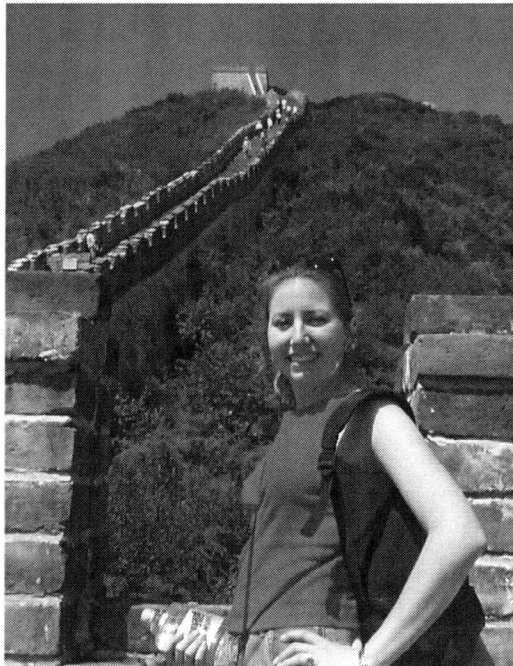

#2 Honeymoon—Sarah Taking a Break—Mutianyu Site

#2 Honeymoon—The Great Wall—Mutianyu Site

#2 Honeymoon—Tower at Mutianyu Site

#2 Honeymoon—View from Great Wall—Mutianyu

#2 Honeymoon—Linda's Son Getting a Kiss from Sarah

#2 Honeymoon—After Wedding Banquet in Nanyang

Second Honeymoon—Amanda and Nick's Wedding
Banquet in Nanyang

Second Honeymoon—Visit to Pushan Power Plant

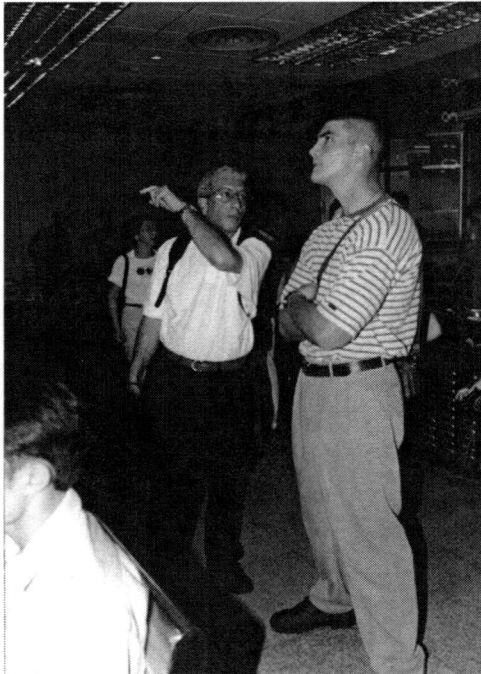

Second Honeymoon—Nick and Ralph at
Pushan Power Plant

Second Honeymoon—Picture Taken with Men Who
Kept Staring at Us in Nanyang

Second Honeymoon—Lunch with Madam Zhang
(Power Plant Manager)

Second Honeymoon—Broken Terra Cotta Warriors in
Pit—Xian

Second Honeymoon—Tiananmen Square

One-Child Policy

I think everyone is aware of the one-child policy in China. At the time we first arrived, the laws were very strict about only one child per family. This was especially true of anyone who lived in a city of any size since these people could be monitored more easily by the officials than those in the villages. But as usual in China, sometimes officials can be bribed to allow a family to have more than one child. After living there a while, I knew that China's huge population caused many problems, and that drastic measures were needed to try to control it; but I struggled with the abortion issue, especially as it was used as a means of birth control.

The one-child policy does not apply to ethnic minorities, however. They are allowed to have as many as three children, and if these ethnic minorities are very small in number, they may have as many children as they wish.

The desire for sons has caused the one son that they have to be pampered to excess. These little boys have come to be called "little emperors" since they are so coddled and spoiled. I would watch some of them who lived in our apartment complex refuse to yield to cars as they played in the narrow streets in their small battery-powered cars (which only the rich could have afforded). When the actual cars would turn to go another way, they would taunt the drivers by laughing openly at the power they wielded. I saw many of these little emperors get fatter and fatter as their demand for favorite foods and treats was constantly met by parents and grandparents.

Many times people in the villages are successful in having several children because it is easier to pass the children around when the authorities come to "count children." I knew of one person whose sister had five children, which only added to the population problem. Not only does the love of children come into play in the desire to have a large family, but they feel they must have a son to take care of them in their old age. Traditionally, the eldest son takes care of the parents when they are old; the daughters have always been considered less valuable because the parents must feed and care for them until the daughters marry and join their husband's family and take care of his parents. In the cities and in the more educated population, many people are satisfied with a daughter and realize the need to reduce the number of people in China. But where the traditional lifestyle is still being practiced, the boy is required.

Many people go to extreme measures to have a son. Linda told me of one instance where a husband and wife had two daughters. Then they made the decision to try once again for a boy. When the wife became pregnant for the third time, they went into hiding to await the birth of the baby. Somehow the authorities found out and went to the village to find them. The mother of the husband was in the family home, and they tried to get her to tell them where the couple had gone. She refused, and they then told her they would pull the house down on her if she wouldn't tell them. Still she refused to reveal their whereabouts, so the authorities made good on their threat and "pulled the house down on her," killing her. Eventually they found the couple and forced the wife to have an immediate abortion. She was eight months pregnant at the time, and the aborted baby would have been the longed-for son.

In the quest for a son, many of China's daughters have been abandoned or given up and adopted by people from other countries. This has helped create a lack of marriageable girls at the present time for the young men in China. It is my thought that in the near future with the limited number of marriageable girls, daughters will be just as valuable or maybe more so than the sons.

The preference for boys has resulted in the stealing of "brides" for the young men in villages. Linda told me another story about a young man living in the city who met a girl and told her he wanted to take her to his mountain village. She thought he was going to marry her and was taking her to meet his family. When they got to the village, he sold her to his old uncle and returned to the city. I asked Linda why the girl didn't just run away from the village, and she said the people were watching her too closely, and they were so far back in the mountains that the girl didn't know the way out.

She had two sons by this man before she finally got her revenge for the humiliating deception. She threw acid on the old man's nephew—I don't understand the logic of this, but I feel it must have something to do with harming the "family line."

Over the years, we saw many baby girls leaving China for their new homes in the West. Once while Ralph's family had come to visit, we were in Xian to see the Terra Cotta Warriors—those lifelike warriors created to guard the tomb of the first emperor of China. We stayed at the usual hotel while there and had the opportunity to see several Americans receive their baby daughters. The excitement of the waiting parents to actually get to see and hold their babies was electric. Finally, in came the caregivers from the local orphanage with the infants, and they proceeded to find the new parents of each baby. As they handed the babies to the anxiously awaiting parents, the babies began crying loudly and reaching back for their caregivers. I'm sure the Americans were the strangest-looking people these little ones had ever seen. Ralph and I had experienced this same thing many times as Chinese parents would thrust their babies at us to hold while they took a picture of us. But the crying had no effect on these new moms and dads as they had been waiting such a long time to meet their new daughters. By the next morning, we saw the babies had already begun bonding with their new parents and found out most of them had all slept in the same bed.

Another story of adoption of little girls in China came as we were on board our plane for a trip back home when a couple who appeared to be in their late forties got on with a small Chinese girl. We began a conversation with the couple and found that they had decided they wanted another child but were not interested in adopting an infant. They learned of this four-year-old girl who had been abandoned by a roadside when she was a baby. An old farmer found her and took her home to raise. As time went on, he realized that he could not handle the task of raising a child so young and took her to an orphanage. She lived there until she was four years old at which time this man and woman from America came looking for a child just like her. The couple was told not to bring anything from the U.S. but to let the little girl continue to have the things she was used to. Of course, they didn't listen to that advice and brought their new child gifts, which she accepted gladly, immediately abandoning her usual clothes and toys. She seemed instinctively ready to adopt another culture as quickly as possible. The plane soon began taxiing down the runway, and the father who could speak no Chinese looked out the window, waved, and said, "Bye, Bye, Beijing!" His daughter who could speak no English did the same—looked out the window, waved, and said, "Bye, Bye, Beijing!" Then she sat back in her seat contentedly, ready to begin a new life in a new land with the first parents she had ever known. Sometime during that long flight, we saw her nestled in her mother's arms, sleeping contentedly. In less than five years, she had gone from abandonment, to a poor farm, to an orphanage, to a five-star hotel, to a first-class airplane cabin, and was now headed to a new home in Naples, Florida.

One last story of adoption came when Bonnie and I were in Beijing, and we were visiting with our Chinese friend Jenny. She had come to the hotel to join us for our planned shopping trip for the day. As we were going down the elevator, we stopped at a floor where a man from Europe was holding two small Chinese girls. They got on the elevator, and Jenny looked at him, the little girls, and then at us with surprise and confusion on her face. I said, "This is the new father of these little girls." She looked even more confused but kept her silence. When we reached the lobby, there were several other Europeans with their Chinese children. Jenny didn't say anything until we got outside the hotel. With total amazement in her voice, she asked, "Why would anyone want a yellow baby?" I replied that when people in the western world want a baby to love, they don't care what color it is. She responded with, "But my father-in-law said that yellow people should marry yellow people, white people should marry white people, and brown people should marry brown people!" I said, "Well, it used to be that way in the west, but things are now changing. Besides, Jenny, we are different colors, and we're still friends, and that's good." She accepted that explanation without another word, but I could tell she really wasn't convinced about it and now had to think "outside the box" of what she had been taught.

At that time, most Chinese people were unaware that their unwanted baby girls were being adopted by people in the western world. I had told Linda this happened, but at the time she didn't believe me. A few months later, when she was on an airplane on the way to a meeting, she saw an American woman with a baby Chinese daughter and had to accept the fact that what I had told her was true. Linda said the woman treated the child better than she herself would have. In the years since we had left Nanyang, Linda wrote to tell me that after her son went to college, she had adopted a small daughter from a "charity."

Before we left China, the laws were changing to allow a family to have another child if the first was a girl and if they lived in the countryside. Not long ago, one of my former students emailed me that she and her husband now have two daughters. I asked her how this was possible, and she said, "The government now allows you to 'donate' money if you want to have another child." So they "contributed money" and had another girl. Another way some people have more than one child is to go abroad to live and work for a while and have their children there. Then they can bring their entire family back with them when they return home. And lastly, sometimes they are able to bribe the officials in order to have more children.

Love and Marriage

In the old days, marriages were arranged by the families, sometimes even before the children were born. Often, the bride and groom did not see each other before the wedding night. Many times, matchmakers were used to find suitable mates for marrying, and fortune tellers would choose the wedding date. In Nanyang, these practices were still used, although not exclusively. I do find it interesting that when the marriages were arranged by the families, the divorce rate was very low. Now that people choose their own mates, the divorce rate has increased dramatically.

I think Linda's parents' marriage was arranged because she said her father did not treat her mother well. He was educated as a teacher and worked away from their home most of the time. Her mother was not considered attractive as was her father, and he evidently held his wife in contempt—although he did manage to father several children with his wife. He was not a good provider for the family, and Linda said her mother had a difficult time feeding her and her brothers and sisters while they were growing up. After her mother died, her father said he was sorry he treated her so badly.

Most people in our part of China did not marry for love but for "suitability." They looked for someone who had the same values, were compatible, and had the same goals for their future together. They used matchmakers to find someone suitable for them and fortune tellers to determine if the signs were right for a good match. They felt that girls must be married by the time they were twenty-eight years old—after that, they would be too old for marriage. I could not convince them that they could wait longer or have a good life as a single person because according to them "people would talk." I took this to mean that it would cause so much humiliation and loss of face that it would be unbearable. So I learned to leave them to the traditions that had worked for centuries in China.

I knew of one young woman who got married and became pregnant before she had gotten the "papers" allowing her to have a child. Since she quit coming to see me for several weeks, I did wonder about her absence because she was one of my most faithful visitors. Linda eventually told me she was recovering from a mandatory abortion. When she finally returned for her weekly visits, she didn't mention her absence and neither did I. Soon after, she brought her husband to meet me and told me he was a doctor (trained in traditional medicine) and worked at a local hospital. I was impressed with him and was very happy for the couple. As time went on, she became pregnant once again, but legally this time, and had a baby daughter. Life seemed good for her. But as the months went by, she began to complain that her mother-in-law would not help her take care of the baby, which is a traditional and proper role for grandparents in China. She said she thought it was because the grandchild was a girl. Her refusal to help with the baby made her angry. I replied that the baby couldn't help she was a girl, and that this reasoning would make me angry too.

Not long after this, Ralph and I moved back to the U.S., and I lost track of her. Then I got an e-mail from Linda telling me the sad news that this woman's husband had not only left her but refused to see her or explain why he had left her and the baby. He even refused to help support the baby. I suppose he eventually divorced her so he could remarry to have a son as so many men do in China.

I lost track of this young woman when we returned home to stay. A few years later, I heard from our friend Roy Wilson from

London who had taught at the Normal School. He had returned to Nanyang for a visit and had met a woman meeting my friend's description in a restaurant. She had a young daughter with her. She asked him if he knew me and if he would give her my e-mail address. Since he didn't have my e-mail address with him, he was unable to give it to her. I still wonder about her and if she ever found the happiness she longed for.

Another story I know personally is about a young couple in Nanyang. The young man was an engineer and worked for the joint venture (NGLE). These two young people appeared to be happily in love and were always smiling. They married and continued their romantic life together. Soon they had obtained the permission to have a child, and we all hoped to soon hear the happy news that she was expecting. A baby daughter was born to them about nine months after completing the legal work. At first both parents seemed to be very happy and content with their baby daughter. But as time went on, the new mother had a difficult time dealing with severe postpartum issues. She had even been found on rooftops getting ready to jump off. She just couldn't shake the depression.

One day, Linda came to tell me that the husband had taken her to her parents' home to see if they could help her. One night, she locked the door to the room where she and the baby were sleeping. When her mother discovered the locked door, she tried to open it but had trouble doing so. As her mother struggled with the door, the young woman called out that it was "too late." Finally, her mother was able to get the door opened, but when she entered the room, there was blood everywhere, the baby was dead, and the young mother was trying to cut her wrists. She had cut her baby's throat and was trying to end her own life. The police arrested her and took her to jail. Knowing how swift and sure justice was in China, I was afraid she was going to be executed for murder.

Linda, who had been a nurse before becoming a translator, knew many people in the medical community and was able to convince them that a mental disorder had caused her to kill her baby. She was put on medication for her depression, and we all thought she was overcoming her problems. The husband didn't divorce her but stayed by her side through the whole time she was on medication and recovering from her depression. They even had a baby boy after it was considered that she was mentally stable once again. However, I was to learn later from Linda that in the end nothing could help this young woman as the depression was too severe, and the young man finally divorced her. He has since remarried, his new wife is expecting, and I was told the son lives with him and his new wife.

Thankfully, Scott's story has a much happier ending. He met a lovely young girl that he tutored at the university, and they became engaged. The courtship was a rocky one as they were arguing all the time and causing everyone to wonder if this relationship was going to work out well. But as soon as the wedding was over, everything changed and they settled into a blissful marriage. After several attempts of paying bribes to find a job for her (which is a normal procedure in China), he was finally successful, and their life together was a happy one. They eventually had a son who looks like Scott, and their lives are now peaceful, happy, and prosperous.

Linda and her husband both grew up in the same village, and she said when they were young he would come to play with her brother, but he also came to "look at her." She said before she married her husband she was working in a hospital as a nurse, and one of the doctors there also wanted to marry her. After comparing the two men, she said she chose to marry her husband and still believed she had made the right choice. I had met him several times and liked him very much. He had a very good job as an engineer with the local cigarette company, which gave him the opportunity to travel to Europe occasionally as well as within China. Sometimes he would go to Beijing on business, and Linda would want to visit him there. Usually, he told her not to come—he was busy. Linda said he was "having fun." I'm not sure what she actually meant by that, but knowing that Chinese men are not very monogamous creatures, it left a lot to the imagination.

Weddings

In such a large country, different customs are observed in different areas for the ceremonies and festivals. Where we lived, it seems that modern weddings are a combination of the old and the new. The first business of a wedding is the approval of the marriage by the two families. Not having this can prove troublesome to the couple. The legal paperwork must also be obtained and is usually done well before any of the festivities take place.

Traditionally, the bride wore a red dress on her wedding day, but now most of the brides at the weddings we attended wore a white dress prior to the banquet, sometimes changing into a red dress before dinner. We attended several weddings in Nanyang, and only Scott's wife wore the traditional red dress from the onset of the festivities until the end of the wedding banquet. Once I found out that white is the mourning color at a death; wearing white on this day surprised me quite a bit. Of course, most of the younger Chinese are striving to be as modern as possible and scoff at the old "superstitions."

Red is still recognized as the lucky color, and not only might the bride wear a red dress, but the gifting envelopes for cash gifts are also red, the wedding invitations are red, and red decorations adorn the home of the bride and groom as well as the banquet room.

The firecrackers would begin early in the day at the home of the groom as most Chinese still love the noise and tradition of using them. The black "wedding car" would be decorated with artificial flowers and usually a plastic bride and groom on top of the car. At the proper time, the bride and groom rode to the banquet in this chariot and were greeted by the guests—who were always armed with tons of firecrackers "to keep the evil spirits away and bring good luck."

The guests would arrive at the designated place for the banquet, which was usually at a hotel. Then the guests would take the red envelopes containing money to those people who recorded into "the book" who gave what amount of money to the bride and groom. This custom is helpful in knowing how much to reciprocate at the weddings of friends and family members at their weddings. I believe this custom is traditional all over China.

After emerging from the wedding car, the bride and groom were sometimes covered with silly string by their friends. Then they would stand for a long time outside the banquet room, allowing the guests to look at them and greet them. When a proper amount of time had passed, the couple would go into the banquet room followed by the guests, with the groom often carrying the bride.

The first custom performed was the traditional bowing (or as they say, kowtowing) to the parents and grandparents of both families, honoring the ancestors. After this ritual, family and friends of the couple tease the bride and groom with games and jokes about the wedding night and also sprayed them once again with several cans of silly string. The one game used at all the weddings we attended in Nanyang involved hanging an apple on a string above the heads of the couple. The couple had to try to take bites out of the apple while the person who controlled the dangling apple made this as difficult as possible. As they eventually ate into the apple, it was intended that the game ended in the couple kissing each other to the immense delight of the wedding guests.

I was told that traditionally, the mother of the bride was not present at the wedding. She was supposedly at home crying at the loss of her daughter who was joining her new husband's family. The banquet finally began after all the games and rituals were observed and everyone was seated at their assigned table. The traditional foods began arriving with eight traditional dishes being served, which included a delicious roasted pork dish in Nanyang. During the banquet, the bride and groom went to each table and performed the ritual toasting with the baijiu. It was customary for the guests to toast the couple by drinking six cups in their honor. In the old days, it was the tradition for the friends to follow the bride and groom to the bedchamber making silly jokes and teasing them. I don't know if this is still practiced in Nanyang as we went home following the banquet.

It was customary in Nanyang for the newlyweds to travel to the home of the bride on the third day to visit her family. There would be a banquet for the couple and for her family and friends. We only went to the wedding day banquets as many of the brides were not from Nanyang, and it could have been a hardship on the family to include more people, especially westerners. It may also have caused the foreigners to get as much if not more attention than the bride and groom.

Mr. Meng's Wedding—Ralph Toasting the
Usual Six Toasts to Bride and Groom

Scott's Wedding—Arriving for Banquet in Wedding Car

Scott's Wedding—Sprayed with Silly String

Scott's Wedding—Jean and Bride, Zhao Jing

Scott's Wedding—Bride and Groom

Scott's Wedding—Amanda with Mr. Meng and Mr. Wang

Scott's Wedding—Ralph with Scott's Relatives

Scott's Wedding—Posing with Scott's Family

After Scott's Wedding—A Baby Boy a Few Years Later

Mr. Wang's Wedding—Before the Banquet

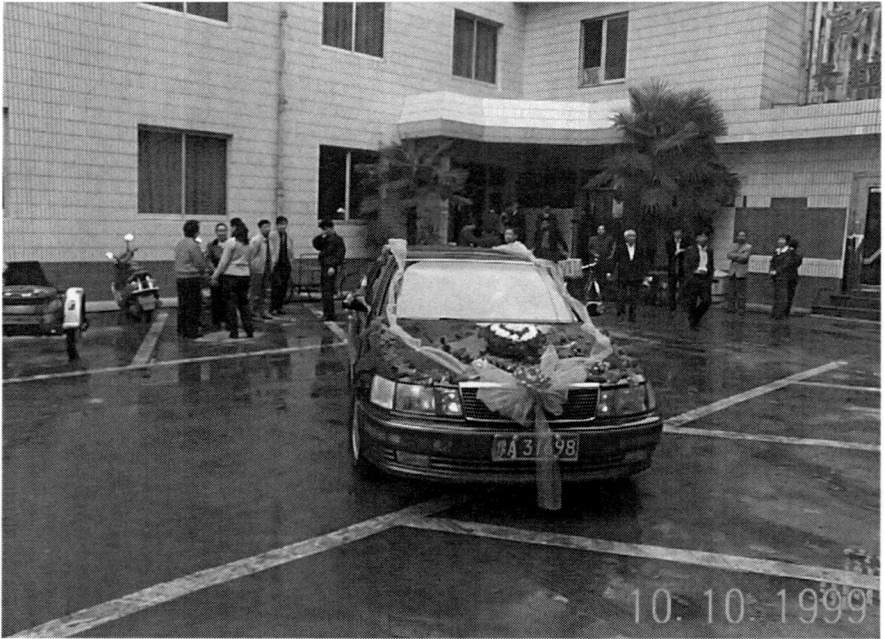

Ms. Feng's Wedding—The Wedding Car

Ms. Feng's Wedding—Banquet

Ms. Feng and Blue Tiger Entering the Banquet Room

Ms. Feng's Wedding—Sprayed with Silly String

Ms. Feng's Wedding—Teasing the Couple with Apple on
a String Game

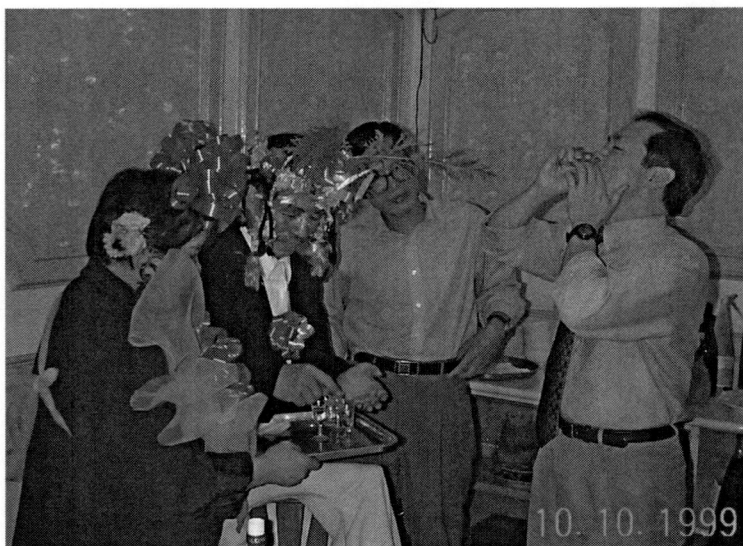

Ms. Feng's Wedding—Eric Toasted by Costumed
Couple—Mr. Kang Watching

Ms. Feng's Wedding—Mr. Guo Drinking the 6 Cups to
the Newlyweds

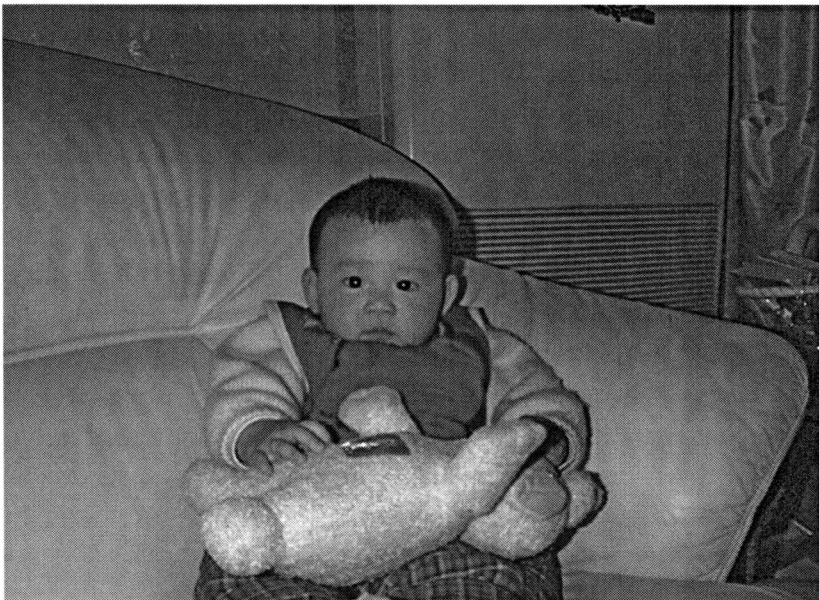

After Ms. Feng's Wedding—A Baby Girl a Couple of
Years Later

Death and Funerals

My first introduction to a Chinese funeral was a truck passing by our first apartment with people wearing white headwear and armbands and riding in the bed of the truck. They were blowing horns and making much noise with sticks and such. I asked Linda why they were making so much noise, and she said, "That's not noise! It's music!" I think I offended her with my question, but I was just beginning to learn how much the Chinese people love loud noise of almost any kind. I later found out the "music" was to frighten away evil spirits.

Some of the customs of burial were bathing the body and putting new clothes on the deceased. The burial clothes were made of silk for families who could afford it and cotton for those who could not. The body was then placed in a coffin as expensive as was possible. Sometimes sons would buy coffins for their parents while they were still living, and these coffins were actually proudly put on display in the home. The food for the dead was prepared, and the rites of the religion the person practiced were observed. All these customs dealt with preparing the dead for the afterlife at the time of the funeral. After three years, it was customary to burn fake paper money called "spirit money," so the dead would have money in the next existence.

Where we lived, people could choose where they wanted to be buried, and so we often would see the cone-shaped burial mounds in the fields as we rode through the countryside. Sometimes these mounds would be in a group, and sometimes they would stand alone in the field. Mao tried to stop this practice as he said it took up too much farmland to bury all the people. He encouraged cremation instead and supposedly wanted to be cremated himself. His body, however, has been preserved and is on display in Tiananmen Square in a glass enclosure. It is on view daily for people to see this man I personally call "The Real Last Emperor of China." He was unsuccessful at stopping burial practices as the people still continued to bury their dead on the farmlands. These mounds were decorated with colorful round objects and covered with artificial flowers. There were shops that sold these decorations and shops that sold burial clothing to dress the dead. In other places in China, people were buried in a mountainside or hillside, which I was told they believed made them closer to heaven. The burial customs for dealing with the dead vary from region to region, with burial done mostly in the rural areas and cremation mostly in the cities. Also, if the family of the dead has religious beliefs, these customs would follow the dictates of that particular religion.

Linda once told me that babies who die are not buried near the family but are "buried in a ditch" since they are not old enough to be part of the family. They are buried in silence since older people in China cannot show respect to a younger member of the family. If an unmarried man dies, there would be no children to show proper respect and offer prayers, so their bodies cannot be brought to the family home but must remain at the funeral home. Scott told me that the Muslims would bury their dead and put a lit candle in the grave. Then they would seal the grave, and the candle would burn up what oxygen was left, which helped preserve the body longer.

The only time we were involved in the funeral process was when we went to Linda's village after her brother died in a motorcycle accident. His body was in a casket in a building with three sides and open at the front. Linda's father was not there at the time, so I asked about him. She said he was resting. I assumed he was abiding by the belief of not showing respect to a younger person, even though the dead person was his own son. The eldest son becomes the head of the family when the father dies, and it appeared that it was up to the eldest son of Linda's brother to do the respectful mourning. Her nephew wore the usual white cloth tied around his head and was energetically kowtowing and mourning at the casket the entire time we were there. We left after staying long enough to pay our respects. That was the extent of my personal observation of the Chinese funeral customs, which in some cases last many days.

A Visit to Scott's School and Village

Rural life in China is much harsher than that in the cities. Most of the people living in the countryside are very poor and so are their living conditions. Once as we were riding past a village on the way to visit a hydroelectric power plant, I was thinking about how terrible it was that the people had to live in these basic and very meagerly furnished houses. About the time these thoughts were running through my mind, our translator for the day spoke up and said, "Since Mao and the revolution, the farmers now have good homes." I did not respond, but other than having a brick exterior, that was about all the "good" I saw in them. Although these houses did have brick exteriors, many people in the villages have houses made of dried mud or mud and rocks. The family home is usually passed down to the eldest son.

Most of the people we knew had at one time either lived in a village or had relatives who still did. Other than visiting a school that AEP had helped finance, we had never visited anyone in a rural area before, so when Scott asked us to make a visit with him to his old high school to give a talk and then visit his village, we readily agreed. Of course, we would have done just about anything Scott asked us to do. We chose a Saturday (and yes, school was in session on Saturday because they only have one day's rest) and left Nanyang at 7:30 AM to make the two-hour drive to the school.

I had purposely chosen to wear a red plaid jacket because red is considered their lucky color and because it would be a novelty to see a woman my age dressed in a bright color. Upon arrival, we were given the usual royal welcome with flowers, banners, smiles, and stares from everyone there. By this time, we were fairly used to being treated as visiting celebrities just because we were foreigners and because of Ralph's position in the province. We were introduced to the faculty, a few of whom could speak a little English, and the inevitable Communist Party Secretary.

After spending about an hour talking with the faculty, it was time to meet the students. We walked out onto a platform in a courtyard that was filled with curious, excited faces—about two thousand of them, mostly students, but there were also some adults standing around the courtyard in whatever space they could find. I assume they were parents of students and most likely wanted to see these foreigners, also. After the vigorous applause ended, Ralph was the first to speak with Scott translating for the crowd. He told them about the joint venture Power Plant, and that it was the reason we had moved to China. Then it was my turn, so I began answering their many questions, some of which were: what is the school day like in America, what about the violence there, how easy is it to find jobs, and the one I had come to dread most—would I sing a song for them? I chose to sing "A Bicycle Built for Two" because (1) It was fairly easy to sing; (2) their main transportation in the countryside, if they were lucky enough to have one, was a bicycle; and (3) the words and tune were both simple, and there were no sexual innuendos in the song. I managed to make it through the song without my voice cracking, and, judging by their smiles, they seemed to be pleased with my efforts. I then went on to tell them about school buses providing transportation, the average length of a school day, and school dances such as the prom and homecoming. They liked hearing about the beautiful dresses and handsome suits the students wear and all the festivity that goes with these occasions.

Finally, after about two hours in the hot sun, we were able to conclude our talks and leave the stage. As we were walking away, we were suddenly surrounded by students and bombarded by the insistent requests for our autographs. We tried our best to sign as many as possible, but there was no way we could sign them all. It was a strange feeling and made us sympathetic for what real celebrities go through. After we were "rescued" by some of the teachers, we were taken to a local hotel for lunch and then a tour of the new school currently under construction.

We left there about 2:00 PM to begin the journey to Scott's village, which was deeper into the traditional heart of China. It took one and a half hours to reach his hometown (which they are quick to tell you is distinctly different from a village) where we met his brother and nephew, and then we continued on farther back into the mountains toward his village. The road became worse and worse—dirt, dust, rocks, and ruts the whole way. We finally reached a huge reservoir by the name of Danjiangkou, and we learned that Scott's father had worked on a construction crew that built this reservoir. Later I found out we were now about one hundred kilometers from Nanyang, which is a little over sixty-two miles—a long way on such roads as we were traveling.

We boarded a ferry packed with carts, trucks, animals, and people. We caused quite a stir among the people as I am certain none of them had ever seen a westerner before, and most were probably getting their first look at an automobile.

After disembarking from the ferry, Scott said we were on the last leg of our journey. About the time he said that, I had begun wondering if we would ever get there. The road was even worse on this side of the reservoir, and after another half hour, Scott said we were getting close. We stopped at a smaller "town," and Scott went into a store that sold the fake paper money that is burned at the proper time after a relative has died. His father had died about three years earlier, and it was now time to burn the "spirit money" at the gravesite to assure that his father will have money in the afterlife. Sure enough, about twenty minutes later, we saw some people walking from a village toward us. We had arrived.

We stopped about five hundred yards from the village. Since Ralph and I were not invited to go with the family, we waited while Scott, his aunts, uncles, and cousins went up the hillside to the gravesite. This gave us time to get out of the car and survey the land and the farming techniques of the area. They had terraced what little land there was that could be farmed. Everything else was just large rocks—everywhere! Their hoes and other implements were mostly simple and homemade, much like those used by their ancestors. Many of those probably had been handed down from their ancestors. We felt like we had stepped into a bygone century, and in the way these people lived, we pretty much had.

Soon the family members returned from their money-burning ceremony and began walking back to their homes in the village. I watched as two of Scott's uncles and a little girl who looked to be about four or five years old came and got into the car. Scott's uncles were very old men but had never ridden in a car before, so they rode with us about five hundred yards to the entrance of the village. This was a very big honor and quite an adventure for them. During our short ride, I tried to make friends with Scott's young cousin, but she was too afraid and would not have anything to do with me. Not wanting to scare her any further with my alien looks, I finally stopped my attempts and let her finish the ride in peace.

We walked through the village amid stares and shy smiles—we were the first foreigners to ever visit here and the first ones they had ever laid eyes upon. On our way to Scott's uncle's house, we noticed that they had made good use of the bountiful rock supply by using them along with dried mud to build their homes. Scott took us to the house where he grew up and proudly showed us a huge flat rock that his father had placed over the doorway when the house was built. There was a crooked tree near the house, and Scott said that was where he spent many hours playing as a child. There was no grass in the "yards," only dirt. Chickens roamed freely, pigs were kept in sties beside the houses, and goats were grazing on the hillsides of the village where the only grass was growing. As we walked along the pathway, we were careful not to fall into a deep hole beside the path that was used for storing vegetables in the winter. When we reached the uncle's house, we were invited inside.

The floors of the house were made of concrete, but the walls were the same inside as they were outside—dried mud and rock—with newspapers covering most of them. There were three rooms: two bedrooms on each side of the "living room." The kitchen was a separate building beside the house. The furniture consisted of a few homemade chairs with slanted backs that sat low to the ground, a table, a couple of trunklike chests, and some beds that were also homemade with the usual board "mattresses" and two quilts—one to lie on and one to cover you. Since it was still warm weather, there was mosquito netting around the beds. They pointed with pride to the single light bulb hanging from the ceiling, which was the only concession to the modern world we saw. We were served huge persimmons and smaller oranges that grew locally, and we were offered the inevitable tea. They were so happy to have us visit their village and kept smiling the whole time. We had brought much honor to the village just by being there. However, though the adults showed their pleasure at our company, the adolescent and younger children were afraid to openly look at us and kept their heads bowed when we tried to talk to them. The adults showed no such restraint, and one old lady who was taking her goats to graze stopped to "chat" with me. Scott translated that she was asking me to visit her home, but he explained that we were leaving soon and did not have enough time to visit with her.

About 5:30 PM, Scott said it was time to leave as we had a long journey back to Nanyang. Of course, we couldn't leave without taking gifts—that is the Chinese Way. They gave us what they had: walnuts, persimmons, hot peppers, and sweet potatoes. We hated to take their food because we knew they had to work so hard for what they had and would need it for the coming winter. But we couldn't refuse, or they would have lost face, so we allowed them to load up the trunk. Scott said goodbye to his relatives amid many tears shed by all. Scott told me later that he loved his entire family no matter if they were rich or poor. We got in the car, waved goodbye, and left the village and these impoverished, yet, happy people of the mountains.

We took a "short cut" back to the main road over the most abusive road I have ever traveled. Mr. Bai, the driver, kept stopping to check the tires and to look under the car. I was praying that we wouldn't break down before we reached the main road because I knew if we did, we would have to spend the night in the mountains—most probably in the car. As usual, during long trips, either Scott or Linda would tell stories to us to pass the time, and so Scott told us stories about his family. As the stories flowed, our respect for these generous, hardworking people grew immensely.

> First he told us about his father who had died of stomach cancer and how he had encouraged his four sons to become educated. His father sacrificed everything he had on their educations, telling them that if they were educated, they would be able to find wives on their own, and he wouldn't have to spend money doing that. However, the daughters were not offered an education, and Scott said they sacrificed themselves for their brothers. They seem to have married successful men, though, and do not live in the village any longer. When his father became so ill that he could no longer eat, he made his coffin and prepared the food for his funeral. Then he lay down on his bed and died. Scott's great regret is that he was never able to share his successful life and money with his father. He brought his mother to Nanyang to live with him when she became ill. Even though her life was of a much better quality since then, she still missed living in the village.

He went on to tell us of his great uncle's wife who had been sold to their village when she was about four years old for marriage purposes. She is an old woman now and doesn't know where she came from originally. Scott said his uncle who was a kind man married her and treated her well, so her life turned out to be a good one.

He also told us of a young boy who was a childhood friend of his. This boy had sacrificed his life to rescue a small girl who had fallen into a sweet potato cellar. Although he was successful in helping the little girl out of the hole, the fumes from the rotting vegetables overcame him, and he was unable to climb back out. He was only twelve years old.

He told us about his school days in a school away from the village. He and his brother lived together, and both lived on about two yuan a week, which only allowed them a diet of vegetables. He said that when he was still young, he sometimes wet the bed, and his brother was kind enough to not scold him about it, even though in the winter this made the bed very cold. When the time came for school breaks, Scott and his brother had to walk many miles from the school back to his village. He said when he came to a certain curve in the road, he became very excited because he knew he was almost home.

He told us that when he was a little boy, he would chase after any bicycle he saw as they were quite a novelty since there were so few of them in the mountain villages. He also said he would look up as an airplane flew overhead, and it became a dream of his that one day he would ride in one of those magnificent machines—which did become a reality when he became a translator for the joint venture.

These stories gave us a glimpse into a life few Americans can begin to comprehend.

I asked him if there was a hospital anywhere in the area, and he replied that there were only local clinics using the traditional Chinese medicines. I asked, "What do the people do when they get really ill?" To which he replied, "They just die." In most situations, there would not be any money for operations and costly treatments. Besides, they are in such remote places that some of them have never gone farther than the nearest small town and if very sick wouldn't be able to stand the rigors of traveling out of the mountains. I then asked him if these mountain villages were too remote to have fought in the Revolution. He replied, "No, the mountains were where the revolution began. The mountain people gave Mao the Revolution." He went on to tell us that when he was a small boy, he and his friends would sometimes find bullets left over from the Revolution when they were out playing. As he talked, I was thinking that although the mountain people were so instrumental in handing victory to Mao Zedong and the Communists, they received nothing to reward them for their efforts. Scott, I'm sure, was invited to become a party member once he proved to be one of the brightest students at the university in Nanyang, or after he was hired by NGLE as a translator. I once told him he would make a good mayor of Nanyang, but he said he hadn't started soon enough to ever accomplish that.

Eventually, we reached the main road and pavement once again. We finally arrived back in Nanyang at nine thirty that night after what seemed the longest and roughest ride of my life. Although I was worn out both mentally and physically, I was not only thankful to be safely back home but also thankful for the experiences of the day—and humbled by it all.

Our experience in Scott's rural village was quite different from that of our friend Eddie. He went home with a student once and spent the night in the home of the student's family. He was given the room where the corn was stored, so consequently, he spent the night wide awake lest the rats who shared the room decided to eat him instead of the corn. He was also given quite an honor by the village—a new toilet had just been dug, and they and named it after him. We all got quite a bit of amusement out of that "honor," all the while realizing how important those toilets are to villages.

Celebrating the Chinese New Year

There are many festivals the Chinese celebrate each year, but the most important one is the Spring Festival, otherwise known as the Chinese New Year. This is as much fun and as important for them as Christmas is for us. This major festival is based on the Chinese lunar calendar and is on the first day of the first month of the year and falls on different dates each year, but it is usually in the first part of February.

Students of all ages get three weeks to a month's holiday from school, and those in college look forward to going home to enjoy some free time, home cooking, and the traditional foods of the festival. This time of year causes all means of transportation to be extremely crowded, especially the trains as this is the way most of the college students travel back and forth to school. People buy their travel tickets early because otherwise they won't be able to get a seat of any kind.

The merchants are busy selling the traditional foods, firecrackers, flowers, door and window decorations, clothing, cigarettes, baijiu, candy, and all the other items needed for celebrating the New Year. The stores and shops are crowded as thousands of people are all out shopping for the same things. Red appears everywhere as that is the lucky color and used in all the decorations for this festive occasion. Everyone is busy, busy, busy getting ready for the celebration, and the closer it gets to the New Year's Eve, the more the excitement mounts.

Some ways people begin preparing for the New Year are shopping; buying new clothes, which are usually red; going to the barber for a new haircut; cleaning their entire house; decorating the house with red paper cuts and the woven red knots; buying flowers, oranges, and tangerines; preparing a candy tray; decorating with the red paper that frames the doorways; and cooking the traditional foods for the New Year's Eve dinner. The food should all be prepared before the New Year's Day since all knives and scissors are to be put away. This is to ensure that the luck of the New Year will not be cut off.

One of the legends of the New Year celebrations was about a beast called Nian. This huge beast would come every Chinese New Year's Eve night to eat humans in a village near his cave, so the people would take their old people and children and hide in the mountains. It was even said that he could swallow the entire population of a village in his immense mouth. One year, an old man came to the village and told them he knew how to scare Nian away and would prove it by staying in the village over the New Year's Eve night. The next morning when the villagers returned, the old man was gone, but he had left the remains of what he used to scare away the beast—firecrackers and red banners. So the villagers knew what to use in the following years, and the practice of putting off firecrackers and using red banners became traditional all over China. It remains the current way of celebrating the New Year's Eve. There are many versions of this legend, but this is the one I was told.

The legend of the Chinese Zodiac was told to me as follows: long ago, the Chinese had no way to measure time. The Jade Emperor, the Emperor of Heaven, lived on an island surrounded by a river. He decided to have a race on his birthday for all the animals, and the first twelve would be included on the Zodiac, which would allow people a system to determine the passage of time. All the animals began the race, and when they reached the river, the ox was in first place. The rat and cat who were once good friends were right behind the ox. They convinced the ox to let them ride across the river on his back since they were not good swimmers. The ox agreed but told them since he had gotten to the river first, the honor of being the first animal in the zodiac would have to belong to him. They agreed to this condition. As the ox swam across the river, the rat, who is clever and ambitious, was worried that the cat might win the race, so he pushed the cat into the river. This explains why cats still hate rats. Just before the ox reached the shore, the rat jumped off the back of the ox and took first place and is listed first in the Chinese Zodiac, leaving the ox the second place. The animals arrived in this order: Rat, Ox, Tiger, Rabbit, Dragon, Snake, Horse, Sheep/Ram/Goat, Monkey, Rooster, Dog, Pig/Boar, all having distinct personality traits. It is thought that people born under the sign of each of these animals has the characteristics of that animal. Each New Year becomes the year of the particular animal chosen in order of their place in the zodiac. It takes five cycles of the twelve-year cycle to make sixty years. If a Chinese person has lived sixty years, he or she has completed a full cycle of the Zodiac. There is usually a banquet to celebrate this occasion.

Ralph spent the first Spring Festival in China without me since I had to remain in the U.S. to finish all the legal work and take care of all the moving to China details. He didn't have to worry about spending it alone, though, as everyone there made sure he was invited to many dinners and other functions. Although he tried to tell me about it, I just couldn't understand since I had never had the experience.

My first Spring Festival was in 2000. We stayed in Nanyang and celebrated with our friends. Linda brought us the red paper to go around our doorway. She asked if I wanted the paper to represent good luck, good health, or good fortune. I chose "good luck" since I reasoned if we had that, the other two would result as a matter of course. Scott furnished us with what I thought at the time was way too many firecrackers. Some students gave us paper cuts (delicate paper cutouts of flowers, zodiac animals, etc.) to decorate our windows. So on that New Year's Eve, we were prepared and ready for the events to begin. Ralph warned me that the firecrackers at 6:00 PM would be deafening and even more so at midnight.

He hung our firecrackers out the window, and we were ready for the explosion to begin. And begin it did at precisely 6:00 PM. Considering I had lived in China long enough to know about the noise of firecrackers at celebrations, I had to admit this was beyond anything I had imagined. It went on and on—the air soon became filled with smoke and the smell of gunpowder. Ralph finally exhausted our supply of firecrackers and closed the window to help block out the cold, smoke, and noise—although the Chinese believe in leaving the doors and windows open to allow the old year to go out. After quite a while, the noise ceased, and we waited for the next onslaught at midnight, which began right on time. **Boom**! Once again, the cacophony was in full force but even more vigorously. I thought it would never end, but eventually it did, and we actually got some sleep that night—until the next morning at about 6:00 AM when it began again, but not nearly at the levels and intensity of the night before. Perhaps they had stayed up too late celebrating or had consumed too much food and baijiu to be as exuberant as the previous night.

The New Year's Eve night is for family members to be together as they enjoy the evening eating a big dinner, putting off firecrackers, and watching TV as there is special programming prepared for that evening. The number of dishes eaten on the New Year's Eve will be an even number such as ten or twelve. This is because the Chinese believe that multiples of two represent double happiness and fortune. The foods eaten that night are symbolic of good luck, good health, and good fortune or prosperity. In our part of China, the most common food eaten at that time is a dumpling called jiaozi (jow'sa) because it resembles the tael (a unit of measure based on the weight of silver). Other foods include noodles that represent long life, spring rolls because their shape resembles gold bars and symbolizes wealth, and tangerines and oranges because the words for them in Chinese sounds like "luck" (tangerines) and "wealth (oranges).

One year, Eric's wife, mother, and children were visiting him, and they invited us to join their family in this special celebration. Among the many dishes at dinner, they served a sweet, sticky, rice dish and a whole fish. Both were the traditional foods in Taiwan. However, we were told we would only be eating half the fish that night because the rest of it would be eaten the next day on New Year's Day. This was done to carry the good fortune over into the following year since leftovers are thought to be a sign of prosperity. Then we sat in the living room with them and watched a couple of hours of the special programming on TV before going across the hall to our apartment to put off our supply of firecrackers at midnight.

On New Year's Day, several of Ralph's coworkers came to our apartment to have lunch with us. They brought the meat and dough to make the traditional dumplings (jiaozi) and all the other foods for the meal. First we made the jiaozi, although I was not very good at sealing the dough around the meat filling. It is not good for the dumplings to break while they are boiling, and I was always afraid that the ones I made would come apart. While I was not proficient in making them, I certainly did enjoy eating them after dipping them in a brown vinegar or garlic sauce. In America, these dumplings are called "pot stickers." As soon as all the food was ready, we sat down to enjoy the delicious foods and toast in the New Year with the baijiu. Everyone then left, and we took a much needed nap that afternoon. In the days following New Year's Day, we attended many dinners with friends, people from the city government, and people who did business with Ralph's company. It was a very happy time in our little city of Nanyang, and we have many good memories of this festive holiday. The next year, however, we traveled to Xian to spend the New Year in a hotel since we wanted our friends to have this special time with their own families and relatives and not have to worry about us.

For the Chinese, the New Year's Eve and the first day of the New Year are spent with families. On the third and fourth days, sons-in-law will take their wives to the home of her parents for him to pay his respects to his in-laws. No visiting to anyone is done on the fifth day as it would bring bad luck, but everyone is free to visit friends and relatives on the sixth to tenth days.

Our last New Year's Day in China was celebrated at the new five-star hotel called the Hyat (with only one "t") that had recently been built in Nanyang. This hotel was by far the most modern and cleanest one in town but would not have been rated as five-star in the larger cities. Many times we would meet our western friends there for lunch or dinner. The most amusing thing to us was the exquisitely detailed sculpture of a bull in front of the hotel. While dining in the lobby restaurant, the sight you could not escape was that of the prominently displayed genitals of the bull, which could be seen from anywhere in the restaurant. We thought we westerners were the only ones who found this funny until one day we saw a table of Chinese people pointing and laughing at it also.

On this last New Year's Day in Nanyang, we went to the Hyat for lunch with our friends instead of cooking in our apartment. We ate in a private banquet room. Along with the traditional foods, we were treated to the new delicacies of camel's meat and camel's "paw"—neither of which I hope to ever have again. I would much rather have viewed the spectacular display of the bull's genitalia than eaten these two dishes.

After two weeks, the Spring Festival was over—just in time for the Lantern Festival to begin. The Lantern Festival is held on the fifteenth day of the New Year, which is the last day of the New Year celebration. There are often parades on this day, which include the dragon dance, performances by marching bands, people beating drums, children showing off their martial arts skills, and other groups displaying their talents for the crowds to watch. There is always a full moon on this night, and beautiful lanterns are hung in a chosen area by individuals or businesses. People and families will gather in this place to see the lanterns, and children will often carry lanterns themselves. Usually, a contest is held to determine the most beautiful lantern. Of course, there are fireworks to add to the festivities. This festival is also known as the Chinese Valentine Day since young lovers enjoy the romantic evening as they walk about in the glow of the lantern light.

Nanyang Lantern Festival—Celebrated the Fifteenth
Day of the First Month in the New Lunar Year

Nanyang Lantern Festival—Dragon Dance

Nanyang Lantern Festival at Night

Nanyang Lantern Festival Parade

Nanyang Lantern Festival Parade

New Year's Day Dinner at Hyat Hotel—2003

New Year's Day Dinner at Hyat Hotel—2003

New Year's Door Decorations

New Year's Eve Spent with Eric's Mother, Wife, and Kids

Kathy at Tiananmen Square

No story about China would be complete without mention of the Tiananmen Square Protests or what others call the Tiananmen Square Massacre of 1989. The Chinese call it the June Fourth Incident. Our friend Kathy had some direct involvement with the events. We had known her for several years, but she never mentioned it while we lived in China, most likely because she didn't want to be overheard talking about it since it was a forbidden subject in China. It wasn't until she came to visit us at our home in the U.S. several years later that we learned of her involvement, and we still would not have heard about it if her husband Edward had not brought it up.

She was studying at a university in Beijing when this tragic day occurred and was working with the Red Cross. That night, she was on her way to deliver meals to the students and sympathizers who were protesting in Tiananmen Square for political, economic, and democratic reform. She was totally unaware that thousands of soldiers and many tanks had arrived to quell the protests at the square. When shots rang out, she didn't realize what was going on, thinking it might be firecrackers. It became a chaos around her as people began running frantically. Suddenly, someone behind her lifted her up and over the wall of a hutong (a hutong is a walled-in long narrow street of houses with courtyards and a gate at one end of the street). Someone on the other side of the wall helped her down and took her to their house. There they dressed her as a peasant and put a red sweater on her. Then they took her to a railway station outside of Beijing since the military was already watching the ones in the city. These kind people then put her on a train to her hometown and safety.

When she arrived at home, her worried parents were happy and relieved to see her. Almost immediately after greeting her joyfully, they quickly sat her in front of the TV and told her to memorize everything that was being said about the events in Beijing. Kathy told them that what was being said on TV was not true, but they told her it didn't matter—she *must* memorize what was being said. So she sat there and tried to commit to memory the information the state-run media was reporting.

When it appeared that things had quieted down in Beijing, Kathy insisted she had to get back to resume her studies. Her parents tried to discourage her from leaving, but she was able to convince them that it was important that she finish her education. Reluctantly, they put her on the train to head back to the university. Soon after she returned to Beijing, the officials at the university began interrogating her about the June Fourth Incident on an almost daily basis. They were trying to catch her in a "mistake" in her remembrance of the events at Tiananmen Square. She eventually went to a trusted faculty member and asked why they continued the questioning and what she should do. He replied, "You have to remember to always tell the same story the same way each time—never change any words or the way you tell it." Kathy took his advice, and soon the intensity and frequency of the interrogations lessened. She then realized why her parents had insisted she memorize what had been said on the TV about the events at Tiananmen Square. They knew this scrutiny would most likely happen if she returned to Beijing because they remembered the interrogations that took place during the Cultural Revolution.

I asked her if she ever returned to thank the people in the hutong who had helped her that day. She said she took the red sweater, went to the hutong, and found the house where the people who helped her had lived, but they were not there anymore. She never did find out where they had gone but will always remain thankful to them that they had most likely saved her life that fateful June day.

The entire time we lived in China, no one ever mentioned what had happened at Tiananmen Square on June 4, 1989. Soon after I arrived in Nanyang, I told Linda our friends and family in America were afraid we would be harmed in China. She was aghast at such a thought! "Why?" she demanded to know. I replied, "Because they remember what happened at Tiananmen Square in 1989." I was met with complete silence on the subject, and it was never brought up again. I don't even think many of the people in China are aware of what actually occurred at "The June Fourth Incident" since I'm sure only the government's position on this protest was broadcast. Also, since it was a forbidden subject, I doubt many of the young people have ever even heard about it.

Behind the SARS Curtain

In the spring of 2003, SARS (Severe Acute Respiratory Syndrome) was beginning to be on the rise in China. There was little concern about it, however, as the number of known cases was not large. The government did not seem alarmed at the time, and most of the people of China didn't panic either. In our city of about a million people, there were only three reported cases, and one of those had already been released from the hospital. It was thought that these cases were contracted in Beijing and brought back from there. Some people in Nanyang became very concerned about this disease, but others didn't seem worried at all, although more and more people began wearing face masks. We found ourselves in the middle of these two extremes—we washed our hands more frequently and tried not to get really close to people, but otherwise, we went about our daily routines as usual. I continued to walk to the supermarket twenty minutes away about twice a week to do necessary shopping but did not wear a face mask. Ralph continued to go to work and didn't wear a mask then either. We saw our foreign friends whenever we wished and still got together on Sunday nights to either go to a restaurant or eat the dinner I prepared in our apartment.

In April, Bonnie and I decided to go to Beijing to shop. David, a young man from Canada who was teaching at a private middle school, decided to go along. We went by train in first-class accommodations. During our two and a half days there, we saw surprisingly few people wearing masks but did notice that there were fewer customers at the Hongqiao Market where we would go to shop and buy jewelry. We also heard that many hotels had closed. Our hotel was operating with a reduced staff, and most of the people staying there were Europeans who had come to pick up their Chinese babies.

On our trip back to Nanyang, we did not go to the waiting area in the train station. Instead, we paid a porter to take us and our luggage directly to the train for immediate boarding. As we quickly passed through the crowded station, we saw that virtually everyone there was wearing a mask.

Upon our arrival back in Nanyang, the fun and games began.

By this time, it was suddenly decided that there was indeed a problem with SARS in Beijing. As usual in China, once the government admits they have a problem, drastic measures are taken. The local school officials immediately took their cue from the firing of the mayor and health administrator in Beijing and began aggressive action with their "war on this disease." They quickly formed an "Anti SARS Leading Group" to do the necessary combat. The officials at the university where Bonnie taught learned that she had gone to Beijing—which by this time had truly become "The Forbidden City"—and slapped a fifteen-day quarantine on her, although she had already taught her classes for two full days by then. She was not allowed to leave her apartment during this time and had to take her temperature daily and phone that in. She also had to provide the school with a detailed list of people she had seen and places she had been while there. Her brother Eddie who lived across the hall from her was also banned from teaching for the fifteen-day period because of his close association with her. They did allow their cook to continue preparing their meals, but Bonnie could not eat with them—the cooking was done in Eddie's apartment, and he had to take her a dinner plate each evening.

On the day after their quarantine, they were taken to the doctor on campus to be examined: chest X-ray, temperature check, and blood work. The only thing they found was that Eddie "had cold in his blood" and told him his cook should prepare foods to correct this. I honestly don't know how the Chinese people ever manage to get sick or die as they have a food or traditional medicine for any illness or injury known to both ancient and modern man. Ironically, Bonnie later saw this same doctor washing his hands in a rain puddle outside one day when the water was turned off—so much for sanitary conditions at the school clinic. They were allowed back in the classrooms to teach their students but were informed that they were no longer allowed to have their cook as long as SARS was a problem. They were told to eat in the dining halls on campus or do their own cooking so that people who lived off-campus would not be exposing everyone to a possible infection of this disease. Now the logic of this was mind-boggling since they would have to go off-campus to buy any food they cooked and then reenter with the possible infection themselves. Besides, the food in the dining halls was brought in by someone from outside the campus gates, which could also expose those on the campus to the dreaded disease. However, the construction workers were somehow exempted from this new rule as they continued to work on campus and leave to go home each evening.

In their zeal to be the best Anti SARS Leading Group in the land, the following decisions were made to halt the dreaded disease:

1. The week-long May Day holiday was cancelled. No students could go home or do any traveling whatsoever.
2. Sports Day was cancelled because the students would have to sit close together. This annual event would have provided fun and exercise during their confinement to campus and would have been held outside. Instead, they had to continue attending classes where they sat close together and continued to sleep in the dorms together.

3. They were restricted to campus. They could not leave campus for any reason unless there was an emergency.
4. Everything in sight was sprayed with vinegar—the disinfectant of choice. Bonnie said they wore white coats and masks, resembling "ghost busters" as they went about their spraying duties.
5. Eddie spied several syringes and bloody waste materials in the garbage can that was outside the foreign teachers' apartment building. This trashcan was under the kitchen window of the two married teachers living in an apartment on the first floor. After Eddie told them about the contents of the trashcan, they called to have it removed. Unbelievable that these health hazards were supplied by the school's health service!

Such reasoning and logic toward solving a medical problem was frustrating to us, and yet we found it humorous too. They were guarding their jobs with gargantuan efforts by appearing to take necessary steps in the War on SARS—all the while keeping everyone confined in crowded conditions, allowing the practice of spitting everywhere and the communal sharing of food from the same dishes to continue.

The students at all the colleges and private schools were getting bored and restless. They began fighting among themselves, and the classroom attention span suffered. John and Heather Pickworth who were teaching at a private middle school had difficulty maintaining discipline and keeping the students focused on learning. The kids were worn out from attending classes from 6:00 AM to 6:00 PM seven days a week with no visits home during this time. Instead of allowing them some recreation time and organizing games for the students, the officials forced more study on them. There was a teacher at this particular school who was married to the doctor who was treating the local SARS patients. She was allowed to continue teaching her classes daily. According to the information I had read, she was what they called a prime example of a person who could spread this killer disease since she spent the nights at home with her husband and returned to the school each morning. Knowing how Bonnie and Eddie were quarantined at the university just for a "possibility of having come in contact with SARS," we shook our heads in confusion at this logic (or lack thereof) that was used. If we hadn't lived there so long, this would have driven us crazy.

A couple of days after this, Ralph and I left on our annual trip with the local insurance company to renew the yearly contract for the joint venture. It is a normal procedure for the Chinese to get lots of traveling done at company expense in order to conduct the business at hand. This year's trip was planned for Southwestern China to the cities of Kunming in the Yunnan Province and Chengdu in the Sichuan Province. Then we were going on to Tibet.

At the airport in Zhengzhou, we donned our masks. Some wore white gloves before boarding the flight to Southwestern China. Upon landing in Kunming, we learned the war on SARS had intensified even more, and all travel was stopped to the other two destinations. That meant we were only going to get to spend four days touring the city of Kunming.

In Kunming, we toured the famous International Agricultural Festival and enjoyed seeing all the garden exhibits of many countries of the world—that is, we enjoyed all but that of our own beloved USA. Whoever was responsible for such a sorry display of our U.S. garden should have been severely punished. It was a poorly maintained replica of a Texas hacienda-style restaurant painted a faded pink and blue. The building sat in a sandy desertlike "garden" of cactus and what appeared to be weeds. This embarrassing display was surrounded by the impressive gardens and beautiful exhibits of Sri Lanka and other smaller, poorer countries. I would have cried if I hadn't been so angry.

Also, we toured the Stone Forrest and went to the villages of some local minority groups. Of course, an inevitable visit to a Buddhist temple was included, also. We did have a nice time and found most of the sights interesting and very beautiful, but traveling with our Chinese friends was done in a much different style than what we were used to. Any sightseeing is done more as a giant photo op than it is an opportunity to learn about the sights you are visiting. They evidently take those pictures to prove they were actually there; but once they get tired, they leave—even if they haven't seen all there is to see. Then it's on to the next place. Much of the day is spent on tour buses or vans going from place to place. I suppose that this manner of sightseeing is due to the fact that the Chinese people have only been allowed to do any touring of their own country since 1987, so they just go crazy trying to cram in as many places as possible when they do travel. When we went to Australia for a board meeting, Ralph asked me to accompany them on a bus tour of Melbourne. They slept the entire time the bus was moving, waking only when we stopped somewhere. I was the only one awake to see all the sights. Scott tried to stay awake in case I needed him, but as I saw him struggle with wakefulness I decided to stay quiet and just let him sleep.

Once we had exhausted the sights of Kunming, we flew back home since the trips to Chengdu and Tibet had been cancelled. In Nanyang, we found the fear of SARS had increased considerably in our absence. Ralph's coworkers were afraid to be around him and Linda, so she stayed home for several days. Ralph went to work but took his own lunch, so he didn't contaminate the others with his presence at lunchtime. The postscript to all this is that the scheduled meeting never happened on the trip because of SARS but was postponed until a later time.

The battle to defeat SARS continued all over China. Eric had gone home to Taiwan during the May Day Holiday and upon his return was asked by the city government to quarantine himself for a week in his apartment. He honored this request and stayed away from everyone. The cleaning lady brought him food, and he cooked for himself that week. That Sunday evening, we had some of our foreign friends to our apartment for dinner and also took a plate to Eric. We talked with him briefly through his screened door every day. He said things were not good in Taiwan concerning

SARS, and since he had gone through Hong Kong on his way to and from mainland China, there was a double concern about his carrying it back to Nanyang.

During this time of quarantines, precautions and fears concerning SARS, I received a call from our friend Chewing Gum. He had previously promised to take Bonnie, Eddie, and me jade shopping and wanted to take us on the following Saturday. We all readily agreed since we wanted to go to the nearby jade market in Zhenping. Saturday morning arrived, and CG arrived as promised. I went down to the car, and I saw that there was a van and two cars waiting. Inside the van were kids of middle school age, and I knew in my sinking heart that we were not going jade shopping that day—at least not right away. We were to spend the day speaking English and interacting with these kids. I tried to call Bonnie and Eddie to alert them of this, but they were already on their way to the gate of the university to meet us. When we arrived at the gate, we waited a while before Bonnie and Eddie got there. Then they put Bonnie in one of the cars and Eddie in the van with me and the kids, and we were off on whatever adventure was in store for us that day. CG was riding in the front seat of the van and soon turned around and said, "Let's go to a beautiful scenery spot this morning." We agreed because what other choice did we have at that point? I knew the plan for the day had already been set in motion. We left the city and traveled about a half hour before we were stopped to have our temperature checked. It was apparent that we were with local high level party members because after this stop arrangements were made so that we could pass all the other temperature-taking stations we saw during our travels that day.

About another half hour passed, and we pulled into a small parking area and got out of the vehicles. We were told we were now going to see a beautiful cave. Dutifully, we followed them to the entrance of the cave and began an instant descent into the bowels of the earth—down, down we went on the built-in ladders. Finally we reached our destination and were proudly shown the pretty rocks and formations in the cave. However, what was not pointed out but we quickly realized was that the cave was populated by hundreds of bats that flew over us the entire time we were there. Bat droppings were not only falling from above, but we were walking in several inches of bat droppings the whole time. My thoughts at the time were "SARS will be the least of our worries if we survive the bat cave without getting a disease."

Finally, we climbed back out of the cave into the sunlight—hopeful that we could now go jade shopping. Instead, CG said, "Let's go have a delicious lunch." By this time, Eddie was becoming anxious to get back to the university since he had an appointment that afternoon. He began trying to explain his situation to CG and company, but they still wanted that delicious lunch to happen. Finally, CG appealed to me to persuade Eddie to eat lunch. I told Eddie that he really had no choice—when "the plan" is in place, you just go along with it, or you risk someone along the way losing face. Eddie finally agreed to lunch, which made CG extremely happy. He told me I was a great negotiator. So we all piled back into the cars and van to head off for our lunch, which did turn out to be delicious.

After lunch, we thought it was still possible to make that jade market if we left soon. That was not to be, though, as CG said we were going on to another beautiful scenery spot—Seven Star Lake. I envisioned a pretty lake with nice trees around it, but when the car stopped, we were in a parking lot with not a drop of water in sight. I thought, "Well, at least there's no bat cave to worry about." It became apparent that Eddie was not going to make his appointment at the university and very doubtful if we would ever get to do any jade shopping that day.

We began to walk—and walk and walk—with no lake in sight. Soon we began an incline that became steeper and steeper, and we realized we were climbing a mountain. The Chinese love nothing better than climbing a beautiful mountain. Just as I thought we would never stop walking up that mountain, we found our lake. It was actually seven pools of water on the mountain top. We sat down to rest, and I told them that I should soon get back to Nanyang since it was Ralph's and my wedding anniversary. Oh, how happy they were to hear that! Instead of understanding that I wanted to have a little time with my husband on this special day, CG's wife Jean Green replied with this remark, "It's so nice we get to spend it with you!"

After considerable resting and admiring the "lake" and the scenery, we began our descent of the mountain. By then my legs were so rubbery I could hardly walk. Bonnie had had the good sense to pick up a walking stick on the way up, and she lent it to me. I wouldn't have made it down without it. As I struggled with the stone steps down the mountain, a Chinese man skipped right by me playing his flute as he practically danced down the mountain. I was in no mood for such behavior and silently wished I could tell him where to stuff his flute and his agility. I finally reached the bottom on my wobbly legs and managed to get into the van. Never had I been so tired! "Okay," I thought, "we're finally headed either home or to the elusive jade market." CG got in the van and told us we were going to pick up peaches on our way home. We inquired about the jade shopping, and he said it would be too dark by the time we got there and the market would be closed. He said we would go another time. Disappointed, but ready to get home, we gave up our dreams of getting any jade that day. We stopped in a town, picked up several boxes of peaches and headed in the direction of Nanyang.

We had traveled about thirty minutes when CG turned around and said, "Let's go have a delicious dinner in Nanyang." I said, "No. Eddie and Bonnie have to get back to the university, and I have to go home." CG turned back around in his seat without comment. By this time, Eddie had a splitting headache, Bonnie was very tired, and I was also. Dinner was not appealing to any of us—we were just ready for the day to be over. Then twenty minutes later, he turned back to us and said, "Let's go have a delicious dinner with Mr. Wang." I had no idea who this was, but it suddenly dawned on me that he was the official that had lent us his van and had arranged for us to have such a "wonderful day" on him.

I realized that someone, most likely CG, would lose face if at least one of us didn't have that dinner with him. I explained this to Bonnie and Eddie and said I would go to dinner, and they could go on back to the university. Eddie was suffering terribly from his headache by now. Bonnie said she would go to the dinner.

We dropped Eddie off at the gate at the university, and we went on to a Taiwan Restaurant in Nanyang that was known for its black pepper steak dish. We met Mr. Wang and tried to talk to the kids in simple English. We all ordered the steak, and we showed them how to use a knife and fork, plus a few other American table manners such as placement of the napkin on the lap. By spending the day with the kids (who didn't really seem interested in us), going to the dinner, and showing them some American ways of doing things, I'm certain we paid sufficiently for our travels that day and dinner that night. Most important, though, was that no one lost face on that long and eventful day.

At last the day came to an end, and we were taken home—minus any jade in hand. Now mind you, those "beautiful scenery spots" had been closed due to SARS, but these people had the power to have them opened just for our pleasure that day, reminding us that once again that there are rules for the masses and other rules for the elite. What a country!

SARS—Roadside Temperature-Taking Station

Kunming—International Horticultural Festival and
Flower Exhibition

Kunming—Garden Outside Stone Forest

Kunming—Large Trees

Kunming—Ethnic Village

Kunming—Getting Ready to Enter Stone Forest

Kunming—Looking Down on Stone Forest

Kunming—Posing for Picture with Children as Parents
Requested

Kunming—After Touring Stone Forest

Home to Stay

In June 2003, we returned home for our summer visit with family and friends. Luckily, travel restrictions due to SARS had been lifted, and we were able to leave for the U.S. As usual, shortly after our arrival, we headed to our dentist and doctors for checkups. Unfortunately, Dr. Lahue, our family doctor, found a suspicious mass in Ralph's abdomen. He sent him to an oncologist immediately who diagnosed that the mass was a lymphoma cancer. He sent him to a surgeon who said surgery was needed. We made the decision not to return to China since the medical situation there was so very different. The hospitals in Columbus are very skilled in the treatment of cancer, and we felt very assured by this. The surgery lasted three hours, twice as long as they had first thought because the tumor was so large and had spread throughout his abdomen. They took out 50 percent of his lower intestine, appendix, and as much of the lymphoma as possible. It was a scary time as we waited to find out the biopsy results. In a few days, we had the answer: it was non-Hodgkin's lymphoma—great news! This kind of cancer was the easiest to treat and cure.

AEP put us up in an apartment where we lived while Ralph had his pre-chemo treatments and then the chemo. I had to make arrangements to return to China to pack up our goods, make the speeches with all the appropriate people, and attend the farewell dinners with business acquaintances and friends. Our daughter Amanda came from Alaska to go with me. Ralph's parents and sister came to stay with him while we were gone. And so we boarded the flight back to China with much on our minds.

We landed in Beijing and caught the flight to Nanyang the next day. A moving company was contacted, and we began packing up the things we were bringing home, attending dinners and making a final visit to the power plant where I met with the plant manager, others who worked in the plant, and the NGLE employees who worked with Ralph. I had my speech all written and thought I would be able to deliver it professionally with Eric doing the translating. Well, it was harder to say goodbye to these people than I thought, and I broke down and cried at the end. They were crying, also, so I didn't feel too badly. I cried again at the dinner with the PICC (People's Insurance Company of China) as we had become good friends with the head of the company, his wife, and his coworkers. Many people we knew among all these people said Ralph was like a brother to them, and that he had taught them a lot.

Several friends arrived as we were finishing up the packing and brought gifts—some of them for our first grandchild to be born in a few months. One such gift was beautiful silk blanket with matching pillow in the lucky color of red. Then I was informed that the pillow was filled with the excrement of the silk worms that made the silk for the blanket and pillow. Although this was supposed to be a healthy thing to do, I was certain that Sarah and Patrick would never let our grandchild nestle its head in a pillow filled with poop. At the time we didn't know that Amanda was also pregnant and was due in May. Had we known, she would have received gifts for her baby also.

Our last dinner was with our friends at the teachers' college, and it was a fun evening spent with friends from different parts of the world—Sandra Bagnall and Michael from Great Britain, Brandon Stoltenkamp from South Africa, Gail Ramroop from Toronto, Natalie from Great Britain, Devi from New York, Bonnie from West Virginia and Eddie from California, Eric from Taiwan, and our young friend Apple from Nanyang, many of whom I will most likely never see again. We toasted each other in the Chinese style with the baijiu and ate the foods of China together for the last time. I met the new teachers who had recently arrived but never got the chance to know well. All too soon, we returned to the apartment to get ready for our return to the U.S.

On the morning we left Nanyang, we were driven to Zhengzhou by Mr. Bai to catch our flight to Beijing—our last trip with him and our last trip traveling on the Suicide Highway. (Soon after we left, a new highway was constructed. When Ralph and I returned to Nanyang the next June, we discovered it is now a four-lane modern highway and a much safer road to travel—but not nearly as interesting as the old one.) On our way through Beijing, we went to see Ding at the Hongqiao Market to let her know how our life had changed. She was very sad to learn we were leaving China. but I told her we would still keep in touch. Then we were soon on our way home—to Ralph and Nick.

In a few weeks, our stuff arrived from China, and we stored it in our apartment garage. In February, we began our search for a house and eventually found the one we currently live in. Ralph finished his chemo treatments in March 2004, and in June, we both returned to China so he could say his goodbyes in person. Everyone was so glad to see him! But once again, it was a seesaw of emotions—elation at being with our friends once more and heartbreak at leaving. We still keep in touch with Eric, Bernard, Linda, Scott, and Xiao Hang.

I continued my relationship with Ding and bought jewelry from her for several years. My mother's health began a rapid decline, and I spent much time traveling the long road back and forth from Columbus, Ohio, to Elkton, Virginia, to take care of her and her affairs until her death in 2007. Then I had to settle her estate, have an auction, and sell her house. Ralph continued working for AEP at the home office in Columbus for a few more years and then retired, only to do some contractual work for other companies and eventually with AEP. He also began working for a catering company called PROM, which is based in Minnesota. He runs a tent that provides food for people attending given golf tournaments for a week at a time—usually doing about five or six tournaments a year. He also plays a lot of golf during the warm months. He has been cancer-free since he completed his chemo treatments and as of 2009 does not require any more CT scans unless future problems appear. He only sees his doctor once a year now. Many prayers were answered, and we feel blessed!

Sarah and Patrick became the parents of Lauren Elizabeth Metzger on December 3, 2003. Then later Kendall Marie Metzger was born on July 6, 2005. Amanda and Nick became parents on May 19, 2004, when Riley Martin Pavlik was born and then again on March 29, 2006, when Jacob Life Pavlik was born. We absolutely love being grandparents of these four wonderful children! They have enriched our lives more than we could have possibly imagined.

As I write this, I am reminded that it has been several years since we made our final goodbyes in Nanyang. I had been warned that repatriating back into our own culture would be more difficult than expatriating. I didn't believe it since we had come home twice a year and thought these trips would keep us current with our own culture. But I did find that it was true. A major part of this feeling stemmed from the events of "9/11," and although we had kept up with the news on that, it was a time we could not personally mourn with those who had lived through the experience. A huge, tragic event that affected our country so horribly had occurred in our absence. Besides that event, as time goes on, things change, and we had to readjust to those changes. There was a definite disconnect—China had left its mark on us. However, it didn't take long for us to completely feel at home once again as we regained our independence, and we weren't the major attraction for so many people so much of the time. Driving ourselves wherever and whenever we wanted to go was so liberating. We joined the Dublin Presbyterian Church and not only have made many new friends there we have also reconnected to old friends from all the places we have lived. We now have busy and full lives on this side of the world once again. It is good to be home.

Ralph with Mr. Bai our driver (on left)
and Mr. Wang—engineer (on right)

Saying Goodbyes—Amanda and Jean at Dinner in
Nanyang

Saying Goodbyes—Amanda and Jean with Mr. Guo,
His Wife, and Grandson

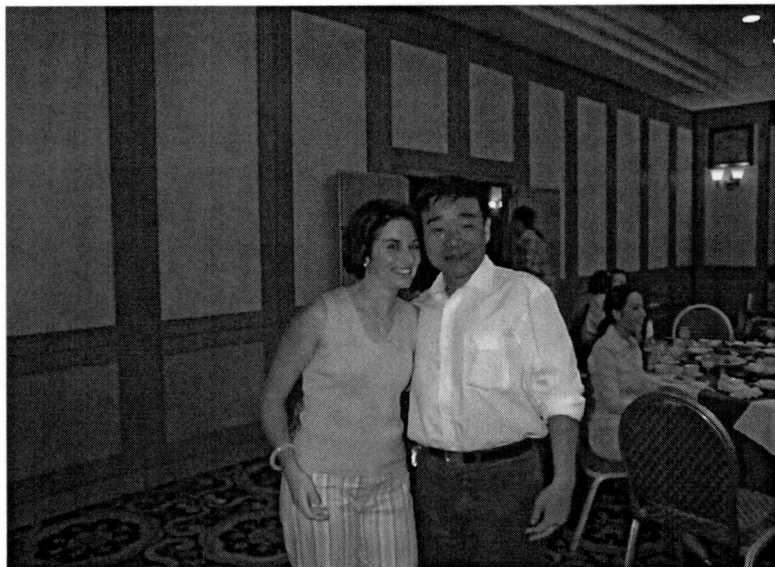

Saying Goodbyes—Amanda with Mr. Bian (a driver)

Saying Goodbyes—Amanda with Scott and Zhao Jin at
NGLE Dinner

Saying Goodbyes—Amanda with Xiao Hang

Saying Goodbyes—Jean at Pushan Power Plant Giving
Farewell Speech

Final Thoughts

This brings our great China adventure to an end—what a wonderfully bizarre experience it was! Four and a half years of our life spent in a country with a culture upside down from what is normal to us. All the fears and apprehensions I had before going were realized—but only for a short time. Once I pulled myself up by my bootstraps, I began accepting things as they were and not comparing them with the circumstances I had recently left. As it became painfully clear that instant gratification was not going to be a major part of my life anymore, it gradually became easier to adapt to the conditions of my new home. I relaxed and gained more patience with an entirely new set of circumstances—these things were not going to go away: the dirt, pollution, lack of conveniences, a loss of independence, and the often exasperating "Chinese Way" of doing things. Also, once I accepted the fact that I was going to constantly be an "object of interest and curiosity," I learned to find humor and pleasure in giving people the joy and amazement of seeing this foreigner up close and personal. I not only found that besides being somewhat of a curiosity, I became a teacher, a public speaker, a model, the subject of a documentary, a friend to not only many Chinese people but people all over the world, and a celebrity as well as the wife of the general manager of the largest project in Henan Province. My life became enriched in ways I could not have envisioned before as I became a part of my new world instead of just an observer.

We arrived in 1999 and left in 2003, and in those years, we saw many changes in Nanyang. Among those changes were NIT attained the status of "university," the streets along the river were cleaned up and developed with more modern buildings, a new five-star hotel was built, a new four-lane highway was constructed in place of the "Suicide Highway," the economy improved to the point of seeing some people getting fat and the children getting bigger in stature from better nutrition, divorces became more common, private car ownership became a rare reality, more modern apartment buildings with a higher price tag were built, and more westerners came to the city to teach or do business, but the longed-for McDonald's and KFC restaurants didn't arrive until a few years after we left. Maybe one day we will be able to return to visit our friends there and see our dear old city again. I'm sure some things will always remain the same such as the "Chinese Way" of doing things and the manner of thinking "inside the box," both of which are so frustrating to a westerner but works very well for them. One thing I hope never changes is the amazing hospitality that they show to guests and that we experienced the entire time we lived there.

We enjoyed the traveling we did with the Chinese people who allowed us to see China through their eyes. They showed us places of historical significance that aren't on the travel itineraries of most travel agencies. We often went to places such as Guilin (gway lin') in southern China, which looks like the earth has turned inside out at some point in time with the magnificent rock formations that thrust through the landscape and the cormorant birds who are trained to dive for fish for their owners, or Harbin (har bin') in the far north to see the amazing Ice Festival sculptures and the Russian influence in past architecture and history, or the island province of Hainan (hi nahn') in the southeast (called little Hawaii) with its tropical climate, palm trees and sandy beaches—and the site of the so-called "spy plane incident."

During our years in China, not only did we have the opportunity to tour much of China, we were able to travel to Singapore,

Australia, Las Vegas, and San Francisco for meetings, places that neither of us had visited before.

We lived there long enough to become comfortable with a culture much different from our own. We became a part of an extended Chinese family with our friends whom we knew from schools and Ralph's work environment. I gained some "adopted" Chinese kids that I have watched become successful adults who were once my students at the Nanyang Institute of Technology. With all we gained from our adventure, I hope I was able to give back to China a portion of what I received from our experiences there. I also hope I was a good ambassador of my beloved USA.

As well as those westerners who were part of our story in Nanyang, I have talked to others who have lived in China, and we all have had most of the same experiences and tell pretty much the same story, especially those of us who have lived in the interior of this vast country. It was my observation that only those going there to live who have a spirit of adventure, a boatload of patience, and an indeterminate amount of adaptability were able to handle the experience of that amazing place that is China.

It took me more than five years after moving back to the States to begin this book, even though I had many people encouraging me to do so. A friend told me about a quote he found in a book by author Cheng Li that was attributed to a western sinologist. It goes as follows:

> If you visit China for two weeks, you want to write a book; if you stay in China for two months, you want to write an article; if you live in China for two years, you don't want to write anything!

This describes exactly the way I had felt in just about the same time frames! When I first emailed our friend Roy Wilson that I was going to begin writing *Life in China,* he wrote back with this:

I think I just could not put pen to paper immediately after returning from China because it was just such an amazing and bizarre experience in some ways. Where would we begin! Perhaps with distance and perspective we can now write about things there.

Again, I found this to be very true in my case. But I finally succumbed to those who kept on saying, "You should write a book!" To all of you who made it through this accounting of our *Life in China,* thank you so much for spending some of your time with me. I have enjoyed telling you my story. I now encourage you to go have your own adventure and make your own story.

Ganbei!

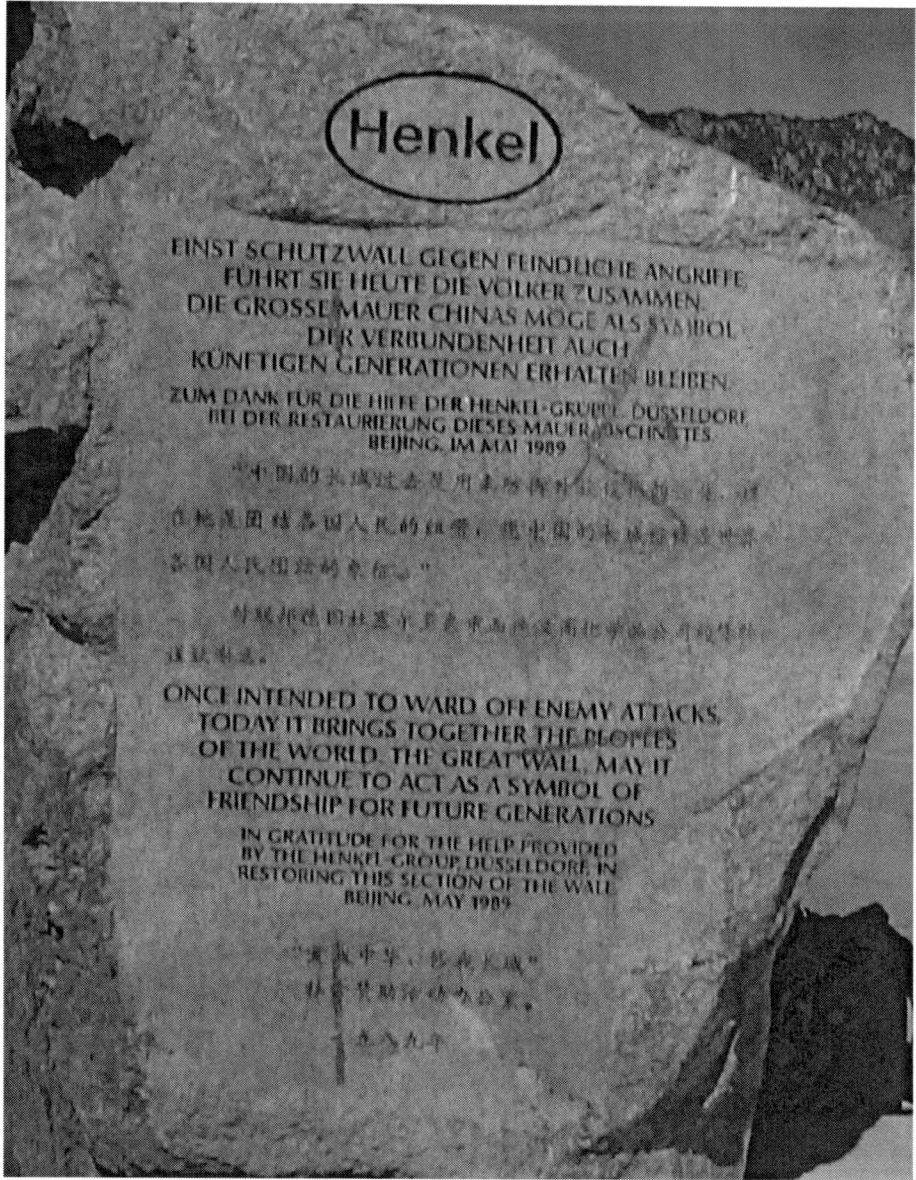

Inscription on rock at Mutianyu—"Once Intended to Ward Off Enemy Attacks, Today It Brings Together the Peoples of the World. The Great Wall, May It Continue to Act as a Symbol of Friendship for Future Generations."

Pushan Power Plant

Pushan Power Plant—Cafeteria

Pushan Power Plant—Coal Truck

Pushan Power Plant—Control Room

Pushan Power Plant—Sculpture in Front

Pushan Power Plant—The Jade Bull

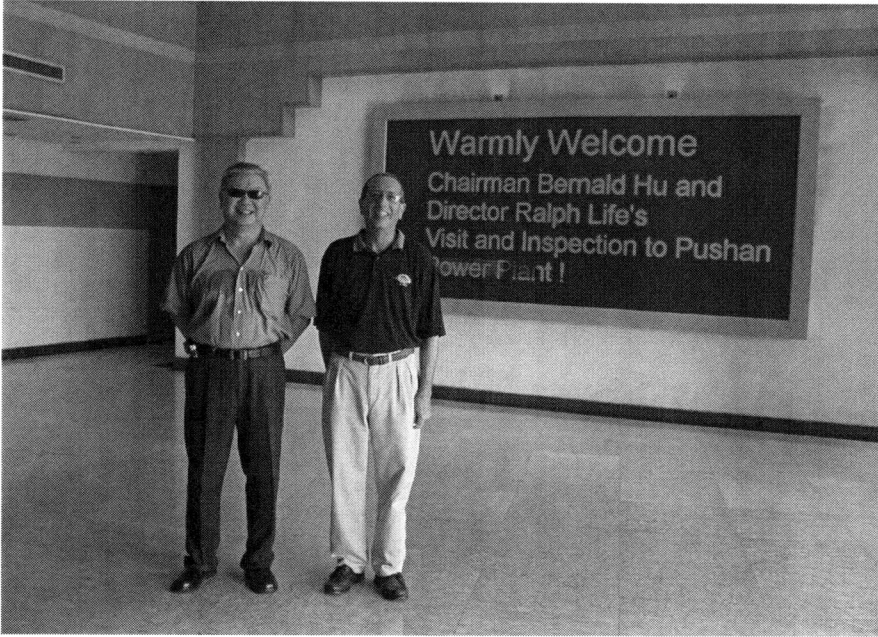

Pushan Power Plant—Bernard Hu and Ralph

Shanghai

Shanghai—Modern Buildings

Shanghai—Older Buildings

Shanghai—Pearl Tower

Shanghai Street

Shenzhen

Shenzhen (2)

Shenzhen Wal-Mart

Shenzhen Sam's Club

Suzhou—Ancient House of Wealthy Man

Suzhou—Ancient House of Wealthy Man (2)

Suzhou—Ancient House of Wealthy Man (3)

Suzhou—China's Venice

Suzhou—China's Venice

Wudang Mountains—Ancient Taoist Temple

Clouds Covering Wudang Mountain Range in Hubei
Province

Beijing—Botanical Garden (2)

Beijing—Botanical Garden (3)

Beijing—HongQiao Market

Beijing—Many Buses to Transport the Masses

Beijing—Marble Boat on Lake at Summer Palace

Beijing—Street with a KFC and a Carrefour Department
Store

Beijing—Summer Palace

Beijing—Summer Palace (2)

Beijing on a Fair Day

Beijing on a Normal Day

Beijing on a Bad Day

Great Wall—Simitai Site (Eric)

Great Wall—Simitai Site (Glenn)

Great Wall—Simitai Site (Not Officially Open to Public)

Great Wall—Simitai Site (Ralph)

Great Wall—Simitai Site
(Unrestored Section of the Wall)

Great Wall—Simitai Site
(Unrestored Section of the Wall)

Guilin

Guilin (2)

Guilin—Musical Show by a Local Minority Group

Guilin—NGLE Trip

Guilin—Camel Hill
(Rock Formation that Resembles a Camel)

Guilin—Elephant (Trunk) Hill (Rock Formation that
Resembles Elephant Drinking Water from the River)

Guilin—Li River Tour

Guilin—Li River Tour (2)

Guilin—Rock Where President Clinton Gave
Environmental Speech

Hainan—Island Province in South China

Hainan—A Ride on the Wild Side

Hainan—Hainan Beach and Hotel

Hainan—Luxury Hotel

Hangzhou—At West Lake with Scott and Zhao Jing

Harbin—In North China Bordering Russia

Harbin—Ready to Go Skiing

Harbin—Ice Festival Sculpture at Night

Harbin—Ice Festival Sculpture at Night (2)

Harbin—Ice Festival Sculpture

Harbin—Creating Ice Festival Sculpture

Harbin—Tigers

Harbin—Tigers (2)

Harbin—A University

Biography

Jean was born in Elkton, Virginia, in 1947. After high school and Business College, she married Ralph E. Life in 1969, and they moved to Blacksburg, Virginia, for him to complete his Mechanical Engineering Degree at Virginia Tech. She worked as head secretary of the Math Department until he graduated. Ralph then began his long career with American Electric Power and they moved to Winfield, West VirginiaTheir two daughters Sarah and Amanda were born in Charleston, West Virginia. In 1979, they began a series of moves that took them to Pt. Pleasant, West Virginia Newburgh, Indiana; Cincinnati, Ohio; Scott Depot, West Virginia; New Martinsville, West Virginia; and finally to the place written about in this book—the city of Nanyang in the Henan Province of China.

Jean and Ralph are now living in Columbus, Ohio, and are the proud grandparents of Lauren and Kendall Metzger and Riley and Jacob Pavlik.

Insert image 246—Jean and Ralph

Synopsis

From the moment I learned we were moving to China to our return home, you will read about our amazing and bizarre experiences. During the years in China, I had sent newsletters to family and friends about our adventures, but upon our return home, many people still wanted me to write a book. Finally, I agreed to begin. I played on our name for the title and then began telling "my story." Not only did I want to write about our experiences, I also wanted it to be a help to those going to live or do business in a very different culture upside down from what we consider normal. Consequently, I have written *Life in China* as a cross between a memoir and a travel book. I hope it is a helpful source for those going there to live or tour and an enjoyable story for those who aren't.

Lightning Source UK Ltd.
Milton Keynes UK
UKOW051940270112

186200UK00001B/262/P

9 781456 898670